Foreign Direct Investment and Development

THEODORE H. MORAN

Foreign Direct Investment and Development:
The New Policy Agenda for Developing Countries and Economies in Transition

INSTITUTE FOR INTERNATIONAL ECONOMICS
Washington, DC
December 1998

Theodore H. Moran, Visiting Fellow, is the Director of the Pew Economic Freedom Fellows Program and is the Karl F. Landegger Professor of International Business Diplomacy at Georgetown University. He is widely known for his work on international economics and national security, political risk analysis, corporate strategy, and multinational corporations. Dr. Moran served as Senior Adviser for economic policy on the Policy Planning Staff of the Department of State (1993-94).

INSTITUTE FOR INTERNATIONAL ECONOMICS
11 Dupont Circle, NW
Washington, DC 20036-1207
(202) 328-9000   FAX: (202) 328-5432
http://www.iie.com
C. Fred Bergsten, *Director*
Christine F. Lowry, *Director of Publications*
Brett Kitchen, *Marketing Director*

Typesetting by Sandra F. Watts
Printing by Kirby Lithographic Inc.

For reprints/permission to photocopy please contact the APS customer service department at CCC Academic Permissions Service, 27 Congress Street, Salem, MA 01970.

Printed in the United States of America
00 99 98   5 4 3 2 1

Library of Congress Cataloging-in-Publication Data

Moran, Theodore H., 1943-
  Foreign direct investment and development : the new policy agenda for developing countries and economies in transition / by Theodore H. Moran.
    p. cm.
  Includes bibliographical references and index.

  1. Investments, Foreign—Government policy—Developing countries. 2. Investments, Foreign—Government policy— Developing countries—Case studies. I. Institute for International Economics (U.S.) II. Title.
HG5993.M667   1998
332.67'3'091724—dc21   97-48803
                                    CIP

ISBN 0-88132-258-X

To three mentors

Albert O. Hirschman
Charles Kindleberger
Raymond Vernon

Contents

Boxes

Tables

Preface

Foreign direct investment has soared in importance over the past decade as a source of capital, management, and technology for the developing world and economies in transition. However, the analysis of policy toward such investment for host countries and potential host countries has lagged far behind. There has been no comprehensive assessment of theory and evidence to clarify which policy approaches are most beneficial, which are counterproductive, and which are genuinely harmful for governments that want to utilize foreign direct investment as part of their development strategies.

This volume on *Foreign Direct Investment and Development* by Ted Moran attempts to fill the analytical gap. It focuses initially on host-country policies that attempt to shape foreign investor activities, especially investment promotion, domestic-content requirements, and export-performance requirements. It turns next to host-country policies that attempt to constrain ownership on the part of foreign direct investors, in particular, joint-venture mandates and technology-licensing requirements. It then examines the special problems of host-country policies toward natural-resource and private-infrastructure investments. It concludes with a "new agenda" of policy recommendations that addresses each of these individual areas of policy debate and then weaves them together in a structure that might take the form of a new international agreement on investment within the World Trade Organization.

Dr. Moran's analysis includes a careful search for indications of market failure, and for signs of externalities, that might justify host country actions that go beyond "getting their macroeconomic house in order" and sitting back to wait for foreign investors to arrive. At the same time, he persistently raises cautions about inappropriate interventions and the danger that host country policy can be captured by special rent-seeking interests. Dr. Moran's evidence is unusual and widespread, drawing upon sources from economics, from political science and political economics, and from the case studies of the international business literature—a multidisciplinary approach that is all too rare in policy research of this sort.

Dr. Moran's proposed "new agenda" of policies toward foreign direct investment suggests that the distinction between investment policies, trade policies, and other policies to influence the location of international companies is becoming increasingly blurred. Indeed, his analysis supports a line of argument—that "trade wars" are coming more to resemble "investment wars"—that he, I, and Thomas Horst first elaborated in our book *American Multinationals and American Interests* some two decades ago (and that I initiated in an article "Coming Investment Wars" in *Foreign Affairs* in 1974). The implication is that developed country authorities, as well as developing country governments and economies in transition, have an interest in working together to eliminate distortionary efforts to compete for international investment or to force international investment within their borders. The book thus includes a set of recommendations for action by developed as well as developing and transitional countries and for self-interested pressure by multinational corporations on policymakers in all three sets of countries around the world.

The Institute for International Economics is a private nonprofit institution for the study and discussion of international economic policy. Its purpose is to analyze important issues in that area and to develop and communicate practical new approaches for dealing with them. The Institute is completely nonpartisan.

The Institute is funded largely by philanthropic foundations and private corporations. Major institutional grants are now being received from The German Marshall Fund of the United States, which created the Institute with a generous commitment of funds in 1981, and from The William M. Keck, Jr. Foundation, and The Starr Foundation. A number of other foundations and companies also contribute to the highly diversified financial resources of the Institute. About 18 percent of the Institute's resources in our latest fiscal year were provided by contributors outside the United States, including about 12 percent from Japan.

The Board of Directors bears overall responsibility for the Institute and gives general guidance and approval to its research program, including identification of topics that are likely to become important to international economic policymakers over the medium run (generally, one to three years), and which thus should be addressed by the Institute. The Director, working closely with the staff and outside Advisory Committee, is responsible for the development of particular projects and makes the final decision to publish an individual study.

The Institute hopes that its studies and other activities will contribute to building a stronger foundation for international economic policy around the world. We invite readers of these publications to let us know how they think we can best accomplish this objective.

C. Fred Bergsten
Director
November 1998

Acknowledgments

Many individuals helped to improve this book in diverse ways, including Steve Beckman, Joel Bergsman, Dennis Lamb, Kenneth P. Thomas, and Louis T. Wells, Jr. I am particularly grateful to Edward M. Graham, Gary Clyde Hufbauer, Robert Z. Lawrence, J. David Richardson, and Raymond Vernon for their careful reading of earlier versions of this work. Myrna Young, Sarah Cleeland, and David Krzywda ably assisted with final editing. With so much support, the weaknesses that remain are clearly my own.

Introduction and Synopsis

The best research on important public-policy issues has several distinguishing characteristics. For policymakers, such research will contain fresh revelations that contradict conventional wisdom. For policy analysts (above all, economists), such research will contain familiar models, familiar analytical techniques, and familiar lines of argument that make the results appear comfortingly obvious, even self-evident. For both policymakers and policy analysts, such research will build its case on new evidence while acknowledging and incorporating much of what is already known. All these are found here.

This study addresses three groups of questions. First, what benefits and opportunities does FDI bring to the development process, and—even amidst today's unparalleled enthusiasm for foreign direct investment (FDI) —what risks and dangers accompany it? When are the benefits and opportunities likely to predominate, and when are the risks and dangers likely to prevail?

Second, how well do international markets function in providing FDI to developing countries and economies in transition, and what have been the principal obstacles preventing them from functioning more effectively? Are there indications of market failure and market distortion that signal a need for individual countries or the world community at large to be concerned?

Third, what policies should host governments and would-be host governments in the developing world and the economies in transition adopt to capture the benefits, avoid the dangers, and maximize the contribution of FDI? In particular, is "getting the fundamentals right" (pursuing sound macroeconomic policies and investment-friendly macroeconomic policies and building reliable legal and other commercial institutions) enough? That is, after getting the fundamentals right, can host authorities simply sit back and expect international forces to deliver appropriate amounts of valuable economic activity to them via FDI? Or do host authorities have a larger role to play—a larger, more energetic, especially vital role to play—to enhance the use of FDI in the development process?

The evidence examined here points to the latter: that there is a larger, more energetic, especially vital role for host authorities in the developing countries and the economies in transition to play—certainly more activist, perhaps more interventionist, potentially more perilous—than waiting passively for international markets to bring foreign investors to participate in the growth of the local economy.

But the agenda for action—how to design policies and where to focus efforts to enlarge the contribution of FDI to development—turns out to differ substantially from the most commonly held beliefs on this subject.

The purpose of this study is to delineate a "new agenda" for action on the part of host governments and would-be host governments in the developing countries and economies in transition. This new agenda aims to maximize the benefits they can obtain from FDI and minimize the dangers. It also suggests how they might best pursue this new agenda, acting singly, acting collectively, and acting (often) in conjunction with home-country authorities, with multilateral institutions, and with the investors themselves.

Chapter 1 introduces the legacy of investigation about the impact of FDI on development. There is a common assumption that if international companies conduct their activities with the same good citizenship standards abroad that they do at home, their contribution to the host economy can only be positive. But this reasoning hinges, implicitly, on the presence of highly competitive conditions that are fundamentally at odds with both theory and evidence about FDI behavior. In fact, FDI typically originates in international industries where there are high barriers to entry and deploys itself in domestic markets in the developing countries and economies in transition where there are high degrees of concentration. Quite apart from important specific harmful activities (such as permitting pollution, carrying out operations with inadequate health and safety standards, or tolerating the behavior of abusive subcontractors) that could be righted by common good citizenship standards for behavior at home and abroad, the possibility that FDI might lead to fundamental economic distortion and pervasive damage to the development prospects of the country is ever present.

Simultaneously, however, the same conditions of imperfect competition that might be so troublesome indicate that FDI may provide rents (including high wages, benefits, and profits), intangible assets (including technology, marketing, best management practices), and potential spillovers and externalities that are highly beneficial for host-country economic growth.

In this precarious setting, three aggregate "net assessments" of the impact of FDI covering 183 projects in some 30 countries over more than 15 years found that a majority of the projects (55 percent to 75 percent) usually had a positive impact on the host national income, but a large minority of the projects (25 percent to 45 percent, and in one of the studies 75 percent) had a clearly negative impact on the economic welfare of the host. The difference between positive and negative impacts was accounted for by policy variables, as subsequent chapters reveal, that the host authorities could control.

The choice of policies to deal with FDI—and the design of the policy environment that surrounds FDI—is crucial, therefore, to ensure that the contribution of foreign firms is beneficial to host-country development.

Chapter 2 reviews theoretical considerations about the pros and cons of host-country policies that guide the activities of foreign firms, such as investment promotion, domestic-content requirements, and export-performance requirements. Under assumptions of perfect competition, these kinds of intervention almost always produce damaging outcomes that distort the allocation of resources, penalize unfavored sectors, create industrial-policy targeting problems, and introduce a rentseeking dynamic into the economy.

Under assumptions of imperfect competition—in particular, within a strategic-trade framework—the outcome from intervention is indeterminate. The prospect of capturing a share of the rents and externalities from the operations of international investors in imperfectly competitive industries raises the stakes for those who are successful in attracting (or holding) them and imposes large opportunity costs on those who are not successful or who do not take part in the competition. But the rationale for activism is matched by equally powerful caveats about the dangers, because improperly constructed public policies may have a magnified negative impact on the prospects for economic development.

To analyze what kind of interventions might be helpful and what kind might be damaging under strategic-trade-type conditions requires, as a consequence, complex and subtle judgments about both the economic desirability and the political-economic feasibility of pursuing alternative paths with consistent success. Depicting the policy ingredients and policy options necessitates, moreover, a broad canvas: investment policy cannot be artificially separated from the provision of grants, subsidies, tax preferences, and other locational incentives to foreign and domestic firms or from the use of investment-distorting measures in trade policy.

Investment promotion, examined in chapter 3, is the first area in which the question arises of whether it is enough to get the fundamentals right or whether a more proactive approach might be needed. Even so seemingly benign an activity as devoting resources and attention to "market" a country as an attractive site for FDI can impose burdens and create distortions for the rest of the economy.

But marketing efforts do yield impressive results. A rigorous examination of the evidence, with appropriate controls for alternative explanations, shows a high payoff for hosts who make aggressive efforts to attract foreign investors, generating benefits with a (conservatively estimated) net present value of almost four dollars for every dollar expended.

What accounts for the high payoff? Marketing theory suggests that the answer could come from the need for product differentiation on the part of the host. Models of search and signaling that embody poor indices of quality differentials among products indicate that hosts may find it beneficial to show that they have superior properties to rival locations. Thus, superior hosts could stimulate more interest among potential investors for their location than those investors would have for the least attractive alternatives.

If strategies of investment promotion could be confined to efforts at product differentiation and overcoming minor information asymmetries —with no larger indications of market failure to contend with or distortionary interventions on the part of others to compensate for—there are relatively unobtrusive, inexpensive, and nondangerous methods to accomplish these goals.

But, to anticipate the analysis in subsequent chapters, such is not the case. Both the imperfect functioning of international markets and the investment-diverting actions of others pose challenges to the design of any given host country's approach to dealing with foreign investors.

After investment promotion, chapter 4 shifts the focus to domestic-content requirements, chapter 5 analyzes export-performance requirements, and chapter 6 broadens the inquiry to what is becoming a global struggle for the location of manufacturing investment. Each of these chapters draws heavily on evidence from three sectors that have been the leaders in the globalization of industry—the automotive, petrochemical, and electronics/computer sectors—cross-referencing these with studies from other sectors. (The special problems of natural-resource and private-infrastructure projects are analyzed in chapter 9). The evidence comes from the economics literature, from the political science/political economics literature, and from business case studies. While some of the data are in fact introduced here for the first time, the degree to which these multiple literatures draw upon each other or even acknowledge each other is so astonishingly small that the majority of the studies are likely to strike any given reader as completely new.

Chapter 4 shows that the intervention most frequently used by host authorities in the developing countries and economies in transition—insisting upon domestic-content requirements in highly protected markets—is not only extremely costly, but also quite ineffective as an infant-industry tactic to demonstrate the underlying appeal of a given host to multinational corporations. Except in the largest countries, economies of scale are seldom realized, and there are weak managerial incentives to upgrade technology, or maintain the highest standards of quality control, or improve human resources. Contrary to conventional expectations, backward linkages to domestic suppliers are less sophisticated and exhibit fewer indications of training, assisting, or providing technological and marketing externalities than are foreign operations with fewer restrictions.

The imposition of high domestic-content requirements in protected markets tends, moreover, to generate a perverse political economy in which the foreign investors themselves frequently join domestic forces in opposing further liberalization of trade and investment. A detailed case study of the IBM investment that marked a turning point in Mexico's approach to FDI shows that Hewlett-Packard and Apple helped, in vain, to wage the fight within the higher echelons of the Mexican political establishment against the IBM initiative and the policy shift it represented. There is similar evidence from contemporary Eastern Europe, where Suzuki (in Hungary) and Fiat (in Poland) have successfully lobbied for continued, even increased, protection to safeguard their small assembly operations. In these countries, the foreign investors have allied with domestic workers and suppliers to slow the prospects for accession into the European Union.

Overall, there is scant justification on infant-industry grounds, strategic-trade grounds, or any other grounds for the use of domestic-content requirements as a sound tool of development policy. Instead of the foot dragging and obfuscation that is taking place in some countries, strict adherence to obligations under the World Trade Organization (WTO) to phase out domestic-content requirements as rapidly and thoroughly as possible makes good sense as a part of host-government development policy.

Turning from domestic content to export promotion, the question of how to attract world-scale operations that are thoroughly integrated into the global/regional networks of international corporations is the most important issue for host authorities intent upon utilizing foreign manufacturing investment to enhance their own development. The assessment of theory and evidence needed to guide host-country policy, gathered in chapters 5 and 6, occupies the major portion of this volume.

The evidence offered in these chapters shows that full-scale foreign plants in the automotive, petrochemical, and electronics/computer industries provide benefits to the economies where they are located far in excess of the capital, management, and marketing commonly assumed. They have, indeed, been characterized by high wages and benefits, high levels of research and development, and sophisticated managerial and marketing techniques. But beyond this—once the parent investors committed themselves to incorporate a host site into their global/regional sourcing network, with the aim of enhancing their overall competitive position in international markets—there is evidence of a dynamic-integration effect, which provides newer technology, more rapid techno-logical upgrading, and greater attention to quality control, cost control, and managerial/human resource development in the local subsidiary than does any other method of acquiring such benefits. The subsidiary enjoys persistent parental supervision in raising the state of play to major league standards, so to speak, and keeping it there.

The energetic advantages that this integration effect brings from the parent corporation may be akin to the commitment to superior perfor-mance that has been observed when domestic firms in the United States are exposed to the challenges of global engagement.

The establishment of integrated production systems that cross bor-ders in the industries examined here—in particular, the automotive and electronics/computer sectors—not only creates a highly potent interaction between parent and subsidiary, but generates abundant backward link-ages. Spillovers and externalities to locally owned suppliers, including coaching in management and marketing, are more evident from foreign investors whose only host requirements involve exports than from for-eign investors operating with other host-country constraints. Indigenous suppliers to these investors often themselves begin to export to other affiliates of the parent and then to independent buyers in external mar-kets. Hundreds of local firms in the countries surveyed here became certified as original equipment manufacturers (OEM) and replacement equipment manufacturers (REM) suppliers, many with sales in the mil-lions of dollars. In addition, measures of capital and technological deep-ening within these local firms have risen.

The investments of large international companies examined here, and the clustering of foreign and indigenous suppliers to serve them, fre-quently exhibit characteristics of agglomeration, specialized inputs and services (many of which enjoy their own economies of scale), labor pooling, and enhanced likelihood of further technological spillovers.

Chapter 5 focuses on the role of export-performance requirements per se in creating such valuable activities, as part of the globalization of the automotive, petrochemical, and electronics/computer sectors. Despite notable differences among the three sectors, these case histories reveal a surprising story: they show export-performance requirements playing a crucial part in impelling international investors (against considerable re-sistance) to establish sourcing networks that included developing and transition economy sites, with results that benefited not only firm and host-country welfare but global welfare as well. These sourcing networks rapidly generated billions of dollars of sustained new output from hosts in Latin America and Southeast Asia—a far different outcome from the weak streams of artificially supported exports usually depicted as emerging from export-performance requirements.

But why should host countries in the developing countries and economies in transition have to engage in any intervention at all to become sites for global production? Should their use of export-performance requirements now be rationalized and expanded, using export-related subsidies to foreign investors as a tool to connect to the externality-rich sourcing networks of the parents? Or should hosts in the developing and transitioning world be willing to control and curtail the use of export-performance requirements (perhaps in return for some larger agreements on investment and trade policies)? These questions are the subject of chapter 6.

A first justification for some kind of intervention might spring from evidence of market failure. A puzzling discovery in all three industries is the reluctance of many firms to undertake export-oriented investments even after they had obtained clear evidence that their overall profitability and competitive position could be improved by doing so. This reluctance would then be punctuated by rapid follow-the-leader behavior on the part of many members of the industry once a first mover established a new sourcing pattern.

Chapter 6 examines two possible kinds of market failure. The stickiness in undertaking new investments appears analogous to the lemons problem in used-car economics, where an investor can evaluate a large, indivisible world-scale-sized export facility only by "trying it out," leading to suboptimally slow learning from the perspective of global welfare (within what the chapter introduces as a framework of irreversible investments under uncertainty). Then, the follow-the-leader behavior may be indicative of appropriability problems, with first movers not enjoying sufficient returns to compensate them for the burden of initial risk.

While neither the identification of possible market failures nor the evidence from the potent employment of export-performance requirements in the cases investigated here suggests that export-performance requirements will always work, they pose a challenge for the design of policy toward FDI. Few authorities in the developing countries and the economies in transition could be expected to ignore that those countries who were able to overcome the international firms' initial reluctance, and trigger a burst of investor response, found that such efforts paid enormous benefits. The cost of remaining passive and simply waiting for international markets to bring world-scale-sized plants to any given economy, in contrast, was appalling. The export-performance requirements themselves may have been cumbersome and inelegant (cumbersome and inelegant in comparison to the straightforward provision of grants and subsidies to hold established investors or entice new ones by countries that are members of the Organization for Economic Cooperation and Development [OECD], considered next), but the payoff was large indeed.

Complicating the task of designing policy toward foreign investment in world-scale manufacturing operations, a second rationale for possible intervention on the part of hosts or would-be hosts in the developing countries and economies in transition, on second-best grounds, comes from observation of the growing effort on the part of home countries, once the process of globalization began, to use economic carrots and political sticks to keep already-present firms from moving and to attract new international investment to developed-country sites. The developed countries have escalated the use of locational incentives to more than $50,000-$100,000 per job, as calculated by the OECD. There are learned disputes about whether Ireland, the eastern regions of Germany, or individual US states lead in this incentive competition.

But the policy options in response are not appealing. Developing countries and economies in transition have tried, mostly ineffectually, to participate in this race, often turning in frustration at their lack of readily available grant monies to the promise of trade rents to match the subsidy packages in the OECD. A case study in box 6.1 documents the negative consequences of even indirect competition for FDI between Germany's grant of more than $250 million for an integrated GM plant at Eisenach in the former East Germany and Hungary's provision of more than $50 million from trade protection for a GM engine plant and associated boutique assembly operation at Szentgotthard near the Austrian border.

A third rationale for possible intervention by developing countries and economies in transition comes from evidence of a counteroffensive on the part of capital-exporting countries against their loss of productive capacity, a counteroffensive that utilizes protectionist and investment-diverting trade measures, most notably rules of origin and antidumping regulations. The deployment of both of these measures has evolved in a discriminatory and demonstrably distortionary manner, skewing trade and investment patterns away from what international comparative advantage would otherwise predict.

Here, too, the temptation to mimic the self-centered and myopic use of rules of origin and antidumping regulations of the developed world does not offer a path that coincides with the long-term interests of the developing countries and economies in transition.

All in all, the setting in which the developing countries and the economies in transition must design policy toward FDI in manufacturing is becoming both more perplexing and more fraught with peril. The evidence from the struggle over valuable externality-rich segments of industrial activity suggests that conventional trade wars are being replaced by investment wars to determine important contours in economic geography around the world.

Extending this perspective, the efforts of diverse countries to hold old or attract new international corporate investment have in fact taken on some of the characteristics of a strategic-trade-like struggle, with less highly stylized visibility than Boeing versus Airbus but no less important outcomes for the countries that are players. The use of a strategic-trade framework is more than a theoretical refinement: this struggle has beggar-thy-neighbor features and escalatory dynamics that require supranational consensus to contain. States acting individually may find genuine justification (beyond pure protectionism) for trying to win battles over the location of international firms.

The strategic trade paradigm points, moreover, to the only viable path for resolution of the inherent policy dilemmas: while developing countries and economies in transition might be justified in intervening to attract world-scale-sized manufacturing plants—with means and methods that include export-performance requirements, escalating locational incentives, and self-centered deployment of rules of origin and antidumping regulations—they would be engaging in a struggle that they cannot win and whose outcome their actions would only be likely to worsen. Chapter 6 concludes that their interests would be better served by devoting their energies to efforts to limit and control all forms of investment-diverting mechanisms by all parties.

Chapter 7 shifts the analysis from host efforts to shape foreign-firm operations to host restrictions on foreign ownership, in particular requirements to enter into a joint venture with an indigenous partner. For many kinds of operations, the joint-venture relationship offers benefits to all parties. When the partnership is imposed rather than spontaneous, however, rates of dissatisfaction and instability within three years of start-up are high. US and European parent firms shun joint-venture arrangements when international sourcing, quality control, rapid technological change, and product differentiation are integral to the operations; Japanese firms may now be exhibiting the same tendency.

As for contentions that joint ventures achieve greater technology transfer, expanded access to external markets, and more robust backward linkages to the domestic economy, none is supported by the evidence. Technology transferred to joint ventures is older and speed of upgrading is slower than that transferred to wholly owned subsidiaries. Affiliates that export a large fraction of their output are more likely to be wholly owned; in particular, affiliates incorporated into the especially beneficial global/regional sourcing strategies of the parent and enjoying the integration effect described earlier, are almost always wholly owned. Joint ventures may source more inputs from indigenous firms, but wholly owned affiliates generate more technological, managerial, and export-marketing spillovers for indigenous suppliers (in large part because of the more intimate relationship with the parent corporation).

Contradicting charges that wholly owned affiliates only engage in low-value-added screwdriver operations or that outsourcing represents no more than a relocation of low-wage production, there is extensive evidence—even in electronics/computer assembly—of substantial value added (including responsibility for design and system integration) by the affiliates themselves and of dynamic coaching, training, and export assistance for indigenous suppliers. Local machine-tool firms working for foreign semiconductor investors in Malaysia, for example, have moved from backyard workshops, through stamping and machining parts, to manufacture of precision factory-automation equipment. These local firms sell first to the nearby investor, then export to other subsidiaries of the same parent, and then export to other buyers in the global industry. Indicators of capital intensity and technological sophistication have risen, and the sales of these indigenous firms, in direct competition with German and Japanese rivals, have increased.

Chapter 8 examines technology-licensing requirements as a substitute for FDI (the so-called "Korea model"). Quite apart from broader questions about the appeal of this development model in light of the Asian financial crisis, the evidence shows that indigenous corporate operations that are built via mandatory technology licensing are likely to suffer the same kind of economic disadvantages as joint ventures: lags in technology acquisition, in best-management techniques, in access to foreign markets, and in development of a competitive supplier base. Even the stylized view of the historical emergence of South Korean electronics firms has to be revised to take note of rather large direct and indirect contributions from FDI and foreign corporate alliances. And enthusiasm for the initial record of South Korean successes must be tempered with consideration of a long history of weak performance in sectors such as chemicals/petrochemicals that have lagged because of the same joint-venture and technology-transfer requirements. Finally, there is the non-trivial issue of diversification, in which the prospects for the South Korean automotive sector, for example, have been tied to the fate of a single national champion, Hyundai (with Daewoo and, as many had hoped, Kia following at some distance) in comparison to the prospects for the Mexican, Brazilian, or Thai automotive sectors where multiple members of the international automobile industry have a large stake.

As for the political benefits from autonomy, the extent to which maintaining ownership in national hands has a legitimate national-security rationale—to avoid monopolistic external suppliers who might delay, deny, or set conditions upon the use of inputs—is quite limited, and the drawbacks in terms of cost and performance that self-sufficiency imposes are quite large.

Protecting and nurturing national-champion firms and industries may be inseparable, moreover, from exposing the economy to the problems of "crony capitalism" that have figured prominently in many Asian countries. Even if political-economic corruption is not evident, however, the creation of national champions as a development strategy is highly problematic. A case study in box 8.1 focuses on Malaysia's national-champion car company, Proton, a joint venture with Mitsubishi, and shows repeated problems of high cost, lagging technology, and weak export performance. This dubious outcome stands in marked contrast to Mexico, Brazil, or Thailand's more favorable record in benefiting from competition among foreign investors in the automotive sector and to Malaysia's own more favorable record in benefiting from competition among foreign investors in the electronics/computer sector.

Chapter 9 devotes special attention to FDI projects in natural resources and infrastructure that suffer from a distinctive kind of market failure involving imperfect contracts. Such projects—involving large fixed investments with long payback periods that make the stability of the regulatory environment paramount for the success of the venture—are vulnerable to "obsolescing bargain" dynamics, in which hosts do not want to pay a premium reflecting initial risk indefinitely (especially host authorities who are successors to those who signed the initial agreements). Here, investors seldom have control over rapidly changing technology and brand-name recognition that manufacturers in other sectors can wield to protect themselves. They suffer from a structural vulnerability to demands for renegotiation of their investment agreements before they are adequately compensated, leading to undersupply of such investment.

Consequently, there has been a growing role for multilateral institutions (in cooperation with private actors) to help to ensure the credibility of commitments, via insurance and guarantee programs, long enough to make up for imperfections in contract markets but allowing hosts some flexibility to adjust investment terms in line with national treatment after a period of time. A case study in box 9.1, on Broken Hill Proprietary's investment in the Escondida copper mine in Chile, details a pioneering effort to build a network of long-term buyers, export-credit agencies, and private and multilateral financial institutions to deter fundamental changes in the initial 20-year investment agreement.

In synthesizing the policy implications of this research, the concluding chapter points out that what is striking about the new agenda of actions needed to incorporate FDI more effectively into the development process is not only what should be included but what should be excluded.

Host authorities in the developing countries and economies in transition have a great interest in three priorities: first, in helping to make transparent and then limiting locational subsidies and locational incentives around the world; second, in mobilizing a campaign to halt and roll back the use of rules of origin and antidumping regulations to protect producers and divert investment flows; and third, in participating in initiatives within the multilateral financial institutions to enhance the credibility of long-term investment agreements for natural-resource and private-infrastructure projects.

Excluded from the list of desirable policies, indeed dismissed from the list altogether, are domestic-content requirements, joint-venture requirements, and technology-licensing requirements.

Reformers in the developing countries and economies in transition who want to pursue this new agenda will face a steep uphill battle, at home and abroad, but they may be able to mobilize powerful allies to help.

Should they proceed individually and unilaterally or as part of a "grand bargain" with reformers in the developed countries to incorporate tradeoffs among the most objectionable investment-related policies of all parties in a Multilateral Agreement on Investment (MAI) that is broader in scope than the current exercise under OECD auspices?

The analysis of costs and benefits of alternative approaches to FDI undertaken here should assist in rendering several of the more contentious issues of a reconstituted MAI more tractable to negotiation, in particular, national treatment, right of establishment, sector-specific reservations, and national-security exceptions.

Combining concessions on these with demands for reform of locational incentives, rules of origin, and antidumping regulations may start a process that, paradoxically, enhances the chances of success on all fronts.

FDI in Developing Countries and Economies in Transition: Opportunities, Dangers, and New Challenges

Introduction

The role of FDI in the developing countries and economies in transition has grown dramatically over the course of the 1990s, from $24 billion per year in 1990 to approximately $120 billion per year by the beginning of 1998. FDI flows remained relatively robust right through the Mexican peso crisis of 1994-95. If history is a guide, international companies are not likely to pause for long with their investment plans as the Asian economies resume their growth.

Private capital flows now total more than four-fifths of all capital inflows to the less-developed countries and the economies in transition. Among these private capital flows, FDI is by far the largest and most stable source of capital, climbing in recent years to near 50 percent (see tables I.1 and I.2).

The distribution of FDI to the developing countries and economies in transition has been quite uneven. The top 10 countries received $89 billion, or 72 percent of the FDI flows, in 1997. Since 1992, China has attracted the largest proportion, reaching a high of $42 billion, or 38 percent of the total, in 1996 (although some substantial component of this represents what is called "round tripping" by indigenous capital holders).

But the potential to attract foreign investors is not a static phenomenon. Over the course of the 1990s, individual countries have improved their prospects considerably, with strengthened performances on the part of Hungary and Poland in Eastern Europe; Argentina and Venezuela in

Table I.1 Aggregate net private capital flows to developing countries, 1990-97 (billions of dollars unless otherwise noted)

Type of flow	1990	1991	1992	1993	1994	1995	1996	1997
Total private flows	41.9	53.6	90.1	154.6	160.6	189.1	246.9	256.
Debt flows	15.0	13.5	33.8	44.0	41.1	55.1	82.2	103.
Commercial bank loans	3.8	3.4	13.1	2.8	8.9	29.3	34.2	41.
Bonds	0.1	7.4	8.3	31.8	27.5	23.8	45.7	53.
Other	11.1	2.7	12.4	9.4	4.7	2.0	2.3	8.
FDI	23.7	32.9	45.3	65.6	86.9	101.5	119.0	120.
Portfolio equity flows	3.2	7.2	11.0	45.0	32.6	32.5	45.8	32.
Aggregate net resource flows	100.6	122.5	146.0	212.0	207.0	237.2	284.6	300.
Private flows share (percentage)	44.1	46.4	62.1	74.1	77.9	77.7	85.7	85.

Source: Global Development Finance, World Bank Debtor Reporting System, World Bank (1998).

Table I.2 FDI flows to the top 10 recipient developing countries (billions of dollars unless otherwise noted)

1991		1994		1997	
Mexico	4.7	China	33.8	China	37.0
China	4.3	Mexico	11.0	Brazil	15.8
Malaysia	1.0	Malaysia	4.3	Mexico	8.1
Argentina	2.4	Peru	3.1	Indonesia	5.8
Thailand	2.0	Brazil	3.1	Poland	4.5
Venezuela	1.9	Argentina	3.1	Malaysia	4.1
Indonesia	1.5	Indonesia	2.1	Argentina	3.8
Hungary	1.5	Nigeria	1.9	Chile	3.5
Brazil	1.1	Poland	1.9	India	3.1
Turkey	0.8	Chile	1.8	Venezuela	2.9
Share of top 10 in FDI to all developing countries (percentage)	74.2		76.1		72.3

Source: Global Development Finance, World Bank Debtor Reporting System, World Bank (1998).

Latin America; Kazakhstan, Uzbekistan, and Azerbaijan in Central Asia; India in South Asia; and Vietnam and the Philippines in Southeast Asia.

Underlying this growing role for FDI in the developing countries and economies in transition has been a transformation in perspective, from critical wariness toward multinational corporations to sometimes uncritical enthusiasm about involving foreign firms in the development process.

Is uncritical enthusiasm warranted? How and where might it have to be tempered? What are the benefits and opportunities that foreign firms have to offer? What risks and dangers might they pose? Beyond improving the micro and macroeconomic fundamentals in their own countries and building appropriate investment-friendly institutional infrastructure, do host countries in the developing countries and the economies in transition need an active (or proactive) policy toward FDI? Where should host authorities focus their attention as they design policies to maximize the benefits, and avoid the dangers, of incorporating FDI into their development strategies?

Chapter 1 provides background on theory and evidence about the impact of FDI on development, as a framework for the detailed studies of individual policies and extensive review of evidence in particular industries that follow.

The Impact of FDI on Host-Country Development: The Heritage of Theory and Evidence

What impact does FDI have on the standards of living and prospects for economic growth of developing countries and economies in transition that receive it?

Two alternative conceptualizations of the impact of FDI guide the understanding of its potential contribution to the economic development of the host country. The first emphasizes the net addition of inputs that foreign investors may bring to a domestic setting of vigorous (if not perfect) competition. The second emphasizes the potentially distortionary impact that foreign investors from imperfectly competitive international industries may have on domestic economies that are themselves riddled with market imperfections.

Both these conceptualizations, or models, are plausible. But they predict widely different outcomes—the first greatly positive, the second much more problematic and (under some circumstances) decidedly negative.

Which structure more closely fits the setting for FDI in the less-developed countries? And how might the potential for negative outcomes be diminished?

The Benign Model of FDI and Development

Perhaps the most prevalent version of the beneficial conceptualization begins with a stylized description of how FDI may help the host country to break out of the vicious cycle of underdevelopment. Here, the potential host is mired in a poverty-laden equilibrium: low levels of productivity lead to low wages, which lead to low levels of saving, which lead to low levels of investment, which perpetuate low levels of productivity.

FDI can break this cycle by complementing local savings and by supplying more effective management, marketing, and technology to improve productivity (Gillis et al. 1996; Cardoso and Dornbusch 1989). The gain in national income depends on the size of the capital inflow and the elasticity of the demand for capital. Furthermore, technological and managerial inputs, and transfers and spillovers to local firms may cause the national production function to shift outward.

Thus, under reasonably competitive conditions—which the foreign presence may enhance—FDI should raise efficiency, expand output, and lead to higher economic growth in the host country. Indeed, the interaction between economic and social development should be positive as well: the additional supply of capital should lower the relative return to capital while the additional demand for labor should bid up the wages of workers, thereby equalizing the distribution of income and improving (quite probably) health and education throughout the society.[1]

The emphasis on the new resources that foreign investors bring to relieve the bottlenecks that constrain development is a common theme among international business groups and multilateral agencies that urge greater acceptance of international corporations within the developing countries and economies in transition. It is the prevailing assumption in macroeconomic growth models that gaps in savings and in foreign exchange set the limits to long-term growth.

The Malign Model of FDI and Development

There is a long history of criticism of multinational corporations. Much of it centers on the possibility that foreign investors will thwart the passage of laws that constrain socially undesirable practices—such as pollution regulations or health, safety, and minimum wage requirements—or ignore laws already enacted. But there is also a strand of criticism that focuses directly on the central relationship between FDI and the prospects for economic growth.

This alternative conceptualization to the benign model (above) emphasizes the potential malign interaction between FDI provided by foreign companies in imperfectly competitive international industries and host economies with imperfectly competitive domestic markets. Here, foreign companies operate in industries where there are substantial barriers to entry, enjoying and perhaps increasing (rather than decreasing)

---

1. For the debate about the assumptions required to generate such a favorable outcome, see Cardoso and Dornbusch (1989).

market concentration (Cardoso and Dornbusch 1989; Grieco 1986). Instead of filling the gap between savings and investment, they may lower domestic savings and investment by extracting rents and siphoning off capital through preferred access to local capital markets and local supplies of foreign exchange. Instead of closing the gap between investment and foreign exchange, they might drive domestic producers out of business and substitute imported inputs. The multinational company may reinvest in the same or related industries in the host country and extend its market power. The repatriation of profits might drain capital from the host country.

Far from generating a favorable impact on income distribution and social development, their operations may support a small oligarchy of indigenous partners and suppliers. Their use of "inappropriate" capital intensive technology may produce a small labor elite while consigning many workers to the ranks of the unemployed (or underemployed) if local labor market rigidities fail to deploy them to more productive occupations. Their tight control over technology, higher management functions, and export channels may prevent the beneficial spillovers and externalities hoped for in the more optimistic scenarios.

Which of these conceptualizations, the first overwhelmingly favorable and the second overwhelmingly unfavorable, better describes FDI in the less-developed countries and economies in transition?

Theory and Evidence about Market Structure and FDI

For either of them to be used as the model of the interaction between FDI and host country development requires a multitude of assumptions, most having to do with how competitive the industry and economy are where the FDI takes place.

In the theory of FDI, the prevalent assumption since the earliest work of Hymer (1976), Vernon (1966), and Kindleberger (1969) has been that barriers to entry and imperfect competition are the sine qua non for the FDI process to be possible. This tradition of analysis postulates that for firms to operate outside their own home economy, they must possess some sort of specific advantages over rival firms in other national markets. These specific advantages may include control over technology, proprietary rights to brand names, economies of scale realized by operating across more than one national market, and other intangible assets derived from organizational and managerial expertise internal to the firm. Such specific advantages are necessary to offset the extra costs associated with communication and coordination among far-flung subsidiaries; they are also necessary to offset the counteradvantages that local firms might have in dealing with local labor, local public relations, local tastes, and local culture.

Absent the specific advantages, one would expect entrepreneurs in each national market to have a superior position from which to recognize nearby economic opportunities and take advantage of them. But possession of one or more of the specific advantages constitutes a barrier to entry into the industry for host-country firms that an international investor can exploit in search of economic rents.

Why should the international company try to exploit the barrier to entry, however, via the cumbersome apparatus of setting up a subsidiary rather than merely licensing a local firm to work on the parent firm's behalf?

Licensing is, in fact, one common method of expanding operations abroad. But it is difficult to protect the ability to extract oligopoly rent via licensing in a world of imperfect contracts and principal/agent problems. In addition, the local firm has a self-interest in learning how to duplicate organizational and managerial skills and to maneuver around proprietary restraints over technology and marketing. These factors lead the parent firm to internalize the rent collecting ability via direct ownership over international operations (for difficulties similar to those of licensing, see the analysis of joint ventures in chapter 7) (Caves 1996; Dunning 1988, 1993b; Buckley and Casson 1976).

FDI therefore becomes a parent-firm strategy to extend or defend the ability to generate oligopoly rents derived from barriers to entry first established in the home-country market in response to conditions there. This model and other variants of it have helped to account for what has otherwise been a puzzle, namely, why multinational manufacturing corporations expanded their operations earliest and most vigorously in countries with similar demand structures (e.g., from the United States into Europe, and vice versa), even though both were regions of relative capital abundance.

FDI (especially manufacturing investment), then, takes two tracks: first, to cater to local markets that have similar demand structures as the developed countries at least among a small elite or middle class (this market is often protected by high trade barriers), and second, to exploit locales that can serve as export platforms to reinforce the competitive position of the parent companies regionally and globally.

As for natural resource industries, FDI is largely driven by geology. But the understanding of FDI in these sectors also derives from the dynamics of imperfect competition (Moran 1974; McKern 1993). At the production stage, there are often barriers to entry, deriving from scale, capital intensity, technology of exploration and exploitation, and intangible assets associated with managing large complex engineering operations on time and on budget. At the same time, factors of scale, capital intensity, and processing technology subject players with high fixed costs at positions upstream and downstream from each other with sudden shifts in monopoly or monopsony power. With profitability extremely sensitive to variations in throughput, the parent firms resort to mechanisms of formal or informal vertical integration, ranging from sole ownership, to joint ownership of various stages, to long-term contracts for large volumes at slowly moving arm's-length price averages. Such mechanisms of formal or informal vertical integration help to insulate them from abrupt price gouging and large fluctuations in volume.

In both natural resources and manufacturing, oligopoly dynamics—including great circumspection about what international rivals are doing, caution about unilateral initiatives, and rapid matching moves to counter the initiatives of others—may figure prominently. Such oligopoly dynamics might show characteristics of deterrence, preemption, retaliation, and hostage exchange (Knickerbocker 1973; Graham 1978, 1996b).

What does the evidence suggest about market structure and FDI? Looking first at the industries in which FDI originates, measures show that imperfect competition is pervasive. There is a strong correlation between high concentration ratios and outward investment for the United States, the United Kingdom, France, Germany, Sweden, and Japan. Outward investment is found in industries in which there are large economies of scale and high advertising and technology intensity (Caves 1996; Frischtak and Newfarmer 1994).

Turning to market structure in the developing-country economies that receive incoming FDI, there is again pervasive evidence of a correlation between market imperfections and FDI (Dunning 1993b; Lall 1978; Blomstrom 1986; Willmore 1976; Connor 1977; Rodrik 1988). In eight regressions using Mexican data, Blomstrom and Persson (1983) found that the foreign firms' ownership of productive capacity in the local market was highly correlated with a Herfindahl index of market concentration. In a similar study on Brazil, Newfarmer and Marsh (1992) also found a high correlation between foreign ownership and industry concentration. Earlier studies of Mexico and Brazil showed that 84 percent of foreign subsidiaries in Mexico and 83 percent of foreign subsidiaries in Brazil were in industries where four-firm concentration ratios exceeded 50 percent, and 21 percent of the foreign subsidiaries in Mexico and 58 percent of the subsidiaries in Brazil were in industries where the four-firm concentration ratio exceeded 90 percent. There are similar correlations between market concentration and foreign-firm presence in Peru, Chile, Colombia, Central America, and Malaysia.

In short, theory and evidence indicate that FDI takes place in a setting with many of the characteristics of the malign model. Such a setting carries threats and dangers, as well as opportunities, for host-country development in the developing countries and economies in transition. At the same time, those characteristics of imperfect competition that are so worrisome indicate that FDI may feature rents (including high profits and high wages), access to privately controlled activities (including technology, marketing, and best management practices), and potential spillovers and externalities that are of high value to host economies.

This is the precarious position in which host authorities find themselves as they try to design policies toward foreign investors with the aim of generating rapid growth and higher standards of living for their populations. What are the most likely results?

There have been three principal attempts to provide an aggregate net assessment of the contribution of FDI to national incomes in the developing world. They offer a useful background for examining host country policy options in the subsequent chapters.

Three Earlier Net Assessments of the Impact of FDI on Development

These three studies cover 133 projects (principally manufacturing, agribusiness, and natural resource processing, rather than mineral or petroleum extraction) in more than 30 countries, plus some 50 proposed projects in one country, over more than 15 years. The studies were undertaken under widely different auspices and with widely different starting perspectives, yet they came to remarkably similar conclusions.

In a study for the United Nations Conference on Trade and Development (UNCTAD), Lall and Streeten (1977) examined 88 foreign-owned and locally owned projects operating in 6 countries, using cost-benefit analysis to calculate national-income effects. For two-thirds of the 88, foreign investment had a positive effect on national economic welfare; for the other one-third, it was negative. The key factor skewing the outcome in one direction or the other was the competitiveness of sales.

In a study for the OECD, Reuber (1973) led a team that analyzed a sample that comprised 45 foreign-owned projects in some 30 host countries. He compared the production costs of the subsidiaries to the production costs of the parents. While not set up explicitly like the study by Lall and Streeten (1977), his methodology approximated a social cost-benefit analysis that assumed that all inputs were valued at local market prices and all outputs were valued at world market prices. He found that over one-quarter of the subsidiaries had production costs that were equal to or lower than the production costs of the parents but that the remaining subsidiaries—almost three-quarters of the entire sample—had higher production costs. Again, the factor that determined whether the social benefit to the host country was positive or negative was the competitiveness of sales.

In a study for the Overseas Development Council, Encarnation and Wells (1986) calculated the contribution that 50 proposed FDI projects made to national income, at world market prices, minus the costs to the national economy, again at world market prices (frequently using shadow prices for labor, energy, foreign exchange, and domestic capital to reflect the opportunity cost of the resources to the domestic market). They found that a majority of the 50 projects (from 55 percent to 75 percent, depending upon the assumptions) would increase national income, while the remaining sizable minority (25 percent to 45 percent) would actually reduce the country's national income, even though they were profitable to the foreign investors that undertook them.

As in the previous two studies, the difference between positive and negative impact was not a close call: the results tended to be overwhelmingly positive or overwhelmingly negative. Once again, the difference came from the competitiveness of the markets in which the foreign investments took place, including the competitiveness of input and output markets, which were often influenced by host-country regulatory policy.

These aggregate studies provide three common conclusions. First, FDI may well have a clear, positive impact on development. In fact, as the evidence introduced in subsequent chapters demonstrates, these three assessments far understate the benefits (static and dynamic) that well structured FDI projects potentially can provide to host country development.

Second is an equally significant obverse observation, namely, that FDI can also have a demonstrably negative impact on the host's prospects for development (sufficiently negative that the host society would be better off not receiving the FDI at all). In fact, as evidence introduced in the subsequent chapters demonstrates, these three assessments far understate the direct damages to and lost opportunities for host-country development caused by ill-structured projects.

Third, a primary factor accounting for whether the impact is strongly positive or strongly negative is the extent of competition in the markets in which the FDI is embedded. In fact, as the evidence introduced in the subsequent chapters demonstrates, host actions in stimulating or retarding competition wherever foreign investors are located will constitute the most important determinant of whether the host benefits or suffers from the presence of foreign firms.

With a perspective toward FDI that highlights the possibility of substantial dangers as well as substantial opportunities, the next chapters turn to the design of specific host-country policies toward foreign investors.

II

Host-Country Policies to Shape Foreign Investor Activities: Investment Promotion, Domestic-Content Requirements, and Export-Performance Requirements

Introduction

The most important step that host governments in developing countries and economies in transition can take to foster their own development is to get the fundamentals right. In other words, they should provide a stable, noninflationary, micro and macroeconomic environment, with appropriate legal and regulatory infrastructure, that rewards both domestic and foreign investment.

Is there a need for further policies to attract foreign investors in the first place, induce them to enlarge the domestic content of their operations, and push them to export to external markets?

Is there rigorous justification for any intervention relating to FDI? What costs or dangers might result from inappropriate or ill-designed efforts to shape the activities of FDI?

The next four chapters analyze the efforts of host countries in the developing countries and economies in transition to influence the operations of FDI. Part III devotes two additional chapters to the efforts of host countries to control the ownership structure of foreign firms via joint-venture requirements and technology-licensing mandates.

2

Theoretical Considerations about Host-Country Intervention in Investment Promotion, Domestic-Content Requirements, and Export-Performance Requirements

Host-country interventions to influence the operations that foreign direct investors engage in carry an array of costs and risks. Do the benefits and opportunities outweigh these costs and risks? What might be the penalty for not intervening? What is the likelihood of being able to carry out appropriate interventions successfully?

This chapter raises theoretical considerations about host-country intervention that will help to illuminate the discussion in the subsequent three chapters on public-sector efforts to attract FDI, on the imposition of domestic-content requirements, and on the use of export-performance requirements.

Even so popular and seemingly benign an activity as investment promotion carries possible dangers for host countries. The expenditure of public revenues to try to attract FDI draws off resources from the rest of the economy, penalizing other industries and making them less competitive. To the extent that FDI promotion programs are selective and concentrated on particular sectors (if only for economy of effort), they lead to industrial-policy problems, placing the government in the position of trying to measure externalities and pick winners and losers better than the market would. FDI promotion programs may create distortions and introduce a rent-seeking dynamic into the economy and potential beneficiaries may use their political clout to influence the targeting process.

Turning to more complex and controversial efforts on the part of host authorities to impose domestic-content or export-performance requirements, the evaluation of public-sector intervention seems deceptively simple.

Under neoclassical assumptions of perfect competition, a host-country requirement that mandates a certain amount of domestic content on the part of foreign investors forces the local subsidiaries to substitute more expensive (by definition) indigenous goods and services for less expensive imports. Like any kind of trade barrier, this generates inefficiencies, diverts resources from more productive uses, raises prices, reduces consumption, and penalizes users and consumers. Protected from cheaper imports, the foreign firms in the sector with the domestic-content requirement may reap high rates of return, resulting in what Brecher and Diaz Alejandro (1977) identified as a special case of immiserizing growth, as foreign corporations siphon off excess profits at the expense of local consumers.

Within the neoclassical framework, a host-country requirement to export exacerbates the difficulties for the host economy. Because production costs in the local market must (by definition) be higher than world prices (or else domestic subsidiaries of foreign corporations would already be exporting on their own), a public subsidy must accompany the export requirement to render the operation viable. In effect, that subsidy levies an implicit tax on the rest of the economy, leaving other sectors less competitive and imposing a drag on the prospects for growth.

As for combining domestic content and export requirements in a trade-balancing strategy to bolster the balance of payments, Grossman (1981) and others (Davidson, Matusz, and Kreinin 1985; Herander and Thomas 1986; Rodrik 1987) have found that the domestic content mandate may reduce a country's export potential so much that it leads to a deterioration in the balance of payments.

In short, under neoclassical assumptions of perfect competition, the imposition of domestic-content and/or export requirements on foreign firms damages the prospects for economic development of the country that adopts them.

The relaxation of the assumption of perfect competition, within the domestic economy and within the industries where foreign investors reside, complicates the analysis considerably.

Infant-industry arguments have traditionally been based on the possibility that imperfections in local capital or labor markets might prevent would-be investors from demonstrating that local operations could in fact be successful. To compensate for such imperfections, according to infant-industry logic, public authorities should intervene to help firms to provide the needed demonstration effect; if the more efficient route of offering subsidies were not available, then trade protection could constitute an alternative.

But there has never been good evidence on how pervasive such hypothetical imperfections in local capital or labor markets might be. And, accompanying uncertainty about the need for public-sector intervention, questions about implementation of an effective infant industry strategy have loomed large: how might a government decide which industries to offer special treatment and which to ignore (leaving the latter to bear the penalty of preferences for the former)? How might the selection process be insulated against capture by special interests? And how could infant industries dependably be pushed toward maturity, so that they shed their need for public support promptly rather than remaining in diapers indefinitely?

Strategic-trade theory gives new life to traditional arguments about intervention on behalf of foreign-investment-driven infant industries. The strategic-trade framework, in contrast to neoclassical analysis, assumes imperfect competition, with barriers to entry into the industry that include increasing returns to scale and that generate rents for the participants (Brander and Spencer 1983; Krugman 1986). Such rents may sometimes emerge in the form of higher than normal profits, but more often they show up in terms of high wages and benefits and strong research and development expenditures (Katz and Summers 1989). The prospects for externalities, that is, spillovers that provide benefits to the domestic economy that exceed those that can be captured by investors themselves, are favorable.

Once such imperfectly competitive industries are in place, the possibility of dynamic learning emerges, giving a purely historical advantage on which to base further growth. "Indeed, by focusing on learning effects," observes Rodrik (1988), "the new literature has provided some of the best arguments for infant-industry protection since Alexander Hamilton and Friedrich List."

Under strategic-trade conditions, relative production costs may still play an important role in the locational decisions of international companies. But the absence of perfect competition means that the pressures that might push firms along the path of international comparative advantage are much less strong and deterministic than the neoclassical model indicates. Imperfect competition provides firms a measure of leeway and discretion on where to locate their activities; they can behave as satisficers rather than profit maximizers. Exactly where international investors choose to produce and the consequent arrangement of trade among nations are not exogenously determined. A semirandom overlay of scale-economy specialization may diverge significantly from the broader structure of international comparative advantage.

In these circumstances, the possibility of capturing a share of the rents and externalities raises the stakes for those authorities who are successful in attracting (or retaining) FDI in their countries and imposes large opportunity costs on those who are not successful or who do not take part in the competition for investment.

Strategic-trade-type competition for international investment requires a broad canvas: investment policy cannot be artificially isolated from grants, subsidies, special tax treatment, and other locational incentives or from investment-distorting aspects of trade policy.

But the rationale for activism embedded in strategic-trade theory is matched by equally powerful caveats about the dangers: whereas under imperfect competition the outcome from public intervention cannot be assumed to be automatically distortionary and harmful, neither can it be assumed to be beneficial or welfare enhancing. Improperly constructed public policies, especially those that perpetuate exclusivity and protection from competition, may have a disproportionately malign impact on the potential for growth and development (Richardson 1989).[1]

Moreover, strategic-trade theory does not allow host-country authorities to escape from the dilemmas already identified in the more traditional infant-industry arguments: How can these authorities choose which industries to target (because rents and externalities are notoriously difficult to isolate and detect)? How can they ensure that the benefits from encouraging the movement of resources into favored sectors outweigh the drag on the rest of the economy? How can they ensure that industries launched with special help subsequently "grow up" to competitive stature instead of remaining dependent on public support? And how can host authorities prevent special interests from capturing the process by which industries are selected to receive special support?

Finally, there are adverse systemic implications to consider. Strategic-trade theory introduces a disturbing zero-sum dimension into the usual win-win structure of trade and investment policy. Strategic-trade theory not only opens the door to rigorous justification for action to influence the decisions made by international firms but also suggests that countries that intervene most aggressively will benefit at the expense of those that do not. How can these beggar-thy-neighbor dynamics—in which all actors are likely to end up worse off—be muted or eliminated?

The dangers of misusing strategic-trade analysis—and the fear that strategic-trade rhetoric could easily be used by special interests seeking protection or privilege for themselves—has introduced considerable wariness into debates about the design of public policy in the developed world. As for developing countries and economies in transition, as one analyst has quipped, perhaps discussion of strategic-trade theory should be stamped "'classified' as 'for economists' eyes only" until we have time to assess the full implications" (Yarbrough 1988).

To what extent, then, should strategic-trade-type calculations influence the design of public policy toward FDI in the developing countries and the economies in transition? To anticipate the analysis that follows in the next four chapters, mild host-country efforts to engage in investment promotion can be justified on the basis of asymmetries and imperfections in information markets, without need to appeal to strategic-trade-policy considerations. But transforming the marketing aspects of investment promotion into hefty grants, subsidies, and incentives as part of the

---

1. Richardson finds that losses in efficiency from constraints on trade are two to three times higher under conditions of imperfect competition than under perfect competition.

promotional package can trap participants in a strategic-trade-like rivalry to influence the externality-rich sourcing patterns of multinational investors. Such rivalry may leave all players—in particular host governments in the developing countries and economies in transition—worse off.

Turning from investment promotion to local-content mandates, the still-popular idea of imposing domestic-content requirements on foreign investors, in contrast, finds little support on infant-industry grounds, strategic-trade grounds, or any other grounds.

The assessment of export-performance requirements, however, poses a much more complicated challenge. Export-performance requirements turn out to have played an important role in correcting for market imperfections and in offsetting locational distortions during the globalization of the major manufacturing sectors examined here—to the benefit of global as well as specific host-country welfare. They have become a tool in the competition for world-scale-sized plants that does fit well—all too well— within the strategic-trade framework, with complex and ominous policy implications for all concerned. A specification of the conditions under which their use might be abandoned by developing countries and economies in transition requires quite careful examination, with consideration of how to eliminate other sources of distortion simultaneously.

3

Foreign Firms and Host-Country Investment Promotion

Investment promotion has come to occupy a prominent place in the development strategies of developing countries and economies in transition. Since 1991, 58 more nations have begun to undertake proactive approaches to attracting FDI, making a total of 116 countries that now do so.

To what extent are proactive efforts necessary? Leaving aside (for now) the question of providing grants and subsidies directly to foreign investors, why should hosts have to expend resources on promotional activities per se? Cannot host countries rely on international market forces to drive foreign investors to them?

The predominant justification for investment promotion comes from the demonstration of positive results. There is a long-held belief that would-be host countries that adopt an energetic approach to investment promotion are much more successful in attracting foreign firms than are those that do not.

To investigate this assertion with some rigor, Wells and Wint (1990) attempted to control for the most common variables that might influence FDI (GNP per capita, growth rate of GNP, inflation rate, survey rankings of political stability) to isolate the impact of a variable associated with investment-promotion effort on attracting FDI.

They discovered that the investment-promotion variable had a strongly significant statistical impact. Promotional efforts were highly cost effective, generating benefits with a net present value of almost four dollars for every dollar spent. Strongest in producing results were sector-specific investment missions that were guided by firm-specific research and featured customized "sales" presentations that matched the presumed needs of the target investors with the alleged ability of the particular host country to meet those needs. Much weaker in producing results were general advertising campaigns on behalf of the host country and general show-and-tell visits to major cities in the developed world. A concentrated proactive approach was particularly valuable for countries that had not been major hosts of FDI in the past or that were trying to change their image as they reformed their domestic policies. Still, investment-promotion activities generated high returns for all hosts that engaged in them.

What accounts for such a strong response? The Wells and Wint (1990) study likened investment promotion to a marketing challenge. It adduced no further evidence of market imperfections.

Relaxing only the most unrealistic of assumptions about perfect competition—instantaneous and cost-free acquisition of information by all parties—it becomes rational for a potential host, like any advertiser, to spend resources to expand demand for its product so long as the returns outweigh the costs. Moving deeper into possible imperfections in information markets, the host might want to differentiate its product, so to speak, as well.

How much effort should the host make, and what might be the prospects for success? To try to judge the effectiveness of expending scarce host-country resources on product differentiation, one might compare investment promotion to economic theories of search and signaling that embody poor indices of quality differentials among products (McKenna 1986). Models of search and signaling are frequently used to assess how job markets function: when workers do not have clearly defined degrees or certified skills, potential employers may regard all workers as being of the same poor quality and bid for their services at the same low level. Workers who believe they are superior in nonobvious ways have an interest, therefore, in expending resources to demonstrate that they have favorable attributes in comparison to their less appealing counterparts; seeking help in preparing a simple resume or soliciting recommendations from past employers are common examples.

By analogy, host countries may find it beneficial to show that they have superior characteristics to those of rival countries, to stimulate more interest among potential investors than those investors would have for the least attractive alternatives.

But firms also have an interest in ferreting out information that may provide them with an advantage over rivals. And, as part of search theory, investors, like employers, have an interest in developing screening devices to sort among potential prospects.

If the investment-promotion task could be limited to efforts at advertising and product differentiation and there were no larger issues of market failure or investment-diverting interventions by others to deal with, then potential hosts could accomplish these goals with only modest expenditure of resources and minimal potential for distortion.

In terms of providing information, the Multilateral Investment Guarantee Agency of the World Bank Group, for example, has established an internet system, the Investment Promotion Network (IPAnet), that offers host countries the opportunity to post economic statistics, legislation governing FDI, other laws and regulations, maps, accommodations, names of current investors and suppliers, and names of relevant officials (with hyperlinks). Innovations like this lower the foreigners' cost of search in comparing alternative investment sites and provide nearly real-time interactive follow-up via internet, email, fax, and telephone.

In terms of projecting a favorable image, Wells and Wint (1990) found that personal contact between host-country officials and individual companies had a substantially larger impact than did impersonal advertising (even advertising in highly visible and expensive outlets). Mixed investment missions, including satisfied private-sector representatives and ministry representatives from the host country, were particularly effective.

In terms of certification, the International Monetary Fund and World Bank Group already serve in this capacity. They are backed by private sector rating agencies such as Moody's and Standard & Poor's and by an array of consultants and evaluation services.

Even such modest efforts pose some threat of distortion to the would-be host country. But the penalty levied on the rest of the economy can be minimized by keeping the resources devoted to investment promotion small. And the dangers of industrial-policy "targeting" errors can be minimized by ensuring that nonpromoted sectors also enjoy investor-friendly treatment.

Many successful FDI projects do emerge independent of the planning of investment promotion agencies: Chilean investment teams concentrated on minerals, timber, fish, wine, and agricultural products; they did not suspect that Santiago would become a center for the development of financial services. Early investment teams from India focused on attracting foreigners to unskilled-labor-intensive assembly operations; they did not immediately assume that highly-skilled-labor-intensive sectors such as software development would be a magnet for foreign investors.

Absent larger justifications for investment promotion, therefore, host-country efforts at advertising and product differentiation could easily be kept within moderate limits. Developing countries and economies in transition would be well-advised to draw a clear line between spending small amounts of public funds for marketing purposes, even for intensive and proactive marketing purposes, and giving marketing teams sizable tax breaks, grants, subsidies, and preferences to bestow upon prospective investors.

In fact, the reverse has been the case: developed countries and developing countries alike have expanded the deployment of expensive incentives and preferences in the effort to attract FDI.

And, as evidence from the globalization of the automotive, petrochemical, and electronics/computer industries examined in later chapters shows, the rewards for a country that is successful in this endeavor can be much larger, and the opportunity cost for a host that lets the opportunity pass by also much larger, than Wells and Wint (1990) indicated.

How should host governments in the developing world and economies in transition respond to this competition for investment? Is the escalation in incentives and preferences that has become a central feature of investment promotion merely driven by the need to match the moves of others? Or are there larger signs of market failure that justify intervention on the part of hosts and would-be hosts in the developing world and the economies in transition? What are the "prisoners' dilemma" dimensions to this process? Finally, should host governments insist upon special performance from the foreign investors, such as high levels of domestic content or high levels of exports, in return for such investment incentives?

Addressing these questions is the task of the next three chapters.

4

FDI and Domestic-Content Requirements

Host governments have imposed domestic-content requirements on the subsidiaries of foreign investors to enhance "industrial deepening," augment "supplier creation," and multiply "backward linkages" in the hope of creating a reasonably vibrant, productive, and, ultimately, competitive indigenous industrial base. They frequently provide infant-industry rationales and sometimes offer sophisticated strategic-trade-policy justifications for these requirements. And almost always, they accompany domestic-content requirements with import restrictions. In spite of WTO obligations to phase out domestic-content requirements on FDI, the speed and transparency of compliance remain controversial and uncertain.

Are domestic-content requirements an effective developmental tool? Does the economic self-interest of host countries lie in prolonging their use?

Evidence about Domestic-Content Requirements

The empirical record of the contribution of domestic-content requirements to the economic development of the host countries that have adopted them, whatever the aim and whatever the purported justification, is decidedly negative.

A survey conducted under the auspices of the United Nations Centre on Transnational Corporations (1991) found high inefficiency and a pronounced tendency toward stasis in industries where hosts imposed domestic-content requirements: effective rates of protection ranged from

50 percent to more than 600 percent, consequent prices were 200 percent to 300 percent higher than the cost for comparable products outside the host country, the intensity of use of those products was reduced to much less than half of what might be expected by international standards, the net social contribution of the investor activities was sometimes far in the negative column, and there was little evidence of dynamic-learning effects or movement toward competitive status. Evidence from the automotive, petrochemical, and electronics/computer sectors demonstrates the adverse consequences.

In the automotive industry, Bale and Walters (1986) found that 16 countries that mandated domestic content from 18 percent to 100 percent on foreign operations with less than 100,000 vehicle-per-year output had to support those operations with ad valorem import tariffs averaging nearly 100 percent. In a classic study of the Indian automobile industry's experience with domestic-content regulations, Krueger (1975) calculated that 27 of 34 assemblers and associated suppliers received effective rates of protection above 50 percent, with almost half of the firms enjoying more than 100 percent protection (the highest figure, for a metal fabricator, was 642 percent). If the effective rate of protection had been limited to no more than 50 percent, Krueger calculated, value added in production would have increased by more than one third; instead, increasing costs and economic losses spawned more protectionist trade and foreign-exchange practices to prop up the uncompetitive plants.

In the petrochemical industry, Gray and Walter (1984) examined 15 representative FDI projects subject to domestic content or export-performance requirements. Two of the projects (in South Korea and in Pakistan) required local production for domestic markets too small to capture all available economies of scale. In each case, the host government awarded import protection and quasi-monopoly status to try to launch the projects successfully; in neither case did the effort lead to efficient and competitive operations. Instead, in both instances, there was a vicious cycle of increasingly intrusive host-government interventions. In the South Korean case, the foreign company, Dow Chemical, finally gave up and sold out.

In the computer/infomatics industry, Frischtak (1986) estimated that foreign computer producers in Brazil, operating with stringent domestic-content regulations and high import protection, charged prices two to three times higher than those charged outside the country (these calculations excluded the area of "market reserve" in Brazil, where FDI was excluded). This price differential resulted in computer use in Brazil that was approximately one-fourth the intensity of comparable experience elsewhere, with a particularly heavy drag on high-tech sectors of the Brazilian economy (Cline 1987).[1] Similarly, in India, government

---

1. Embraer, the aviation enterprise, became a vocal critic of the state's infomatics policies.

insistence on local production has a long history of hindering both the domestic expansion and export potential of foreign computer companies and other foreign investors in electronics.

Why are the results for host countries that try to use domestic-content requirements on foreign investors, backed by straightforward or hidden trade protection, so dismal in laying the base for internationally competitive industries?

Reasons for the Adverse Impact of Domestic-Content Requirements

Domestic-content requirements have an adverse impact not because labor and capital markets in host economies in the developing countries and economies in transition already function perfectly on their own, but because attempts to "improve" the functioning of markets by imposing domestic-content requirements on foreign firms generate technical, economic, managerial, and political-economic problems for the investors and for the host country. These problems interact in a perverse manner and tend to reinforce each other toward inefficiency and stasis rather than lead to some new level of dynamic learning, enhanced efficiency, or accelerated growth.

Perhaps the most prominent reason that domestic-content requirements have an adverse impact is that it is difficult for projects that do not capture full economies of scale to become globally competitive.[2] In the automotive sector, estimates of the optimal scale for an integrated auto plant, or the point at which additional cost savings from increased production fall off, hover around 200,000 units per year. The principal components also have large economies of scale: in the range of 200,000 to 450,000 units per year for engines and for power trains (Shapiro 1993). A survey of 16 countries with subscale automobile assembly operations, compiled by Bale and Walters (1986), found that domestic-content levels as low as 18 to 20 percent generated price differentials 1.5 to 2 times as high as the cost of imports. In the General Motors plant in Hungary, which produced 15,000 cars per year, Hungarian workers managed to win EU-wide intrafirm quality awards but could not reach output-per-day levels as much as one-tenth of full-scale operations in Antwerp (Klein 1995).

In petrochemicals, the cost penalty for operating subscale plants varies: it is highest in primary products such as ethylene, propylene, and benzene and intermediate organic derivatives and lower in downstream products such as fertilizers, pesticides, paints, and pigments (although

---

2. Eastman and Stykolt (1970) demonstrate that protection leads to excessive entry into a given industry and results in inefficient plant size.

scale factors in some synthetic fibers, synthetic rubber, and plastics are also large). In their survey of FDI in 15 petrochemical projects—involving primary, intermediate, and product plants—Gray and Walter (1984) found that scale of output was the decisive factor in the ultimate success of the operations.

Even in electronics/computers, where economies of scale are less important, Cline (1987) found that production of less than 50,000 microcomputers per year inflicted a penalty that accounted for some substantial portion of prices that were 2 to 3 times the international norm.

Besides the higher costs involved in subscale units, there are technical issues of whether boutique plants can become the building blocks for full-scale production facilities. In automobile assembly, plants that put together knock-down kits are sufficiently different from full-scale assembly as to require a completely new investment evaluation about whether to move to the latter rather than merely decide whether to add on. The prior existence of a small plant may actually constitute a hindrance in the selection process. Chemical and petrochemical plants can sometimes be installed in modular sequence to bring them up to full scale. Most often, this is an expensive way to expand in comparison to designing an operation that captures all economies of scale from the beginning. In the sample of Gray and Walter, the subscale plants did not transform themselves from infant-industry building blocks to a full grown competitive industry through dynamic learning. Two of the six projects came to be considered failures by the parent companies, and the prospects for the other four, absent on-going trade protection, were not favorable.

But failure to achieve economies of scale in production is only one aspect of the difficulties caused by domestic-content requirements. There is evidence of lags in the introduction of new technology to projects with high domestic-content mandates, independent of scale; that is, both for projects where economies of scale are large (autos) and where economies of scale are smaller (such as many segments of the electronics/computer industry), the pace of technological upgrading of local operations is slower than in countries/projects that lack domestic-content requirements.

Grieco (1984) found that the technological lag in the computer industry in India—measured as the interval between the introduction of a system in the developed countries and its adoption in the host country—was greatest when markets were highly protected, but fell steadily as authorities eased domestic-content requirements and import controls. Borrus (1994) found that Japanese electronics/computer firms met domestic-content requirements in East Asian markets with simple labor-intensive processes and lower-end assembly while US and European firms, more oriented toward production for external sale, upgraded both the products and the processes in their East Asian operations much more rapidly to match the pace of change in international markets (see also Guyton 1996).

Krause (1985) observed the same phenomenon in Latin America, where small-batch production of computers for the domestic market in Mexico involves hand soldering and old-fashioned (and more expensive) cabinets, while larger volume export operations utilize more automated, precise, and cheaper construction methods.

In the automotive sector, Doner (1995b) found similar delays in the introduction of new technology in the high-domestic-content (80 percent), highly protected Malaysian automotive market (although whether this was also due to the absence of the stimulus from international competition or to the requirement of operating with local Malaysian partners, is not clear).[3] There are similar reports from Latin America, where Ford, behind ad valorem tariff walls of more than 50 percent, produced the Falcon from the 1960s to the 1990s with 80 to 90 percent domestic content but very few design changes (*New York Times*, 16 May 1997).

In addition to delay in the introduction of more sophisticated technical processes, Ernst (forthcoming 1998) observes a lag in the utilization of more advanced management systems, including quality control circles and just-in-time inventory control.

Without economies of scale, cutting-edge technology, or best-practice management, the likelihood that there will be spillovers associated with the foreign investor's presence is not large. And, in marked contrast to cases in which domestic operations are part of the parent company's export-oriented, global sourcing strategy (introduced in chapter 5), the prospects for agglomeration effects of scope and specialization are not promising. In line with that, these FDI projects do not benefit from Krugman-Helpman interactions between final-goods and intermediate-goods suppliers that often form the basis for the construction of giant industrial complexes with abundant externalities for the rest of the economy.

The more clever strategic-trade negotiating strategies, which shift rents from foreign investors to host players, turn out in practice to be complex and arcane (Rodrik 1988; Davidson, Matusz, and Kreinin 1985; Richardson 1993). The end result is that foreign corporations, domestic firms, and a labor elite from the population at large receive trade rents created at great cost in terms of inefficiencies for the economy as a whole.

The Adverse Political Economy of Domestic-Content Requirements

At the same time, domestic-content requirements on the local subsidiaries of foreign firms introduce an adverse political-economic dynamic into

---

3. On lags in the introduction of new technology in joint ventures, see chapter 7.

the strategy of the external investors and open the door to fundamental conflicts with the host authorities.

The incentive structure for the foreign investor is skewed toward preserving a low-volume, high-profit position in the small protected market. The host authorities, having "captured" the foreign investor and "created" jobs, then try to correct the problem of high costs with further, more burdensome interventions. Gray and Walter (1984) found a vicious cycle in the 2 of 15 petrochemical cases that were oriented toward a protected domestic market rather than exports (in South Korea and Pakistan): foreign firms pushed for higher prices and higher profits while host authorities undertook increasingly intrusive countermeasures to fight inflation, monopoly, and "exploitation." In the South Korean case, the foreign company, Dow Chemical, which had been the country's largest single external investor, ultimately sold its holdings and withdrew (Schwendiman 1984). In the extreme, this "adverse" political economy may give foreign investors incentive to oppose a transition toward greater openness and economic liberalization rather than incentive to support such a transition.

As examined in detail in the next section, in the mid-1970s US automobile investors mobilized US government support to maintain their established positions in highly protected markets in Mexico and Brazil in the face of efforts by host authorities to push them toward a more global sourcing pattern. In East Asia, Japanese investors have routinely imposed export prohibitions on the operations of electronics and automobile companies set up to supply local markets, and, until the yen appreciation after 1985 forced a change in parent company strategy, these investors joined with domestic producers to preserve lucrative subscale operations oriented toward protected domestic markets. In Eastern Europe, a similar dynamic may be emerging as labor groups, political supporters, and, in some cases, foreign investors whose operations were originally oriented toward still-protected domestic markets, have pushed to delay reducing import barriers in the accession process with the European Union. In Hungary, Suzuki—intimating that it might call in a $134 million loan if its small assembly operations were exposed to competition—demanded higher customs duties on cars and a prohibition on importing used cars in 1993. Budapest responded with a ban on imports of cars older than six years. In Poland, Fiat successfully lobbied Warsaw in 1994 to levy excise duties of 15 percent on imported cars and 10 percent on domestic cars costing more than $12,000, leaving the under-$10,000 Fiat automobile untaxed. (For another example of the impact of domestic-content requirements on foreign investors, see box 4.1.)

In short, the imposition of domestic-content requirements on foreign investors—far from generating a dynamic learning process in which foreign subsidiaries, local suppliers, labor, and host authorities work together to grow from infant industry status to internationally competitive operations—contains multiple sources of breakdown and stagnation.

Box 4.1 Foreign investors, domestic content, and the political economy of protectionism: Apple and Hewlett-Packard versus IBM in Mexico

Mexico's negotiations with IBM for a major export-oriented investment in Mexico in 1985 constituted a turning point in Mexican informatics policy. In place of the prior import-substitution strategy, which required domestic production of mini and microcomputers by joint-venture firms (in subscale plants) with 25-35 percent local content, IBM presented a proposal offering full-scale production of 100,000-180,000 microcomputers, 90 percent of which were destined for external markets, in return for the right to operate a wholly owned venture with much greater control over its sourcing of inputs.

The debate about the IBM proposal and the decision by the Mexican government to accept it helped to precipitate the reorientation of the country's entire approach to trade and investment in a more liberal direction. What is less well known is that Hewlett-Packard and Apple helped wage the fight within the upper tiers of the Mexican political establishment against the IBM proposal and the policy opening that it represented.

Prior to the IBM proposal, mini and microcomputers were protected by import quotas, with local content rising from 25 percent (for minis) and 35 percent (for micros) in the first year to 50 percent and 60 percent by the third or fourth year (respectively). Apple had a market share of 58 percent, selling the Apple Iic-II with a markup 74 percent over the US price. Hewlett-Packard had a market share of 18 percent, selling the HP-150-II with a markup 61 percent over the US price. Production runs for computer assemblers ranged from a few thousand per year to perhaps as many as 15,000, all below minimum efficient scales that begin at 20,000 units annually.

The components produced in Mexico prior to the IBM venture included cables, resistors, keyboards, cabinets, and other passive components. Imported components included integrated circuits, hard disks, videos, and active components.

When the IBM proposal first surfaced, the domestic producers, including Hewlett-Packard and Apple, organized a special interest-group association, AMFABI, which took out ads in major newspapers and lobbied the Ministry of Commerce to block the IBM project. They argued that an investment of the size contemplated by IBM would crowd out existing producers and monopolize the market. They added that granting IBM wholly owned status was unfair to them, because they had complied with the requirement of minority foreign ownership. In a letter to President Miguel de la Madrid, AMFABI called for endorsement of the existing informatics regime.

Instead, President de la Madrid stood up to this opposition and approved the IBM proposal. Within a short period of time, both Hewlett-Packard and Apple, along with other foreign firms, reversed direction and approved investment-expansion packages large enough to meet three-to-one export-to-import requirements that qualified them to operate with wholly owned subsidiaries (Apple subsequently was unable to meet its commitments and had to withdraw). From this burst of new foreign investment, exports of computer parts, components, and finished equipment (including typewriters/printers by IBM) grew more than 10-fold over the next 4 years, from $21

(*continued on next page*)

million to $252 million, with IBM and Hewlett-Packard accounting for shares of approximately 60 percent and 20 percent respectively.

Allaying fears that the informatics sector in Mexico might become merely a screwdriver industry, the degree of integration in the sector increased, imports as a percentage of production dropped (IBM's domestic-content levels rose), and the technological sophistication of the components industry increased as the scale of production of final producers expanded. Within the domestic industry, competition intensified (multiple full-scale-sized producers that were oriented toward external markets prevented the much-feared monopolization of the domestic market by IBM), prices moved toward world levels (although the Mexican government did maintain a system of tariffs and quotas in the sector), and the technological lag between the introduction of new models/upgrades in the United States and deployment in Mexico shortened appreciably (to about 12 to 18 months).

Sources: Harvard Business School (1990); Cline (1987); Peres Nuñez (1990).

The operations they spawn systematically lack what the next chapter will describe as a kind of externality that comes with FDI operations that are integrated into the larger strategy of the parent firm, exposed to competitive pressures in international markets, and backed by the parent firm's commitment to provide the technological upgrading and quality control needed to enhance the corporation's position in international or regional markets.

But it would be a mistake to conclude that, absent domestic-content requirements, the FDI process will provide a smooth and appropriate allocation of local value added, industrial deepening, and technological and managerial spillovers to the developing countries and economies in transition along the lines of international comparative advantage.

To understand why this is not so requires a more detailed analysis of export-performance requirements and the problems of breaking into international markets via FDI in manufacturing.

5

FDI and Export-Performance Requirements

In light of past Asian successes with export-led growth and the reorientation of countries in Latin America and elsewhere toward the penetration of external markets, one might suppose that the imposition of export-performance requirements on foreign investors would fit well with the development objectives of host countries.

Further, once foreign investors are launched on an export trajectory, perhaps the key ingredient that was so frequently absent in the domestic-content-requirement-in-a-small-protected-market setting—full economies of scale—provides auspicious starting conditions for ongoing success.

But using export requirements to launch that export trajectory imposes a burden on other sectors of society that have to supply the resources and/or pay for the subsidy. And special treatment for foreign-owned exporters, like special treatment for domestic-owned exporters, opens the door to interest-group politics and rent seeking by those who want to get or keep privileges.

Why must host countries provide scarce resources and run the political-economic risks of rent seeking by special interest groups to force or entice international investors to engage in such export operations? Shouldn't the profit motive and self-interest of the foreign investor be sufficient, without the expenditure of public resources?

To begin to provide answers, this section looks in some detail at the three largest industrial sectors in which FDI has come to provide a channel for host countries in the developing countries and economies in transition to penetrate international markets—the automotive, petrochemical, and electronics/computer sectors.

Drawing out policy conclusions from the examination of these industries is a challenge: the evidence in these sectoral cases is dense, confidential, episodic, incomplete, and not structured with sufficient controls and precise comparisons to isolate the impact of export incentives/requirements from other influences on firm decision making. The individual industries differ among themselves in many ways, as do the processes by which they have spread, and are spreading, into the developing countries and economies in transition.

But despite these drawbacks, the examination of the globalization of these three sectors (automotive, petrochemical, and electronics/computers) provides important insights for less-developed countries and economies in transition about the difficulties of using FDI in manufacturing to penetrate international markets.

These investigations are the longest and most complicated in this book. The results are also the most surprising. The evidence presented here shows export-performance requirements playing a crucial role in pushing global corporations (against considerable resistance) to incorporate developing- and transition-economy sites into their international sourcing strategies. It shows forceful interventions on the part of host authorities leading to bursts of investment by major companies in each industry that generate exports sustained in the billions of dollars per year. It shows cumbersome combinations of carrots and sticks used to force exports helping (and often appearing necessary) to create new patterns of international production that enhance not only the welfare of the hosts that deployed them and the firms that obeyed them but global welfare as well.

Does this mean that export-performance requirements of the kind deployed in the automotive, petrochemical, and electronics/computer industries should now occupy a legitimate place in the policy toolbox of contemporary less-developed countries and economies in transition? Should their use of export-performance requirements be enlarged and rationalized, or should they offer to cut back and control the use of export-performance requirements as part of some larger package of policies to govern international investment?

To assess these policy choices requires moving beyond the examination of export-performance requirements per se, to ask three broader questions: First, how well do international markets work in apportioning FDI in line with comparative advantage? Second, what obstacles inhibit international markets from functioning more effectively? And third, what investment-diverting actions are other countries taking to shift the location of international manufacturing production in their own direction? These larger questions are the subject of the next chapter. Only after addressing them will it be possible to assess under what conditions host authorities in the developing countries and economies in transition might reasonably abandon the use of export-performance requirements altogether.

This chapter, on export-performance requirements, lays the groundwork, therefore, for the broader analytical investigations of market failure, investment-distorting interventions of other kinds, and, ultimately, the global strategic-trade struggle to attract international investment, which is the subject of chapter 6.

Before embarking on these great analytical investigations and trying to draw the implications for home, host, and collective public policy, it is necessary, first, to examine the interaction between export requirements and foreign-investor behavior in each of these three sectors in some detail—perhaps too much detail for some, doubtless not enough for others.

FDI and Exports in the Automotive Sector: Mexico, Brazil, and Thailand

Despite contemporary preoccupations with a "great sucking sound," "runaway plants," and a possible "hollowing out" of the industrial base—in which home-based firms presumably rush to set up production in lower-cost sites abroad—the task of enticing or pressuring the major automotive firms to establish export-oriented production facilities in Latin America and Southeast Asia turns out to have been, in retrospect, remarkably difficult.

The would-be hosts faced dedicated opposition from home-country labor, home-country governments (national and subnational), and, perhaps most surprisingly, from the parent corporations themselves. The economic and political-economic dimensions of this struggle continue today.

Automotive Investments in Mexico and Brazil

US and European automobile firms initially considered the idea of creating a competitive automotive industry in Mexico and Brazil completely far-fetched. They cited a long list of impediments to ever having successful operations, led by derogatory references to the culture and work ethic of the indigenous labor force ("siesta culture" in Mexico and "tropical influences" in Brazil) (Shapiro 1993).

Such characterizations persisted as long as subscale plants with high domestic-content requirements were the predominant form of production.[1] Mexico, with a smaller internal market, set the domestic-content

---

1. There is an interesting parallel evolution in the foreign firms' evaluation of obstacles to investing in Eastern Europe and the former communist states, whose populations are sometimes alleged to have lost their "work ethic" under socialism. For subscale protected

requirement in the 1960s and early 1970s at 60 percent, which allowed body stampings to be imported but required the power train (engines and transmission) to be manufactured locally. Brazil, with a larger internal market, set the domestic-content requirement at 90 to 95 percent, which meant that all the major components had to be produced internally.

In each country, however, as the size of the domestic market began to be large enough to support plants with full economies of scale, the costs and quality in manufacturing principal components at a number of individual sites began to rival or surpass home-country alternatives. Small levels of exports of automotive parts appeared in the mid-1970s, and within the corporate hierarchies of General Motors, Ford, Volkswagen, and Fiat, at least, there were advocates for export expansion from Latin America (Samuels 1990; Shapiro 1993, 1994; Bennett and Sharpe 1985). Engine plants in both countries showed cost advantages over production in Michigan, Ohio, and upstate New York.

The idea of expanding sourcing patterns to include lower-cost off-shore production sites became more urgent in the United States as Japanese imports put increasing competitive pressure on parent operations in the home country. Imports from Canada, Germany, and Japan had been growing steadily for more than a decade, but Japanese import growth started a double-digit climb after 1974 that did not flatten out until the mid-1980s (Nelson 1996, figures 3.12 and 3.15).

Rather than a smooth spread of international investment along lines of international comparative advantage, however, the notable feature of this period was in fact the stout resistance that the parent companies, in conjunction with home-country political authorities, mounted against the host-country desires for exports.

Some of the opposition was quite straightforward: organized labor in the United States, Germany, and Italy, for example, pressured the parent companies, local governments, and national governments to keep jobs in place. In this process, they used sticks as well as carrots. Sticks included German laws that forbade firms to relocate production if it resulted in layoffs, Italian government threats to withhold subsidized credit if Fiat moved production abroad rather than building new plants in the Mezzogiorno, and electoral and campaign finance penalties from the United Auto Workers in the United States for officials who failed to protect jobs. Carrots included what became a sharp escalation of investment subsidies in the United States, Canada, and Europe to maintain existing production sites or attract new investment.

---

plants, the workers appear substandard; but once workers from the same identical cultural background find themselves in full-scale export-oriented plants, they suddenly begin to win international intrafirm prizes for performance. See box 6.1 on General Motors' 1992 investment in Szentgotthard, Hungary.

Other aspects of the opposition are more opaque, in particular the motivation of the parent companies themselves. To be sure, within the firms there was bureaucratic opposition to global/regional sourcing strategies on the part of managers for whom such strategies posed a threat (e.g., from plants in Lima, Ohio, against imports of four-cylinder engines in the case of Ford and from plants in upstate New York, against imports of two-cylinder engines in the case of General Motors/Pontiac). But one strategic task of headquarters is to ensure that myopic managers do not jeopardize the long-term competitive position and profitability of the firm, a task all the more important as Japanese imports surged and "big three" market share dropped after 1974. There remain, therefore, important questions about the behavior of international investors, about possible market failures and appropriability problems, and about the welfare effects of delay in making what will be characterized as "irreversible investments under uncertainty" (which will have to be addressed later).

Foreign Investors and Global/Regional Sourcing from Mexico

Concerned about a growing trade deficit in the automotive sector, the Mexican government passed a resolution in 1969 and a decree in 1972 explicitly requiring that foreign auto firms increase exports. Exports grew from $26 million in 1970 to $122 million in 1975, but the auto trade deficit surged toward $1 billion.

Frustrated by the reluctance of the automobile investors to source more vigorously for the US market from across the border, Mexican authorities decided in 1977 to make access to the protected Mexican market contingent upon export expansion: they adopted a trade-balancing Trade-Related Investment Measure (TRIM) that established a foreign-exchange budget for each producer of finished vehicles, requiring that imports be matched with exports. Although the trade-balancing TRIM was much more cumbersome than what was becoming the norm for the industry in the developed countries—namely, multimillion dollar investment-subsidy packages, largely in the form of up-front grants, for plants whose scale was frequently larger than the market in which they were located (after 1977, the so-called "Irish model")—it generated a similar impact on the corporate bottom line, as the next chapter will show (Bond and Guisinger 1985).

In response, the US companies mounted a campaign within both Mexico and the United States, with a puzzling goal. Puzzling, because the campaign's objective was not to reshape the Mexican proposal to increase the credit toward the Mexican government's foreign-exchange requirement that they received from complying in those subsectors where production in Mexico already offered cost advantages nor to accede to Mexican export demands in return for augmented import liberalization in the automotive sector.[2] Instead, the US companies sought to pressure the Mexican government into abandoning the push for exports altogether.

Ironically, for students of comparative advantage, it was Ford—which had the longest and clearest record demonstrating the lower costs of producing engines in Mexico and which had a market share that was beginning to drop more precipitously than that of General Motors and Chrysler in the face of Japanese imports (Nelson 1996, figure 3.12)—that led the effort against the export requirements. Henry Ford II took his opposition to the Mexican program up personally with then-Secretary of State Cyrus Vance, then-US Ambassador to Mexico Patrick Lucy, and then-Mexican President Lopez Portillo. Ford prided himself on enjoying particularly smooth relations with the United Auto Workers (UAW) Union and bore the brunt of the UAW pressure not to invest further in Mexico.

Undeterred, Mexico persisted in using what carrots and sticks it possessed to prod the international automotive companies to expand exports.[3] The turning point in the parent companies' strategy came only in 1979, led by General Motors, not Ford. Weighing the appeals of senior managers who advocated "extreme" cost-cutting efforts so as to remain competitive with the Japanese in the US market against the opposition of entrenched parts producers to displacing established production sites (General Motors had the largest degree of vertical ownership of parts suppliers among the big three), General Motor's chairman finally sided with the former. The company announced its hitherto largest-ever one-time investment, the simultaneous construction of four new engine plants in Mexico, designed to expand exports from that country by a factor of 20.

With this break in the ranks of foreign-investor opposition to the Mexican export program, Ford, Chrysler, and Volkswagen followed suit within months, establishing export-oriented expansion plans of similar dimensions. Nissan joined them in less than a year.[4] The result was not

---

2. The US companies enjoyed the rents generated in the protected market; indeed, Chrysler's Mexican affiliate was then its only profitable subsidiary and, as a senior financial executive explained, the parent needed to protect this "cash cow" (Samuels 1990, 148).

3. It is not clear from the case studies of investment decision making in the auto companies to what extent the managers in the Mexican subsidiaries who knew the comparative cost structures in the two countries and who were lobbying the parent for expansion of the Mexican operations might have shared some of their knowledge with senior Mexican officials.

4. Mexico, like Brazil, consistently left the choice of exactly how to meet a subsidiary's export requirements up to the parent firms themselves, rather than insisting that fully assembled cars be sold abroad. This allowed the international companies to make their own calculations of comparative advantage, rather than having the specifics imposed

at all like the case of a small country using a few trade rents from import restrictions to subsidize the creation of inefficient export-oriented jobs within its borders. Instead, like the globalization of the petrochemical and electronics/computer sectors analyzed next, this change in Mexico (and a nearly simultaneous shift in Brazil) represented the beginnings of a vast restructuring in the international industry.

In engines alone, the new capacity in Mexico from this single burst of investment grew in less than three years (by end-1981) to more than one million units per year, with 80 to 90 percent destined for foreign markets. Overall, automotive export levels passed $1.5 billion per year in the first five years after the reorientation of foreign investor strategy, with direct employment of some 121,000 workers concentrated in three geographic areas (in the north, center-north, and center of the country). Wages and benefits in the collective labor contracts were among the highest in the country, second only to those of the large state-owned enterprises (Peres Nuñez 1990).[5] Outsourcing, as confirmed in subsequent studies by Feenstra and Hanson (1995a, 1995b), employs (comparatively) high-skilled workers in (comparatively) high-skilled jobs in the host country.[6]

The presence of the large auto investors stimulated complementary investments by foreign parts firms, of which Clark, Dana, and Eaton were the largest (Booz, Allen & Hamilton reported that Mexico's joint-venture requirement inhibited an even greater number of foreign component producers from setting up plants in Mexico).[7] The creation of backward linkages within Mexico was extensive: within five years, there

---

upon them by host authorities. This strategy helped make the Latin American experience more successful than similar efforts in Southeast Asia (especially Malaysia). See the case study of the difficulties of Malaysia's effort to launch a "national champion" car firm with exports of a national car in chapter 6.

5. More broadly, Aitken, Harrison, and Lipsey (1996) find that—after controlling for size, geographic location, skill mix, and capital intensity—foreign-owned firms pay higher wages than do domestic firms in Mexico (as well as in Venezuela and the United States). They argue that these wage differentials, together with productivity differentials, are consistent with greater human capital formation in foreign firms and with lower worker turnover. They highlight the importance of this evidence in the context of Lucas's argument (1993) that on-the-job training is by far the most important avenue for human capital formation and Grossman and Helpman's description (1991a, 1991b) of the linkage between on-the-job training and higher rates of growth.

6. Outsourcing is defined by Feenstra and Hanson as the share of imported intermediate inputs within industries. For criticism of this expansive definition, which mixes home-country firms that are merely shoppers abroad with home-country firms that operate factories as direct investors, see the discussion of the globalization of the computer/electronics industry later in this chapter.

7. In addition to citing the Booz, Allen & Hamilton study, Peres Nuñez (1990) reports interviews with companies making the same assertion.

were 310 domestic producers of parts and accessories, of which 110 had annual sales of more than $1 million.

The foreigners introduced industry best practices, such as zero-defects procedures and production audits, in weekly meetings with Mexican suppliers. Such behavior was clearly self-interested: one GM plant that featured coaching assistance for its suppliers achieved the lowest number of quality-related rejects in all GM operations worldwide, 1.7 percent, due in large part, in the judgment of one of the participating Mexican firms, to the technical assistance and team spirit that the subsidiary imparted during these sessions (Peres Nuñez 1990, 129-30). Such behavior also benefited domestic suppliers. The spillovers of export-related marketing expertise to domestic producers, for example, were impressive: an analysis of the 10 largest auto parts exporters in 1987 (excluding engines), which accounted for $461 million in sales and 59 percent of total auto-parts exports, found foreign ownership in only four of the firms (Booz, Allen & Hamilton in Peres Nuñez 1990).[8]

The evidence of externalities for the local economy from FDI in the automotive sector fits with the discovery by Aitken, Hanson, and Harrison (1997) that foreign manufacturing investors in Mexico, in general, act as export catalysts for domestic firms. They found that the probability of a Mexican-owned plant engaging in exports is positively correlated with its proximity to multinational investors but uncorrelated with the concentration of overall exporters. The externality between the presence of foreign plants and exports on the part of domestic plants is independent of proximity to international borders or to the capital city. They conclude that the export spillovers they observe must spring, directly or indirectly, from ways in which the foreign investors act as a conduit for technology, management, distribution services, and information about foreign markets (Aitken, Hanson, and Harrison 1997).

The combination of export-oriented foreign investors and export-oriented domestic suppliers gave rise to what might be considered a political externality as well: both groups exercised their political voice on the side of greater openness and less protection in the subsequent policy debates, which ultimately led to the revolution in liberalization after 1985.

With the automotive export base firmly established after 1979, Mexico has grown to become the largest developing-country exporter in this sector in the world, with exports of $14 billion and employment of 364,000 by the mid-1990s.

---

8. There is evidence that foreign investors helped local suppliers to become more productive and more sophisticated and helped them to penetrate external markets (Peres Nuñez 1990). The growth in exports from Mexican firms over time suggests a valuable feed-back loop in which contact with foreign buyers challenges the indigenous firms to enhance the competitiveness (price and quality) of their products. For a skeptical view of the learning-by-exporting hypothesis, however, see Roberts and Tybout (1997).

Foreign Investors and Global/Regional Sourcing from Brazil

In the Brazilian case, the shift of parent-company investment strategy toward incorporating host production sites that had originally been oriented toward domestic production into a global sourcing network was slightly less abrupt than in Mexico. Nonetheless, it illustrates many of the same dynamics of struggle between old and new, and developed- and developing-country production locations.

With a larger domestic market in Brazil, the attempt by the international auto companies to comply with early domestic-content requirements led to a larger number and greater array of full-scale-sized operations there than in Mexico. By the mid-1970s, there were plants turning out machined castings, forgings, transmissions, and engines more cheaply than could US and European sites. The result was a gradual buildup of exports, passing $200 million by the middle of the decade.

To try to stimulate exports further, Brazil launched the Special Fiscal Benefits for Exports (BIFIEX) Program. Under the program, foreign firms committed to specific dollar values for total exports and net foreign-exchange earnings. In return, they received one dollar of duty-free imports for every three dollars in exports. Federal and state value-added and sales taxes were waived on exports and turned into a credit that could be used toward tax obligations on production for the domestic market. (The BIFIEX Program was not unique to the automotive sector.) As in the Mexican case, the parent companies in the United States and Europe had to weigh the advantages of expanding exports from Brazil against pressures from labor and local political constituencies in the home countries to maintain production there. The tensions were particularly acute for Fiat.

For more than a decade, Fiat had been maneuvering between enjoying state support at home and asserting its independence abroad, a balance made particularly difficult in light of the demands of the Italian state to support regional development in the Mezzogiorno.[9] In 1976, lured by extensive infrastructure support from the state government of Minas Gerais (which wanted to develop its own industrial base as a counterpoise to Sao Paulo), as well as the BIFIEX incentives from the federal government, Fiat created its first wholly owned foreign subsidiary and its most extensive automotive investment outside Italy. Within five years, it exported 40 to 50 percent of production and became Brazil's largest private exporter.

This posed a threat to the domestic market shares of the other major auto investors, because BIFIEX allowances for duty-free imports might have enhanced Fiat's internal competitive position. To forestall

---

9. For background, see Prodi (1974) and Wells (1974). See also Bergsten, Horst, and Moran (1978, chapter 11) and Rogers (1979).

this eventuality, Volkswagen, Ford, and General Motors, within a 12-month period, each signed commitments to try to export $1 billion each over a 10-year period.

But once again, it was General Motors' decision to move toward global/regional sourcing in 1979 that triggered the actual "burst" of export-oriented investment that extended to all of the rest of the firms besides Fiat.

The cost advantages of producing engines in Brazil had become increasingly clear during the mid-1970s, and executives from General Motors do Brasil had been pressing headquarters for a more central role for their operations in the face of declining market share in the US market. But, as Shapiro (1994, 230) observed, "although internationally competitive production costs might be a necessary condition for a firm to begin exporting from a country, it is not a sufficient one."

As pressure to cut costs to try to compete with the Japanese in the US market intensified after 1974, supporters of export expansion in the General Motors do Brasil offices grew more vocal. They offered a double justification: the expansion of engine capacity in Brazil could be used both for export and for the introduction of the new J car series in the Brazilian domestic market (Chevrolet Cavalier, Opel, and Monza). They lobbied the Detroit headquarters without success, however, until 1979. Then, following closely upon the parent company's shift toward an international sourcing strategy in Mexico, the company decided to produce engines for its US Pontiac division in Brazil.

The other producers expanded export-oriented operations in step. Ford, like General Motors, concentrated on producing engines and other components in Brazil.[10] Fiat and Volkswagen, in contrast, began to use Brazil as a site for sourcing finished vehicles, with the former exporting back to the home market in Italy and the latter exporting the Beetle and other models to developing-country markets. Over the next three years alone, the value of automotive exports jumped by a factor of three, to $1.5 billion.

The inclusion of Brazil in the global sourcing strategies of the parent firms had a favorable impact on unit costs and on quality control, similar to the Mexican experience. Within four years of the inception of the new export-oriented investment programs, the World Bank found that the prices of Brazilian auto parts and vehicles were on balance competitive with or below those of comparable products elsewhere. At the same time, with fewer restrictions on foreign ownership than Mexico, Brazil gradually built up a larger and more sophisticated supplier network of both foreign and domestic participants. By 1988, automotive exports approached $3 billion.

---

10. Ford faced protests about its expansion of production in Brazil not only from the UAW union in the United States, but from European unions as well (Shapiro 1993, 220).

General Motors began to rank several of its Brazilian plants as having the highest productivity in the company's entire portfolio of operations. Helped, not hurt, by import liberalization in the automotive sector after 1990, Brazil climbed to 10th in the world in vehicle production by the middle of the decade and stood poised to move higher with $12 billion in new investment.

Foreign Investors and Global/Regional Sourcing from Thailand

In Southeast Asia, the obstacles to using foreign firms to penetrate international markets in the automotive sector were even more formidable than in Latin America and contained some novel elements.

Japanese automobile firms insisted that their investment agreements throughout Southeast Asia contain explicit export restrictions, a phenomenon Borrus, Ernst, and Linden also record for Japanese firms in the electronics/computer sector and Frank (1980) has found for Japanese and European firms in other industries as well.[11]

In the hierarchical and centralized Japanese decision-making structure, moreover, there is no documented analogue to the bureaucratic aggressiveness of regional managers eager to expand exports even if it meant displacing established production at home, as discovered by Samuels (1990) and Shapiro (1993, 1994) within the US and European auto companies in Latin America.

Finally, there were numerous alliances and joint ventures among the principal Japanese auto investors in Southeast Asia, reinforcing the solidarity among them. This type of arrangement was largely (not totally) absent among the big three and their European and Japanese rivals in Latin America.

At the same time, however, Southeast Asian markets gave smaller Japanese companies (Isuzu, Mazda, and Daihatsu) a chance to steal a march on the larger firms (Toyota, Nissan, and Mitsubishi), and host efforts to stimulate rivalry among them, when successful, have proved as potent in stimulating matching moves as were similar efforts in Mexico and Brazil. Thailand provides the clearest example of a host using such rivalry to break out into international markets (for contrasting evidence on Malaysia, which was not as successful in breaking into international markets, see box 8.1 on that country's attempt to create a "national champion" car company as an exclusive joint venture with Mitsubishi).

As in other countries, Thailand's development strategy for the automotive sector focused first on generating employment via domestic-content requirements in the late 1970s and early 1980s, ranging from 45

---

11. For an analysis of Japanese investment in the electronics/computer sector, see Borrus (1994), Ernst (1994), and Linden (1996).

percent to 62 percent for passenger cars and light/heavy trucks. Even as operations grew large enough to begin to capture economies of scale in production, however, exports by Japanese firms remained practically nil (less than $10 million per year in the same period that Mexican and Brazilian exports of auto parts were surpassing the multibillion dollar mark), partly because of Japanese claims of inferior quality on the part of Thai producers (Doner 1991).

The miniboom of exports in the automotive sector in the early 1980s began, in fact, with indigenous firms (not Japanese investors) penetrating international markets, first with simple products such as oil tanks and radiators, then more complex items, such as wiring harnesses, brake drums, stamping dies, jigs, and molds. These exports, and achievement of OEM status by some Thai firms that became suppliers to external buyers, undermined the Japanese assertions that Thailand was incapable of generating products of sufficient quality and reliability for international use.

The resolution of the battle between the Thai government and Japanese manufacturers over the construction of diesel-engine plants for one-ton pickup trucks launched Thailand as a major export platform in the automotive sector. Manufacture of the engines for these small trucks required plants with economies of scale too large for domestic consumption alone. Output, consequently, had to be incorporated into the regional/global supply network of the builder. In 1985, as in the earlier Mexican case, Thai authorities used a combination of carrots and sticks to prod the Japanese parent companies. Lacking funding for grants of the kind that were becoming increasingly prevalent in the investment promotion packages of the developed countries, the carrots included tax breaks plus reduction in domestic-content requirements for the firms that built diesel engine plants. The sticks included limiting approval to three projects in a market dominated by four principal foreign investor groups (three Japanese and one European).

The result was unprecedented rivalry among the four (even "home-based" Toyota, the firm most opposed to global sourcing) (Doner 1991, 216).[12] All four submitted bids that included large new export commitments, and, ultimately, Thai authorities allowed all four to build plants. From the resulting inflow of investment came a rush of externally directed production: automotive-sector exports from this first round of outward-oriented projects rose by a factor of eight over the next five years, approaching $2.5 billion annually.

As in the cases of Mexico and Brazil, the backward linkages from the major auto investors have been large and the spillovers in performance

---

12. As Doner points out, this competition among the four investor groups, and the consequent commitment of each to export expansion, took place *prior* to the Plaza Accord of 1985 with its subsequent exchange-rate incentive for Japanese producers to move production to lower-cost sites offshore (see also Lim and Fong 1991).

and quality to domestic Thai firms extensive. Seventy-nine Japanese investors in auto components and parts followed the principal firms into the market (more than twice as many as in Indonesia, Malaysia, Singapore, or the Philippines) (Doner 1995a). As in Mexico, were it not for a requirement that foreign firms find a local partner rather than set up wholly owned subsidiaries, the numbers might well be higher (for more details, see chapter 7). The pace at which the foreign parents introduced new technology into products and processes oriented toward external markets turned out to be faster than that for purely domestically oriented operations.

The Japanese parent companies were particularly active in organizing "cooperation clubs" of the kind that are widespread in Japan to enhance quality control, product improvement, cost reduction, scheduling and delivery, and technical performance among suppliers (Institute of Developing Economies 1995). Within 10 years, 150 local firms qualified as OEM components producers; fewer than half of these firms (67) included any Japanese FDI in the plants. Forty-two of the wholly owned Thai firms received technical assistance from Japanese buyers. The remaining 41 wholly owned Thai companies acquired OEM certification on their own (Institute of Developing Economies 1995, 19-20, table 4). An additional 200 to 250 Thai firms qualified for REM status.

With the decision by the Japanese parent firms to make a dedicated shift toward a regional sourcing strategy came a political-economic "externality" as well: it altered the way in which the Japanese firms wielded their political clout in the host-country and international arenas. Once launched beyond the borders of protected individual markets, the Japanese auto firms became a force for an Association of Southeast Asian Nations (ASEAN) complementation scheme, which was initiated in 1988.

Export-Performance Requirements for Foreign Investors and Global Sourcing in the Automotive Sector: A Preliminary Assessment

The behavior of the auto firms examined here introduces some puzzles about the role of price signals in the FDI decision-making process. Why were the companies so sluggish in responding to cheaper cost-production opportunities, especially for engines, even as evidence that it was in their interest to do so became clearer and clearer and even as the need to cut costs in the home market grew after 1974?

Part of the explanation must come from the political pressures applied by labor leaders and elected officials in the home country. These political pressures were reinforced by economic inducements as well, in particular the sizable buildup in developed-country locational incentives over this period. As documented in the next chapter, from the late 1970s into the mid-1980s, 9 of the European Community (EC) members, Canada, and 37 US states began to offer significant assistance to attract new investment or retain existing facilities, with grants in the EC case reaching up to 60 percent of the cost of the project. The automotive sector has been the leading recipient of such locational incentives in the developed countries.

Even independent of such incentives, some hesitation about reorienting corporate strategy and changing production patterns is quite rational: firms want to minimize lump-sum start-up expenditures and exit costs and they may value delay as they gain more information (as Dixit-Pindyck models of "irreversible decisions under uncertainty" predict—see chapter 6).

But it is hard to conclude that the firms would have been better off, or that global welfare would have been improved, if the Mexican, Brazilian, and Thai authorities had not intervened with their export-performance requirements—cumbersome though they were—to jump-start the outward-oriented investment process. The extent to which firm calculations of firm welfare and objective calculations of global welfare diverge will receive further scrutiny after data from the petrochemical and electronics/computer industries are added to the debate.

Moreover, the pattern of great hesitation about making new investments, followed by rapid follow-the-leader behavior in all three countries (Mexico, Brazil, and Thailand), demands careful examination for signs of market failure, in particular, signaling difficulties (asymmetric information) and appropriability problems.

As for the stakes in attracting world-scale-sized plants, the globalization of the automotive sector provides a first look at three kinds of benefits to hosts such as Mexico, Brazil, and Thailand that are successful in triggering a burst of export-focused investment—the provision of rents and externalities, the generation of agglomeration effects, and the creation of political-economic interest groups favoring further liberalization.

As evidence of the rents and externalities found in imperfectly competitive industries, the international companies paid relatively high wages, offered relatively high benefits, and provided training to highly mobile managers and workers. They formed strong backward linkages to domestic suppliers and generated spillovers in the form of coaching to domestic firms about management practices, quality control, and export marketing. They brought with them second tiers of foreign investors who did the same. Their contribution was dynamic: the hard-won strategic decision of the international automobile companies to integrate a given set of Mexican, Brazilian, and Thai production sites into their global/regional network carried with it a dynamic commitment to keep technology, management, and quality at the cutting edge needed for the parents to compete in international markets. The age of the technology employed was on the order of one-third more recent than any other method of acquiring such technology (Doner 1991, 1995b; Mansfield and Romero 1980; Blomstrom and Kokko 1997; Blomstrom, Kokko, and Zejan 1992).[13] The value of this "parental supervision"—of this "integration effect"—will become even more evident in the petrochemical and electronics/computer studies that follow.

The evidence on agglomeration effects is not sufficiently detailed to judge for sure whether scope, scale, and specialization are extensive enough to qualify as Helpman-Krugman "industrial complexes" and "economic poles," although the aggregate size of the automotive sector in Brazil (10th largest in the world), in Mexico (largest auto exporter among the developing countries), and perhaps in Thailand ($6 billion output) suggests so. There are overlapping economies of scale in assembly, in components (engines, chassis, drive trains, brakes, and ignitions), and in related supplier industries (steel, glass, tires, and electronics). The subsequent economic geography of Monterrey, Matamoros, Sao Paulo, Minais Gerais, and Bangkok can hardly be separated from the hosts' breakthroughs in provoking General Motors, Ford, Chrysler, Nissan, Fiat, Volkswagen, Toyota, Mitsubishi, Isuzu, Mazda, and Peugeot to make the decision to set up export facilities.

Finally, there was the political-economic "externality" of putting into place powerful actors with a major interest in further liberalization of trade and investment and with the political clout to help bring it about.

But the battle to secure the spread of export-oriented facilities along the lines of international comparative advantage was not "won" in the course of the cases examined here. The developed countries have launched a counterattack against the globalization of the automotive sector with the increasingly vigorous use of locational subsidies, whose value per job created (as documented in chapter 6) has climbed more than 10-fold over the past decade and a half. In addition, the effort to influence the placement of automotive facilities has been reinforced by manipulation of rules of origin and antidumping actions, which will feature prominently in the next studies of the petrochemical and electronics/computer industries.

FDI and Exports in the Petrochemical Sector

Despite the ostensible differences between the automotive and the petrochemical industries, the globalization of these two sectors demonstrates similar challenges to would-be host countries that wish to insert themselves into the global sourcing arrangements of the international companies that dominate each sector.

---

13. See the detailed discussion in chapter 7.

The analysis of FDI patterns in petrochemicals also introduces one prominent new tool in the struggle to maintain old or capture new productive capacity around the world, namely, the use of antidumping regulations as a protectionist and investment-shifting mechanism. These regulations are deployed more frequently in petrochemicals than in any other industry, and their impact will reappear in the examination of the electronics/computer sector that follows.

The petrochemical industry emerged between World War I and World War II as oil and natural gas began to supplement coal tar as a raw material for organic chemicals. The industry consists of three stages: primary building-block petrochemicals such as methanol, ethylene, propylene, butadiene, and benzene; intermediate petrochemicals, comprising more than 100 more complicated organic derivatives; and petrochemical products, such as synthetic fibers, fertilizers and pesticides, paints, pigments, plastics, and synthetic rubber.

During World War II, the demand for synthetics that could substitute for natural materials, especially rubber, led all the major industrial states to take an active role in financing the buildup of a domestic petrochemical industry. After the war, the United States government sold its facilities, already embedded in infrastructure, to private companies. European and Japanese authorities assisted in rebuilding the petrochemical industries in their countries. Along with aerospace and steel, public-sector actions have made the location of the petrochemical industry among the most "path driven" of all sectors.

The petrochemical industry is one of the most capital- and energy-intensive industries in the world, with economies of scale larger than in the automotive sector: gross capital stock per employee is more than three times that of the manufacturing average and typical capacity in a contemporary ethylene plant is 300,000 to 400,000 tons of output per year (Chapman 1991; Chemical Manufacturers Association, *U.S. Chemical Industry Statistical Handbook*, 1996). Historically, there has been a comparative advantage for locations where availability of capital, infrastructure, and natural gas converged, including the United States, Canada, the United Kingdom, Holland, and parts of the former Soviet Union. Natural gas provides methane, ethane, and propane, which must be shipped under pressure and/or at low temperatures if the petrochemical facilities are not contiguous. Absent natural gas, the colocation of petrochemicals and oil refineries—in which naphtha that is generated as a byproduct of producing gasoline can substitute as a feedstock—has provided alternative production sites in Europe and in Japan.[14]

---

14. While both naphtha and natural gas/ethane prices vary as a function of crude-oil prices, Chapman (1991, 174-75) shows that ethane prices have tended to be lower, giving petrochemical producers relying on natural gas an advantage.

Until the oil crisis of 1973-74, national-security concerns about denial of supplies in time of war tended to predominate over the search for scale efficiencies and the minimization of transportation costs in the location of production. Twelve of the fourteen European nations provided support for private or state-owned operations after the end of World War II. In many cases, they supported small-scale plants that proved particularly vulnerable to international competition in subsequent years (Bower 1986). Prior to 1974, the distribution of production reflected a desire to maintain petrochemical operations close to final markets: a survey of 537 plants producing the 9 most widely used petrochemical products in 1974 showed that 536 of them were placed to supply nearby industrial consumers, with subsidies and tariffs used to compensate for size and transportation penalties. Only one plant, in Trinidad, was built outside of the industrial world to optimize on scale and transportation savings, utilizing indigenous crude oil as an input and exporting to the United States (Stobaugh 1988).

FDI in Export Facilities in the Hydrocarbon-Rich Countries

The internationalization of the petrochemical industry came in two waves, the first after the oil crisis of 1973, the second after the oil-price surge in 1981. Hydrocarbon-rich host governments, led by Saudi Arabia, Iran, Indonesia, Venezuela, Mexico, Algeria, and Canada, insisted that more value added be created near the source of supply, via new petrochemical investments on the part of oil and chemical firms. Their carrots included cheap natural gas, public expenditure on surrounding infrastructure, and (occasionally) preferential access to petroleum output. Their sticks included reduced access to petroleum and the threat of bestowing what favors they had on rival firms. Their strategy relied on savings in feedstock and transportation costs, with a sudden availability of capital from the oil boom, to make up for weakness in the third variable (infrastructure)—taking full advantage of economies of scale in the process.

This assertiveness on the part of the new petrochemical hosts (old hosts to oil/gas companies) generated the beginnings of a massive redeployment of investment in the industry. In 1978, the Fluor Corporation calculated that new petrochemical plants worth a total of some $14 billion were concurrently under construction in developing countries (*The Wall Street Journal*, 19 September 1978). Chapman (1991, chapter 9) identifies Shell, Exxon (oil companies with large positions in the petrochemical industry), Dow, ICI, and BASF as leaders in the internationalization of the industry, but the participation in new ventures near the sources of supply was so broad as to make identification of first movers and followers difficult. Stobaugh (1988, chapter 9) reports that 18 new plants to produce 9 basic petrochemicals were launched between 1974 and 1985 in locales where they could optimize savings in feedstock and transportation costs, in marked contrast to the single such plant in existence prior to 1974.[15] Of these, 14 were plants for converting hard-to-transport methane to methanol, accounting for approximately half of the 27 methanol plants built in the noncommunist world during this period.

As a result, the share of noncommunist world methanol capacity built to serve export markets grew from negligible amounts to 45 percent. Looking at both ethylene and methanol production complexes, the largest gainers were Canada, the Persian Gulf (in particular Saudi Arabia), Indonesia, Mexico, and Singapore, where ethylene prices were roughly half those in the United States and one-third those in Europe and Japan and where methanol prices were roughly one-third those in the United States and close to one-fourth those in Europe and Japan (US International Trade Commission 1983).[16] In a detailed study of the economics of plants in two of these areas (Saudi Arabia and Mexico), Gray and Walter (1984) calculate that world welfare as well as host welfare was improved by the new investments because the natural gas inputs (which otherwise would have been flared or reinjected in the fields) were provided at a cost of collection that included an appropriate return on the capital employed. The findings of Gray and Walter are supported by Chapman (1991).

Once the fundamental building blocks of primary petrochemicals began to be set in place, engineering synergies and interlocking economies of scope/scale followed. The economics of cracking operations are much more favorable if a full range of coproducts can be fully produced for subsequent commercial sale. Once the parent firm makes a strategic decision to commit to the initial investment, argues Chapman (1991, 134), there follows "a momentum of development which tends to promote further agglomeration in massive industrial complexes." Stobaugh (1988, 138-43, table 9.1) identifies two chains of interlocking products, in particular, that have come out of the installation of new capacity near the sources of supply. From methane—the most expensive feedstock to transport—comes methanol, ammonia, urea, and finally fertilizers, which have higher levels of value added and larger transportation savings at each stage. More than a dozen such methanol-ammonia-urea-fertilizer complexes were constructed in the hydrocarbon-rich countries during this initial period of globalization. From ethylene—the next-most expensive feed-

---

15. Even for more advanced products made from these ingredients, transportation costs may be a large fraction of a product's value; they are 40 percent of the final price of vinyl chloride, for example, based on a trip across the Pacific.

16. Chapman (1991, chapter 8) presents a survey of relative feedstock cost estimates that suggests even larger advantages for hydrocarbon-rich developing countries. This advantage continued after the fall in oil prices in the mid-1980s. In all cases, the United States falls in the mid-range of input costs, with Europe and Japan at the high end.

stock to transport—a complicated array of organic derivatives follow logically, including polyethylene, ethylene glycol, ethanol, styrene monomer, ethylene dichloride, vinyl chloride, and polyvinyl chloride. Saudi Arabia has launched the largest integrated production facilities for of these products (Stobaugh 1988, 138-43, table 9.1).

This redeployment of global investment led to large-scale shifts in the distribution of production capacity in the industrial states. Surveying the US market in 1978, Salomon Brothers reported that "for the first time in the history of the industry" there was "not a single new announcement of a large US chemical plant costing $25 million or more" (*The Wall Street Journal*, 19 September 1978). US capacity for methanol declined by almost one-quarter, and Japanese capacity by as much as one-half. Overcapacity in ethylene production in Europe ranged between one-quarter and one-half. Public authorities in Europe and Japan encouraged large-scale consolidations in the industry. In the United States, the number of US producers of the 8 petrochemicals in the Stobaugh survey declined by 44 percent (the plants that were shut down had, on average, one-half the capacity of those that continued to operate).

Recalling the reaction of home countries and parent corporations to the pressures for global sourcing in the automotive sector, one might ask why there was less evidence of pressure to keep existing production in place during this period, at least initially?

Five factors help to explain the smoother shift of productive capacity along lines of international comparative advantage in the petrochemical sector. First, the petrochemical industry is much less labor intensive than is the automotive industry (less than one-third as labor intensive), and the unions representing petrochemical workers were less potent politically. Second, as noted above, the hosts that insisted on establishing new facilities in their hydrocarbon-rich states were ready to bear much of the cost and risk of infrastructure-related expenditure in the rationalization of production.

Third, the new petrochemical hosts (old petroleum hosts) proved particularly adept at playing the US, European, and Japanese parent firms against each other in arranging for the awarding of investment contracts. Stobaugh (1988) reports that the Saudis, for example, managed to select partners and award contracts to firms that agreed to close some of their own home-country capacity to make way for the petrochemical exports from Saudi Arabia. Fourth, the home governments in the developed world were anxious to please and fearful of antagonizing the energy-rich states during this period.

Finally, the petrochemical industry was split, with price controls on natural gas in the United States providing US producers with a competitive advantage over rivals in Europe and Asia, allowing the former to watch with equanimity as a disproportionate share of the restructuring fell on the latter.

The ultimate distribution of international comparative advantage has remained an open question, however. Input costs and transportation savings alone have not dominated the equation, especially as energy prices have declined since the mid-1980s. Construction costs in some of the new areas have run 1.3 to 1.5 times higher per unit of installed capacity than those of the US Gulf coast, and managerial weaknesses have added further penalties (Sonatrach's state-owned petrochemical facilities in Algeria, for example, have consistently failed to achieve design performance, according to Papageorgiou, due to limitations in management and labor) (Fayad and Motamen 1986; Papageorgiou cited in Chapman 1991, 182).

With the dissipation of concern about access to oil, therefore, the established sites began to wage a battle to prevent further decay in their position, via trade restraints on petrochemical imports. Contrary to initial expectations that Saudi petrochemical products would enter Europe duty free, the European Community restored tariffs on petrochemical imports, as did Japan, as part of government-led efforts to manage an orderly downsizing of the industry. For US producers, the calculus toward trade barriers has been more complex. Of the nine principal petrochemical products, the United States maintained a positive net trade balance in all except methanol, even after the end of the artificial advantage generated by price controls on natural gas. This export posture of the US producers has led them to be cautious about trade restraints at home.

The split in the interests of firms from the United States, Europe, and Japan (matched by splits between the more efficient producers and the less-efficient producers in the developing world) made lowering trade barriers in the chemical/petrochemical sector one of the more problematic tasks when the Uruguay Round trade negotiations began in 1986. The chemical/petrochemical industry became one of the holdouts in the drive for zero-for-zero tariff negotiations that was accomplished in nine other manufacturing sectors.

Instead, basic tariff levels that ranged from 10 to 25 percent, with tariff escalation and higher effective rates of protection on many particular products, were "harmonized" when the round ended in 1994. The stated goal was to reach a level of 6 to 7 percent within 5 to 15 years. Important less-developed countries—including Argentina, Brazil, India, Indonesia, Thailand, and Venezuela—refused to participate in the resulting outcome, provoking the major petrochemical firms to urge at the Singapore WTO Ministerial in 1996 that no further tariff reductions be considered in the chemical sector until the holdouts sign on (International Council of Chemical Associations 1996). As a result, protectionism in developing countries and economies in transition has provided developed-country producers with a rationale (and an excuse) not to further liberalize themselves.

Perhaps more important than tariffs in determining the course of globalization of the industry, the petrochemical sector has become a particularly easy target for a newer form of investment-diverting trade protection: antidumping regulations.

As chapter 6 demonstrates, antidumping procedures have veered sharply away from legitimate concerns about preventing international price discrimination and predatory behavior. As currently construed and now incorporated into the WTO, antidumping regulations are inherently protectionist and discriminatory. Antidumping actions are particularly easy to launch and win against industries with high fixed costs, such as petrochemicals.

The struggling petrochemical industry in Europe, led by two of its less-efficient companies (Montedison and ENI of Italy), became a particularly heavy user of antidumping actions over the course of the 1980s.[17] From 1980 to 1990, the European Community initiated 904 antidumping investigations. According to Messerlin (1990a, 1990b), 40 percent of the cases targeted petrochemical imports. Of these, two-thirds were brought against producers in the developing countries and economies in transition, with between 65 and 90 percent won by the plaintiffs, resulting in either antidumping duties or "price undertakings" (voluntary export restrictions) (Eymann and Schuknecht 1993; Olechowski 1993).[18] While the United States has been a vigorous initiator of antidumping actions in various sectors (documented in chapter 6), petrochemical imports have not been as frequent a target for US producers as they have been for European producers.

Simultaneous with antidumping protectionism and investment diversion, the attraction of new chemical plants has become, with autos, one of the highest-stake games in the investment-incentive contest. In their examination of 15 investment decisions in the petrochemical industry, Gray and Walter (1984) found that location of a facility in Germany and Belgium) was highly sensitive to the provision of cash grants and other direct subsidies. "On purely commercial grounds," they concluded (307), the latter "would be marginal without the backward-area incentive package that was granted." The largest subsidy packages ever approved by the European Commission have been in the petrochemical sector, to Elf Aquitaine and to Dow, to renovate an eastern German petrochemical complex. In the latter case, the European Commission reduced the German government's offer of $7.8 billion by $1.0 billion, but the final $6.8 billion/$800,000 per job outcome still dwarfed other investment packages.

---

17. Montedison was party to 37 percent of all EC chemical cases initiated between 1980 and 1985, ENI to 32 percent. Next came Hoechst with 24 percent and Alusuisse with 22 percent (Messerlin 1990a, 1990b).

18. Messerlin's analysis of the relationship between antidumping and antitrust cases in the European Community shows that the petrochemical producers used antidumping procedures to keep out suppliers that threatened their market-sharing and price-setting practices (Messerlin 1990a).

While investment incentives for failing industries are not directly compa-rable to greenfield investment—because the former may involve extra costs for cleanup and downsizing—the package was estimated to give Dow new capacity for more than half a billion dollars ($550 million) below the cost of building additional capacity from scratch, adding 11 percent to the parent's annual profits (Dow Chemical Gets Go-Ahead in East Ger-many, *New York Times*, 9 November 1995).

Meanwhile, in the overall competition for chemical and petrochemical operations, the less-developed countries have become not insignificant participants, with one East Asian nation spending about $100 million in subsidies to attract a new chemical plant to its territory (Graham 1996a).

FDI and Exports in Petrochemicals: A Preliminary Assessment

In comparing the globalization of the petrochemical industry with the automotive industry, one might first be inclined to dwell on the differ-ences between the two industries: the greater weight of home-state public-sector investment in the post-World War II period to build up the local petrochemical industry; the unique force of the oil crisis in providing new hosts with an opportunity to upset the equilibrium in the petro-chemical industry; and the greater role of input costs and transportation savings in establishing the new pattern of comparative advantage in the petrochemical industry. More than in the automotive sector, the evolu-tion of the petrochemical industry highlights the somewhat arbitrary placement of production for highly capital intensive industries with large economies of scale.

But there are important similarities as well. For both industries, there has been a need for would-be hosts to intervene to generate exports on the part of international investors and global welfare, as well as indi-vidual host welfare, has benefited as a result. Specifically, in both indus-tries there has been

- a proclivity toward stasis and stickiness in international investment behavior;

- a major role played by home-country authorities in reinforcing this stasis and stickiness (in the petrochemical case, a role inspired by national-security planning on the part of central governments rather than by lobbying on the part of subnational political authorities and labor groups, as in the automotive case);

- a need for shock treatment to propel international companies in a new direction that ultimately matched their own self-interest;

- a subsequent burst of moves and matching moves by the major firms in establishing a new pattern of international investment once the departure from the old distribution of production got underway; and

- an enhancement of efficiency in the industry and, in the principal cases, of global welfare from the new pattern of production.

And, as in the automotive industry, the payoff to would-be hosts from success in triggering new investment, and the opportunity cost of waiting for such investment to occur on its own, are substantial. The payoff extends beyond the obvious benefits of establishing this or that plant. In addition, the provision of common infrastructure introduces economies of scope and scale, and there are technical synergies among complementary products in both the ethylene and methanol chemical chains that enhance the scale effects and transportation savings from the construction of large integrated petrochemical complexes.

As for obstacles to the ability of host countries with comparative advantage on their side to use FDI in petrochemicals to penetrate international markets, there is the by now familiar battle of locational subsidies, plus an additional distortionary vehicle to attract/preserve internal capacity—an intense deployment of antidumping actions to keep out exports and induce investment in the domestic industry.

Consideration of how easy such antidumping cases are to initiate, how effortless they are to win, and how substantial they can be in inhibiting export-oriented investment in developing countries and economies in transition will follow the analysis of globalization in the electronics/computer industry (where antidumping actions also figure prominently). But a further worrisome trend has already emerged; in both the battle of locational subsidies and the imposition of antidumping duties, any given host now has to be wary not just of actions by developed-country authorities but increasingly of those by fellow members of the developing countries and economies in transition.

FDI and Exports in the Electronics/Computer Sector

The electronics/computer sector is so different from the automotive and petrochemical industries—much less capital intensive (in most stages), highly sensitive to assembly costs, driven by rapid changes in technology—that it might seem at first glance to have little complementary contribution to make in addressing questions of market function and the possible justification for host intervention.

But, like the other two sectors, the electronics/computer sector has proved to be a particularly rich target for host countries eager to obtain "rents" from investors, eager to obtain backward linkages, spillovers, and externalities for supplier industries, and eager to obtain the "integration" effect that comes when parent firms align domestic operations with the pace of change that they face competing in international markets.

And despite the ostensible ease of new hosts in attracting export-oriented investors (a process more fraught with difficulty than is commonly appreciated), there has been a vigorous counter effort on the part of developed countries to rearrange international production patterns at variance with comparative advantage. In addition to locational subsidies and antidumping actions, this counter effort features a further tool of investment-diversion—manipulation of "rules of origin"—that is more prominent in this sector than in the others (although present to a certain degree in all three).

In comparing the globalization of the electronics/computer sector with the globalization of the automotive sector, the roles of Southeast Asia and Latin America are reversed, with the former being the pioneer in harnessing FDI to penetrate international markets and the latter only recently trying to play catch-up.

Since the late 1960s, the sharp upward trajectory of FDI in electronics/computer production in East and Southeast Asia (first South Korea, Taiwan, Singapore, and Hong Kong, then Malaysia, Thailand, Indonesia, the Philippines, and China) has been concentrated in two broad product categories: consumer electronics (televisions, radios, electronic watches, video cassette recorders, and radio cassette recorders, including major components such as picture tubes); and office automation equipment and industrial electronics (computers and peripherals, communications equipment, telephone sets, mobile phones, answering machines, and semiconductors, including major components such as disk drives, printers, switching equipment, and printed circuit boards).[19]

Here, at last, one might expect to witness the smooth workings of comparative advantage in international markets. But the story turns out to be much more complex.

Foreign Investors and Global/Regional Sourcing from East/Southeast Asia

Beginning in the late 1960s, Japanese imports put US electronics/computer firms under the same kinds of competitive pressures in the US home market as they put US automobile firms under almost a decade later. From this very early period, therefore, US electronics/computer firms' FDI strategies for East Asian production (like the FDI strategies of some European firms, most notably Philips) anticipated the US automakers' strategy after 1979: abandoning initial resistance to moving abroad, they

---

19. Dividing the electronics/computer industry into these two subgroupings is the convention for studies of this sector (see Ernst and O'Connor 1992).

began to devote their creative energies to figuring out how to integrate offshore sites into an international sourcing system that strengthened their competitive position at home.

Demonstrating follow-the-leader investment dynamics similar to those of the auto companies, the major US firms in the electronics/computer industry set up Asian operations in close succession—first in Singapore and then in Malaysia (Encarnation 1992; Ernst 1983). General Electric opened its first foreign television-parts plant in Asia in 1968. RCA and Zenith followed with offshore assembly operations the next year. Semiconductor producers exhibited the same behavior: Fairchild set up operations in Asia in 1968, Texas Instruments in 1969, National Semiconductor in 1970, and Motorola in 1973. The export-performance requirements of the host countries showed a lighter touch for the electronics/computer sector than for the automotive sector—similar to what chapter 6 will call the Irish model—combining locational subsidies and grants, preferential ownership and labor regulations, training assistance, and tax rebates in return for export operations, often with low-cost or public-supplied land in special free-trade zones. Despite rising labor costs and an appreciating yen, the burst phenomenon for Japanese investors (commonly referred to as "fish" behavior, as when a school of fish changes direction) came later, after the Plaza Accord of 1985. Over the next four years, Urata (1995, table 5) shows, the number of offshore units of Japanese parents in East and Southeast Asia doubled, with the number of subsidiaries in Malaysia and Thailand approximately tripling.

But there has been a clear divergence in strategy between US and Japanese parent firms. Whereas US investors incorporated East Asian output into an effort to maintain their competitive position at home, Japanese investors used East Asian production sites largely to supply local markets while apparently being careful to protect established facilities at home. Shipments back to the United States home market have accounted for more than 60 percent of the total sales of US electronics/computer subsidiaries in East Asia. For Japanese investors, the comparable figure for shipments back to the Japanese home market was no more than 25 percent (Encarnation 1992).[20] East Asian subsidiaries of Japanese firms concentrated on assembling knockdown kits produced in Japan for sale in protected local markets. In contrast to their US counterparts, Japanese affiliates were not a powerful vehicle for penetrating the Japanese market in the electronics/computer industries.

One might suppose that this divergence merely represents the Japanese economy's own comparative advantage in electronics/computer production.

---

20. Moreover, in each segment of the electronics/computer market, Japanese firms have maintained bilateral trade surpluses with the East Asian countries where their subsidiaries are located, while US firms have consistently maintained bilateral trade deficits (Borrus, Ernst, and Haggard forthcoming 1998).

But the fact that this pattern is not at all unique to the electronics/computer industry, but is mirrored in the behavior of Japanese manufacturing investors in general, casts doubt on this explanation.

From 1977 through 1985, US manufacturing investors in East and Southeast Asia sold, on average, approximately 40 percent of their output in local markets and exported 60 percent, with 35 to 40 percent coming back to the US home market. For Japanese manufacturing investors, the figures were reversed: 55 to 68 percent was destined for the local economy, with 30 to 40 percent exported and 10 to 16 percent of that coming back to the Japanese home market (Encarnation 1994, tables 3 and 5).[21] Along the same lines, Campa and Goldberg (1997) have found that "outsourcing" (the share of imported intermediate inputs within industries) increased over the course of the 1980s in the United States, Canada, and the United Kingdom but not in Japan, where the share of imported intermediate inputs was smaller at the beginning and declined during the 1980s. The behavior of Japanese subsidiaries in East and Southeast Asia mirrors Japan's more general outlier status as an importer of manufactured products (Bergsten and Noland 1993).

What is striking, as Encarnation (1994) points out, is that the Japanese firms' practice of keeping their home-country market as a kind of preserve for home-country production did not change noticeably after the Plaza Accord in 1985 drove up the value of the yen nor after the burst of outward investment that Urata (1995) subsequently recorded.

In 1977, prior to the Plaza Accord, US manufacturing investors brought 34 percent of their East Asian production back to the United States home market; the Japanese brought 10 percent back to the Japanese home market. By 1988, the comparable figures were 40 percent and 14 percent, respectively, and by 1991 they were 36 percent and 16 percent (Encarnation 1994).

Besides alerting would-be hosts to the costs of intra-*keiretsu* protectionism,[22] this contrast between Japanese firms more focused on production for local Southeast Asian markets and US/European firms more focused on production for international markets (especially the home market) provides a useful test of the "integration effect" hypothesis: did this

---

21. This difference in orientation helps to explain the greater tolerance of Japanese investors and the lesser tolerance of US investors for joint-venture arrangements. As analyzed in chapter 7, joint-venture partners can assist with domestic-market penetration, but they frequently constitute a hindrance to export operations because the latter require higher standards of quality control and more rapid introduction of (valuable and sensitive) technology that might be misappropriated.

22. As part of Japan's protective trade strategy, argues Encarnation (1994), the obstacles to FDI in Japan faced by US and European firms have also served, indirectly, to hinder Southeast Asian access to the Japanese market; a greater corporate presence on the part of Americans and Europeans in Japan would provide multiple channels for goods and services brought in from Southeast Asian affiliates.

difference in strategic orientation have a significant impact on how the parents treated their affiliates and on the kind of supplier relationships they developed in the indigenous economy?

The evidence shows the impact of the "integration effect" quite clearly. As in the case of US automotive investors, once the US electronics/ computer firms instituted global sourcing, they began a process of systematically upgrading the technology, enhancing the quality control mechanisms, and expanding the managerial responsibilities of their subsidiaries—a notable difference from the Japanese investors.

Borrus (1994), Ernst (1994), and Linden (1996) document a progression in which US parents moved their affiliates from simple hand assembly of items such as printed circuit boards, to hand-and-automated assembly of more complex subsystems, and to responsibility for process and even product design (see also Lim and Fong 1991). Motorola's Southeast Asian subsidiaries evolved from rudimentary printed circuit-board assembly for pagers and private radio systems to worldwide responsibility for design, development, and automated manufacture of double-sided six-layer printed circuit boards and for design and development of integrated circuits for disk drives and other peripherals. Hewlett Packard's plants in Southeast Asia progressed from the assembly of calculators to manufacture, tooling development, process design, and even chip design for portable printers, desktop personal computers, and servers. Compaq upgraded its regional operations from printed circuit board assembly to overall corporate responsibility for design and manufacture of notebook and portable personal computers.

Japanese firms, in contrast, maintained higher-value-added operations at home while transferring only lower-end processes to their East and Southeast Asian subsidiaries. They did move large segments of labor-intensive assembly offshore (including cassette recorders, headphones, low-end tuners, cameras, calculators, some VCR models, under-20-inch televisions, and microwave ovens), reaching local-content levels near 60 percent. But the local content contained few sophisticated components. For personal computers, Borrus (1994) finds that (in contrast to US producers) Japanese subsidiaries sourced memory, drives, power and mechanical components, plastics, and printed circuit boards from Japan. In audio equipment, core components such as magnetrons, chips, and recording heads originated exclusively in Japan. Unlike US firms, global responsibilities were not given to the managers of Japanese subsidiaries for production of advanced products, let alone for their design. The Japanese parents maintained control over high-value-added system integration and design functions in Japan.

"Because their Asian affiliates were integrated into production operations serving advanced country markets," Borrus (1994, 134-35) concludes, "US firms upgraded their Asian investments in line with the pace of development of the lead market being served, the US market. In essence, they upgraded in line with United States rather than local product cycles. By contrast, Japanese firms were led to upgrade the technological capabilities of their Asian investments only at the slower pace necessary to serve lagging local markets."[23]

Moreover, as in the automotive sector, not only did the US subsidiaries that were tightly integrated into the parents' global/regional sourcing networks receive higher-grade operations and higher-grade responsibilities, but there is evidence that the US subsidiaries have been transferring more advanced technological and managerial responsibilities to local suppliers.

Rasiah (1993, 1995) examined the evolving relationship between nine local machine tool firms and seven foreign electronics firms (five American, one Canadian, one Japanese) in Malaysian free-trade zones over more than two decades. The early links between the foreign investors and their local suppliers consisted of the latter carrying out simple machining and stamping. From this elemental base, the Malaysian suppliers moved up to contracts for precision tooling and parts fabrication. At the beginning of the relationship, the foreign subsidiaries developed machinery prototypes before subcontracting the work to the indigenous firms, often with the engineers of the former supervising and monitoring the work of the latter. Later, engineers on both sides drafted plans for the machinery together (Rasiah uses the example of an auto-wafer mounter), which the local suppliers then produced on their own.

Over the course of time, all nine of the local machine-tool firms began to export, via channels provided by the foreign firms, to Thailand, the Philippines, Singapore, South Korea, Indonesia, and the United States. Seven of the nine limited their exports, at the time of the study, to sister plants of the foreign investors outside of Malaysia; two had also built up subcontracting orders from independent purchasers abroad. Eng Technology, for example, founded in 1974 as a family business to repair and maintain the machinery of foreign integrated circuit companies, began to export on its own in 1984 and ultimately came to send more than half of its output of precision parts to disk drive buyers outside of the country (Linden 1996).

---

23. To integrate host subsidiaries into the global competitive strategy of the parent, US and European investors have strongly preferred to operate with wholly owned or majority owned affiliates, giving an advantage to countries such as Hong Kong and Singapore that did not insist upon joint ventures. In this context, it is instructive to contrast Malaysia's extraordinarily successful experience in the electronics/computer sector with its weak performance in the automotive sector. In the former, Malaysia allowed foreign investors to operate in free-trade zones such as Penang with wholly owned subsidiaries; in the latter, Malaysia insisted upon creating a "national champion" automotive company as a joint venture with Mitsubishi. Box 8.1 provides a case study of this "national champion" joint venture, where there have been repeated lags in the introduction of new technology and difficulties in penetrating external markets.

In short, Rasiah traces a pattern in which, as part of their relationship with the foreign companies, the indigenous machine-tool suppliers moved from "backyard workshops," to stamping and machining parts, to manufacture of precision computer-numeric machine tools and factory-automation equipment for the international and domestic marketplace. The owners of seven of the nine local machinery manufacturers had had prior work experience at one of the foreign firms before starting their own operations; 10 percent of the employees of the local machinery manufacturers had had prior work experience with one of the foreign firms as well.[24]

By 1990, this first generation of indigenous suppliers had delegated many tasks to a second level of local firms; this second level often took on orders beyond its capacity, forcing it to subcontract the excess to a third tier of local firms.

Many local companies became high-volume exporters, in some cases sending more than half of their production abroad. The export composition of all local firms in the machine-tool industry in Malaysia rose from 0.4 percent of output in 1984 to 31.6 percent of output in 1990. Their major competitors in the markets they served were from Germany, Japan, and Taiwan. Using growth rates for the number of manufacturing machines and machinery structure as proxies for capital widening and capital deepening, Rasiah (1995) concludes that the local firms underwent considerable capital widening and deepening during this process.[25]

Focusing in more detail on the spillovers to domestic suppliers from a single outward-oriented foreign investor, Linden (1996) highlights two cases involving Motorola. In the first, Motorola transferred surface-mount technology for printed circuit boards to a Malaysian firm, Bakti Comintel,

---

24. This finding is similar to Katz's observation (1987) that managers of indigenous firms in Latin America often began their careers after being trained by the affiliates of foreign investors. Isolating pure externalities (benefits generated by foreign firms that do not accrue to owners or workers in the form of higher profits or wages or to users of the firms' output) from other beneficial spillovers is an arduous task. For a discussion of the concept and measurement of externalities, see Graham (1996a).

25. The evidence from Rasiah (1995) and Linden (1996) indicates that foreign firms help local suppliers to become more sophisticated and more productive, and help them to learn how to export. Does the process of exporting, and the contact with external buyers, stimulate or teach the local firms how to remain at the cutting edge of product development, quality, and price? The detailed case studies here suggest that the answer is affirmative. So do other studies: Blomstrom and Persson (1983) find that foreign firms help developing-country firms to enter world markets by providing links to final buyers in the developed economies. Keesing and Lall (1992) argue that foreign investors provide knowledge about design, packaging, and product quality that is used in local companies' operations beyond their role as suppliers to those investors. Kokko, Tansini, and Lejan (1996) find a significant relationship between the presence of foreign investors and the likelihood that local firms in Uruguay export to world markets. These findings run counter to the more doubtful perspective of Roberts and Tybout (1997).

which developed the capacity over time to supply not only Motorola-Malaysia but to ship finished products to 11 Motorola sites worldwide. In the second, Motorola farmed out "flex circuits" to a local Malaysian company, QDOS Microcircuits, which used the contract to grow beyond an exclusive-supplier relationship with Motorola to become a contractor to Siemens and Hewlett-Packard in Penang and to 10 international corporations outside of Malaysia.

For Japanese investors that did develop regional and international ties (albeit seldom with the home market), rather than concentrating exclusively on production for the local market, there appears to be similar potential for spillovers. Linden (1996) follows a Malaysian metal stamping firm, Atlan Industries, which started as a supplier to Sharp, added other customers, including Sony, NEC, Toshiba, and Casio, and grew to be a regional and international exporter. Sony helped one Atlan subsidiary, Cirrus, to learn how to use automated transfer-press technology supplied by other Japanese firms, and then invited Cirrus to build a plant in Jakarta to supply Sony's Indonesian operations.

In the aggregate, by the early 1990s the electronics/computer sector grew from virtual insignificance in 1968 to become the leading generator of employment, fixed assets, output, and exports in the Malaysian manufacturing industry. The phrase "outsourcing" hardly captures the dynamism of the interaction between parent and subsidiary or the magnitude of direct and indirect benefits for the host economy.[26]

But producers in the United States and Europe, as well as Japan, have not been content simply to let the globalization of the electronics/computer industry proceed along lines of international comparative advantage. Whereas Japanese firms have used intra-*kereitsu* ties to maintain production sites in the home market, US and European firms, workers, and public authorities began a battle of their own in the mid-1980s to divert investment and maintain or expand production at home. This battle employed two familiar weapons, locational subsidies and anti-dumping cases. It also featured a new kind of investment-diverting trade restriction that has proved to be particularly effective, the distortionary use of rules of origin.

Turning first to locational subsidies, the electronics/computer sector has been the focus of intensive activity within the OECD. Recent packages of grants and subsidies in the developed countries have included a $320 million investment-incentive package for a semiconductor plant in the United Kingdom and a $289 million investment-incentive package for a microprocessor plant in the United States (see figure 6.1).

---

26. Following Feenstra and Hanson (1995a, 1995b), "outsourcing" has come to be defined as the share of imported intermediate inputs within an industry. This characterization does not distinguish between home-country firms that are simply shopping abroad for components and home-country firms that are setting up overseas production facilities explicitly to produce them.

Looking next at antidumping restrictions, of the 1,558 antidumping cases initiated between 1980 and 1989, those involving electronic products were the fourth most likely to result in restrictive arrangements. For the European Union alone, consumer electronics and office/computing machinery were the second-largest target, behind only chemicals/petrochemicals, with more than a third of the cases brought against exports from the developing countries (Eymann and Schuknecht 1993; Finger 1997).

Rules of origin constitute the novel element that this examination of FDI in the electronics/computer sector introduces into the depiction of the battle for the location of production (however, rules of origin have also figured prominently from time to time in the struggle for automotive production). As chapter 6 will point out, rules of origin can be manipulated, like antidumping regulations, to force investment and thwart the more general liberalization of trade and investment. Rules of origin determine how much domestic content a product must have to qualify as an internal product in a preferential trade agreement. In semiconductors, for example, in 1989, the European Community unilaterally declared that the process of diffusion, or wafer fabrication, had to be performed in the European Community for integrated circuits to be considered of local origin. Otherwise, the integrated circuits would be subject to the European Community's 14 percent semiconductor tariff. Even though wafer fabrication was not cost-competitive in Europe, compared to Asia or the United States, Dataquest recorded the construction of 22 new fabrication facilities within two years of the change in the rule of origin. The largest directly attributable to the change was a plant expansion by Intel in Ireland.

The European Union also established product-specific rules that require printed circuit board assembly within Europe and set high value-added requirements for photocopiers. It has negotiated association agreements in Central and Eastern Europe that require 60 percent domestic content for products to qualify for entry into the European Union.

As chapter 6 spells out in some detail, the European Community's aggressiveness on rules of origin in the late 1980s spurred various industry groups in the United States, in particular some segments of the electronics/computer sector, to follow the same path in the North American Free Trade Agreement. There, the United States used rules of origin to extend an umbrella of trade-protection-cum-investment-diversion to telecommunications, computers, color televisions, fax machines, and photocopiers (Jensen-Moran 1996a, 1996b).

With regard to telecommunications, the NAFTA rule requires that 9 of every 10 printed circuit board assemblies, the essential component of office switching equipment, be packaged within the NAFTA countries. In response, ATT shifted some production from Asia to Mexico, and Fujitsu and Ericsson brought new investments to Mexico as well. As for color televisions, NAFTA required that television tubes be produced within the region to qualify for preferential status. Prior to NAFTA, there was no North American manufacturer of television tubes; in the first two years after NAFTA's passage, five factories took shape within the NAFTA region, with investments from Hitachi, Mitsubishi, Sony, and Samsung.

In the case of computers, the US negotiators proposed a rule that would have required two of the three key components (the motherboard, flat panel display, and hard disc drive) to be North American in origin. With forceful opposition from IBM and other companies that wanted to maintain their more flexible international sourcing patterns, the negotiators settled on a final rule requiring "only" the motherboard to be North American.

NAFTA also tightened origin rules for printers, photocopiers, and fax machines, requiring more components to be manufactured locally. For printers and photocopiers, all major subassemblies have to be produced in North America (equivalent to an 80-percent domestic-content requirement). According to Xerox, this rule was instrumental in motivating its competitor, Canon, to construct a plant costing more than $100 million in Virginia, rather than in Malaysia or in China, where the production costs would be lower (Jensen-Moran 1996b, 985).

Exports, Global Sourcing, and FDI in the Electronics/Computer Sector: A Preliminary Assessment

The globalization of the electronics/computer industry, like the automotive industry, highlights the role of competitive pressures in the home markets in pushing international firms to invest along lines of comparative advantage. For US firms, under heavy competitive pressures at home, the export-performance requirements of host countries in Southeast Asia merely seemed to speed them in the direction they were headed anyway. For Japanese firms, with a home market more protected from electronics products produced offshore, the export-performance requirements of host countries in Southeast Asia only achieved results after the Plaza Accord revaluation of the yen. Even then, exports were still largely oriented toward third markets. The host authorities devoted considerable public resources to the creation of free trade zones—following the Irish model of grants and subsidies—and enjoyed enormous economic returns from the subsequent investment activities. They probably played a less decisive role in altering parent corporate sourcing strategies in the electronics/computer sector than in the automotive and petrochemical sectors.

The initial payoff from attracting export-oriented facilities was substantial. Moreover, once international investors incorporated new production sites abroad into their global/regional sourcing strategies, the electronics/computer firms, like their automotive counterparts, generated the dynamic integration effect of keeping their subsidiaries close to the cutting edge of technology and best-management practices.

The benefits that host countries received from FDI in the electronics/ computer sector again included valuable spillovers to indigenous suppliers and associated industries. The technological and managerial coaching described by Borrus (1994), Ernst, Linden (1996), and Rasiah in helping to generate robust, internationally competitive indigenous firms is reminiscent of similar evidence of external stimulus for the supplier base found by Peres Nuñez (1990) and Doner in the automotive industry. The desire to use offshore sites to enhance their own competitive position worldwide led the electronics/computer companies to engulf the suppliers, as well as their own plants, in a continuous flow of technical and management improvements, which was notably absent from indigenous and foreign-owned plants that were focused exclusively on selling in the domestic market.

Once again, there is evidence of agglomeration properties of scope and scale among external investors and indigenous suppliers in the clusters or poles where the foreign firms settled. There is also the political "externality" of pressure for further liberalization from the outward-oriented foreigners and the local firms that followed them into international markets.

Despite the sensitivity of the electronics/computer sector to competitive pressures, however, there is extensive evidence here, as in the automotive and petrochemical sectors, of intrusive efforts by firms, workers, and public authorities in the developed countries to capture and/or preserve such valuable conglomerations of economic activity, particularly thick in technological spillovers, at home.

Locational incentives and antidumping regulations again played a role; so did the intra-*keiretsu* protectionism of Japanese parent firms. But the study of globalization in the electronics/computer sector highlights an additional policy tool deployed in the struggle to divert investment in one direction or another—the manipulation of rules of origin.

This completes the list of ingredients, or at least provides a reasonably logical cutoff point, necessary to begin assessing what might be the most appropriate and most effective way for hosts and would-be hosts in the developing countries and economies in transition to construct their own policies toward export-oriented FDI.

Export-Performance Requirements and the Globalization of the Automotive, Petrochemical, and Electronics/Computer Sectors

The examination of the globalization of these three sectors (automotive, petrochemical, and electronics/computers) provides interesting and useful but also perplexing results for less-developed countries and economies in transition that want to use foreign manufacturing investment to penetrate international markets.

Perhaps the first and most important discovery is that the benefits for those countries that have managed to attract such investment, and the costs (or opportunity costs) for those countries that have failed to secure such investment are much more significant than conventional calculations suggest.

Not only do the export-oriented facilities in these three sectors bring the usual list of capital, technology, and management skills to an operation enjoying full economies of scale, they also provide an incentive structure between parent and subsidiary that ensures rapid technological upgrading, managerial upgrading, continuous pressure for quality control, and timely and cost-efficient production. Indeed, the decision to incorporate a plant into the global sourcing strategy of a multinational firm appears to have a dynamic "integration effect," whereby the parent seeks to maintain peak standards in the subsidiary.

At the same time, all three industries (especially the automotive and electronics/computer industries) show much greater likelihood of providing spillovers and externalities for local suppliers if plants are thoroughly incorporated into the global/regional sourcing network of the parent instead of oriented primarily toward the domestic market.. These spillovers would come in the form of management training, technical coaching, technology transfer, and export assistance.

Further, there is often a political-economic "externality" as well, because foreign investors stop using what clout they have in the political arena to preserve their own protected status and shift their attention to leading the fight on behalf of greater liberalization against protectionist opponents in the polities where they operate.

The second discovery is more surprising, namely, that the efforts of host authorities to entice foreign investors to develop export-oriented facilities have not proceeded easily or smoothly, even (oddly enough) when there were increasingly clear indications that the establishment of such facilities coincided with the long-term self-interest of the parent corporations. Instead—despite mounting competitive pressures to cut costs in the home market—there is considerable evidence of reluctance, hesitation, and "stickiness" associated with the decision to invest in new export-oriented operations.

Then, however, in multiple cases in each of these sectors, once a leading company was pushed or enticed to establish an export base, the action of the "first mover" provoked rapid matching moves on the part of other investors (and component supplier firms) in the industry. To cope with this stickiness, host authorities had to intervene (forcefully in the case of the automotive and petrochemical sectors, more lighthandedly in the case of the electronics/computer sector) to trigger a response on the part of major investors in the industry to begin a process of regional or global sourcing from their country. Success from such intervention, in the cases examined here, paid huge benefits and set in motion a "burst effect" among other members of the industry that launched the country on a new trajectory of industrial development. The result in each case was a far cry from the usual depiction of export-performance requirements as using public monies or trade rents to generate a weak, uncompetitive, and heavily subsidized stream of exports.

The stakes in attracting foreign investors to move to new locales, on the one hand, and in keeping them in place where they already operate, on the other, are high. In response to globalization in these three industries, developed-country authorities have themselves been intervening in important ways both to prevent exit and to capture new investment. Their principal tools have been locational incentives, grants, subsidies, and investment-diverting protectionist measures such as rules of origin and antidumping actions.

Success or failure in this pulling and tugging over the location of world-scale production facilities involves not just the individual decisions of individual companies with regard to individual plants. In the major automotive, petrochemical, and electronics/computer cases examined here, it also determines what is sometimes grandly called the "configuration of economic geography," with features such as agglomeration of specialized suppliers (many of whom also enjoy economies of scale), labor pooling, and a high potential for technological and human resource externalities (Marshall 1920; David and Rosenblum 1990; Krugman 1991; Helpman and Krugman 1985).

The role of international comparative advantage in determining the ultimate pattern of production is not unimportant, but neither is it decisive. Instead, the grappling over the locational decisions of international companies does resemble a strategic-trade struggle over the distribution of highly valuable economic activity (inframarginal activity). It is a contest that is much more complicated but not less serious than the stylized strategic-trade battles pitting the respective home countries of Boeing and Airbus against each other in a fight to capture aerospace and related "rents."

What are the implications for the design of public policy toward FDI in the developing countries and economies in transition? One cannot conclude from the success stories in these three industries—however broad a portion of international industrial investment they cover, across quite diverse industries and countries—that the use of export-performance requirements will always produce as favorable or as powerful an outcome as witnessed here. But few hosts or would-be hosts would conclude, after studying these industries, that their wisest course is to rest passively and wait for world-scale manufacturing investments to arrive on their own. The rewards for action are too great, and the costs or opportunity costs of inaction may be too severe.

Is the appropriate conclusion, therefore, that export-performance requirements should be considered a legitimate tool of public policy for developing countries and economies in transition? Should their use be rationalized and expanded—enlarging the subsidy component and making any foreign investor eligible, for example, as a transitory way to lock into the parent's externality-filled sourcing network (differentiating this approach, therefore, from simply subsidizing all exporters)? Or should developing countries and economies in transition be willing to control and limit the use of export-performance requirements as part of some larger policy bargain among nations?

To begin to answer these questions requires a more in-depth look at possible indications of market failure in the investment process in manufacturing industries such as these and at the investment-diverting and investment-distorting activities of the countries struggling to capture or retain these externality-rich segments of economic activity. These are the tasks of chapter 6.

6

Comparative Advantage and the Globalization of Manufacturing Industries: The Struggle to Tilt the Playing Field for International Investment

Chapter 5's studies of host-country efforts to use FDI in manufacturing industries such as automobiles, petrochemicals, and electronics/computers to penetrate international markets raise fundamental questions for the design of contemporary policies that go well beyond the pros and cons of export-performance requirements per se. They require examination of the questions introduced at the beginning of this volume, namely, how well do the international markets where FDI takes place function? What are the principal obstacles to the more effective functioning of these markets? Are there rigorous reasons for host authorities in the developing countries and economies in transition to intervene to influence foreign-investor behavior? Or should they simply improve micro and macroeconomic fundamentals in their own countries with the expectation that international investors will then deliver appropriate amounts of economic activity to them along lines of comparative advantage?

There are three kinds of possible justification for host-country activism to push or pull international investors to locate full-scale-sized manufacturing operations in their economies: (1) to correct for market failures; (2) to compensate for the interventions of others on "second best" grounds; and (3) to weigh in as a player in a strategic-trade struggle over the distribution of rents and externalities that accompany the activities of the companies.

What light does the evidence from the globalization of the automotive, petrochemical, and electronics/computer industries in chapter 5 shed on these overlapping but analytically distinct rationales for possible intervention? And what kind of policy responses might be most appropriate and least dangerous?

Market Failure Rationales for Host-Country Intervention

Chapter 3, on investment promotion, drew on models of information gaps, asymmetric information, and signaling to suggest the need for light-handed intervention (i.e., advertising and product differentiation) on the part of potential host governments to attract FDI. The goal would be to highlight obscure or hidden advantages for investors from operating in the host country, so as to make up for lack of enthusiasm that might spring from foreign firms being unable to distinguish any particular site from those at the very bottom.

These sectoral studies support the contention that would-be host countries need to fill in information gaps and market themselves as favorable sites for international operations. The behavior of the international automotive, petrochemical, and computer/electronics firms is not filled with evidence of aggressive search and abundant eagerness to try out new production possibilities. Quite the opposite: these sectoral studies reveal that parent companies are reluctant to consider new production sites.

But what is striking is that in all three industries the "stickiness" in the parent firms' behavior continues even as information gaps are filled, even as new hosts distinguish themselves as cost-effective production sites, even as competitive pressures to alter old production patterns mount, and even as indications that change would be in the firms' own long-term self-interest become apparent.

What explains the reluctance of US automobile investors to invest in sourcing from what they had discovered were cheaper locales in Mexico and Brazil, despite the need to meet the competition from Japanese imports in the US auto market that been growing for a decade but sharply increased in 1975? What explains the reluctance of Japanese firms to invest in sourcing from Malaysia and Thailand for the home market as well as third-country markets despite rising labor costs for Japanese electronics firms in Japan? And what explains the reluctance of oil and petrochemical firms to locate ethylene and methane plants near inexpensive feedstock sources despite technical synergies and large transportation savings?

Equally notable, however, is how reluctance could be transformed into enthusiasm. Once the first movers in each industry shifted direction, after much hesitation, there was a remarkable follow-the-leader response: Ford, Chrysler, and Nissan abandoned their resistance and followed General Motors in Mexico; Ford and Volkswagen abandoned their resistance and followed Fiat and General Motors in Brazil; Mitsubishi, Isuzu, Mazda, Nissan, and Peugeot abandoned their resistance and followed Toyota in Thailand; Apple and Hewlett Packard abandoned their resistance and followed IBM in Mexico; methanol and ethylene production was redeployed to hydrocarbon rich countries after 1974; General Electric, RCA,

Zenith, Fairchild, Texas Instruments, National Semiconductor, and Motorola matched each others' moves in Singapore and Malaysia; and the Japanese electronics firms followed each other like schools of fish into Malaysia and Thailand.

Might this pattern of stickiness in the FDI process, followed by rapid bursts of new investment, be indicative of broader market failures? And, if so, what are the implications for host welfare, and for global welfare?

Stickiness in FDI and the Welfare Effects of "Irreversible Investments under Uncertainty"

Looking first at the stickiness in the FDI process, it is important to proceed with caution. After all, part of the hesitation and reluctance to change patterns of investment may not necessarily be evidence of any kind of market failure. It may simply reflect what modern investment theory, associated with the work of Dixit and Pindyck (1994), considers under the rubric of irreversible investments under uncertainty.

In the Dixit-Pindyck framework, investors are more cautious about constructing a new facility than abandoning an old one. The "asymmetrical caution" in this model goes beyond the simple desire to avoid repeating start-up costs over and over again; it is similar to acquiring a financial option and springs from attributing value to delay in making large new investments (quasi-irreversible commitments) as the firm receives new information that might either confirm or contradict whether the new pattern of production is superior to the old.

In this model, the delay while new information piles up retards the investment process well beyond what conventional capital-budgeting calculations predict. It explains, in the calculation of Dixit and Pindyck (1994), why investment decisions by firms often require "hurdle rates" three to four times the cost of capital.[1]

Does firm behavior of this kind justify some kind of public-sector intervention to trigger or speed the investment decision?[2] Within the Dixit-Pindyck framework, what may be optimal for the private investor is not necessarily optimal for any given host. The investor values the possibility of delay; the host prefers a commitment to proceed. A good

---

1. It is little wonder, therefore, that the offer of trade protection is such a powerful tool in attracting FDI, because it provides profitability and stability to the investor. Launching an export project, in contrast, especially where economies of scale are large, requires making a sizable (indivisible) lump-sum investment without any opportunity to fill such information gaps incrementally.

2. Dixit and Pindyck (1994) point out that the idea of endowing the postponement of action with "a financial option value" (because the firm receives additional information with which to make the investment decision) is compatible with both perfectly competitive and imperfectly competitive settings for firm behavior.

example of such divergence, according to Dixit and Pindyck, can be found in pricing offshore oil leases. Conventional finance theory would lead firms and governments to time the development of a new field as a function of the current price of oil, the expected rate of change of the price, the quantity of production, and the investment cost. Discounting these numbers forward and summing would then generate a value for the reserve.

But it would be erroneous for either party to make the calculation this way, according to Dixit and Pindyck, because it ignores the value to any firm bidding for the property of having flexibility about when it might actually develop the reserve; that is, the conventional financial approach ignores the option value of possible delay as the firm observes what transpires in international oil markets.

To induce the firm not just to acquire the right to invest but actually to undertake development promptly, therefore, public authorities should expect to receive less in terms of bids from lease auctions, or to give away more in terms of royalty and other tax regulations, than otherwise would be the case. And, in fact, government bodies in oil and gas bearing regions, in developed and developing countries alike, insist upon "relinquishment requirements" that limit the amount of time a company can hold a tract before developing it, to force the firm to move more quickly than its own incentive structure might dictate. And government bodies must expend resources (accept lower lease bids and lower royalty and other tax rates) to compensate the investor for the promise of prompt exploitation.

Similarly, a host government trying to convince an international investor to commit capital to develop a new production site would have to expend more resources than conventional finance theory would suggest to trigger the firm's commitment to production.

What is best for the world at large? Is there a possible divergence between what is optimal for the individual investor and what is optimal for global welfare?

From the point of view of global welfare, what is socially optimal depends upon whether and how fast "learning" would take place in the absence of investment.

On the one hand, what Dixit and Pindyck call a "global social planner" might not want to stimulate new patterns of investment too fast; the world as a whole might gain from delay as new information is acquired. On the other hand, if new information does not emerge, or emerges too slowly (suboptimally slowly), while less-efficient patterns of production remain in place and new patterns of investment are delayed, the world is worse off for allowing the firms to do what best suits their self-interest.

Does information about new sites for world-scale-sized plants that can be integrated into the parent firms' global/regional sourcing strategies emerge fast enough, or too slowly, from the perspective of global welfare? It is instructive to look at what kind of information investors identify as most valuable to them in assessing such investment possibilities.

Investor surveys consistently include five broad categories of concern (among others) in the developing countries and the economies in transition:

- cultural factors (worker motivation, absenteeism, alcoholism, cultural preparation, etc.);

- labor regulations (flexibility in hiring and laying off workers);

- responsiveness of the surrounding economy in providing supporting goods and services;

- credibility of public-sector commitments about taxes, infrastructure, and other regulatory issues (often extending beyond the probable duration of any given government); and

- institutional base of commercial law (case law or common law) to provide precedent when disputes arise.

All five are well represented in the automotive, petrochemicals, and electronics/computer industries:

- cultural factors (from the concern about workers in "tropical" or "siesta" environments in the Brazilian and Mexican auto industry in the 1970s, to worries about alcoholism, absenteeism, and lack of a work ethic in former communist states in the 1990s);

- labor regulations (flexibility of hiring and firing in the automotive and electronics/computer plants and questions about the supervision of large, predominantly female workforces in the Malaysian and Thai cases);

- responsiveness of a given local economy in providing goods and services upon which the success of a new foreign investment would depend (from the concern about the functioning of built-from-scratch petrochemical complexes in Saudi Arabia, Indonesia, and Mexico in the mid-1970s to the ability of ASEAN firms to qualify for OEM status for automotive or electronic/computer components in the 1980s);

- credibility of host government promises (from input prices for feedstock and local utilities to provision of infrastructure in all three sectors); and

- institutional factors (from interpretations of commercial law to independence and reliability of the judicial system itself).

These are the kinds of information gaps, so to speak, that international companies find most desirable to fill in order to evaluate the risks associated with an investment opportunity. They have a common characteristic: the information can only be acquired via learning by doing. "Paper investigations," even with expert consultants and extensive site visits, can only take the potential investor a short way toward evaluating the feasibility of a project. Ultimately, the initial investor is left with no way to reduce uncertainties except by making the financial commitment and managing the operation.

The discovery that information gaps associated with identifying new sites for global/regional sourcing can be filled only by "trying out" the site for an extended period of time fits with one of the more complicated areas of asymmetric information and signaling, namely, how to distinguish good buys from lemons (Akerlof 1970; McKenna 1986).

Analogous to the buying and selling of used cars, the lemons model features important potential differences between products, and there are sizable benefits to buyers (investors) that make the right choices and sizable advantages to sellers (hosts) that can demonstrate their status as superior suppliers. Identifying which products are good and which products are defective, however, is extremely difficult for the buyers unless they actually use the product for an extended period of time. This drives buyers toward a common "too low" price for all such products, or, in the investment case, toward a common "too uninterested" stance toward new production possibilities—appropriate only if all used cars or all new production sites are the equivalent of a lemon.[3]

What are the implications for world welfare? In the world of used cars, imperfections in information markets can be smoothed over by developing cadres of certified mechanics who have credentials that satisfy both buyer and seller to take the auto apart and run tests on its individual components. However, in the world of FDI, the imperfections are likely to remain.

This introduces an important element of catch-22 into the FDI process: if the only way that the information gaps can be closed is by actually making the investment, no information will be forthcoming until the first mover moves. Left on its own, "learning," and consequently investment, will be undersupplied.

---

3. Under these conditions, host countries, like sellers of other hard-to-evaluate products, have an interest in expending resources to differentiate themselves; they may demonstrate their confidence in their ability to create superior business conditions ("better than the worst") by bunching benefits to investors up front and showing self-assurance that such superior business conditions will allow them to recoup these benefits later. They may also have an incentive to share the investor's risk by offering a warranty. For more thorough examination of the "extended warranty" option, in terms of mechanisms to increase the credibility of host-country commitments toward particularly vulnerable investments, see chapter 9, on FDI in natural resources and private infrastructure projects.

In the sectoral cases traced above, a "global social planner" with a Dixit-Pindyck (1994) orientation would have to assess whether global welfare would have improved or worsened if the hosts had not forced the issue and the international auto firms had been even slower in exploring the possibilities of Mexican, Brazilian, or Thai sourcing for autoparts, or if the hosts had not forced the issue and the international electronics firms (especially Japanese electronics firms) had been even slower in moving toward assembly operations in Malaysia and Thailand, or if the hosts had not forced the issue and the international petrochemical firms had continued to transport bulky feedstocks to Europe and Japan while hydrocarbon-rich producers flared their natural gas.[4]

Quite likely, a global social planner would conclude that world welfare would be enhanced by multilateral mechanisms to facilitate the experimentation of foreign firms in locating internationally competitive, world-scale-sized plants in new sites, not by retarding the process. The optimum playing field would be tilted slightly in favor of less-developed countries and economies in transition, not sharply inclined against them (as explored more fully later in this chapter). A global social planner might look with concern at the methods that less-developed countries and economies in transition have employed, and are likely to continue to employ, to improve the functioning of the markets in which international investment is found, but the planner would not likely be critical of the effort itself.

Evidence that "bureaucratic politics" played a key role in some of the most important investment decisions in the automotive, petrochemical, and electronics/computer sectors further undermines the attribution of delay in international investment behavior to some kind of optimal information-gathering behavior (Helleiner 1981). Under perfect competition, bureaucratic politics have no place: a firm behaves as a rational unitary actor, responding, like its rivals, to exogenous price signals. Strategic management literature modifies this picture for imperfectly competitive industries but without changing the outcome. One of the functions of headquarters is to adjudicate among subunits whose managers want a greater share of the firm's resources to expand and enhance their own activities. Firm decision making may be the outcome of clashes between and bargaining among subunits that are within the hierarchy of the firm and that pursue their own interest or their own particular conception of

---

4. There is an additional problem with the way in which Dixit and Pindyck (1994) use their model. They take full account of the sensitivity of firms to exit costs and the desire of public authorities at the sites where the firms are located to avoid the pain of adjustment should the firms move elsewhere. But they fail to note that delay in redeploying assets to new production sites may leave resources in those new locales suboptimally employed, creating possible penalties for global welfare as long as the firm postpones the investment decision. The social dimension of exit costs should properly be appraised, but so too should the opportunity costs of leaving resources maldeployed elsewhere. A global social planner would want to take both into account, not just the former.

the firm's interest. But the strategic objective is to maximize the long-term competitive position and long-term profitability of the entire corporation.

The histories of globalization in the three sectors examined in this book do not fit this picture well. Even without the benefit of hindsight, the strategic management of the firms did not energetically search for and try out new courses of action that (on the basis of the evidence available at the time) would probably have been, and ultimately did turn out to be, in the long-term best interest of the firm. Instead, the common reaction was that new low-cost production sites were a threat to managers that had a vested interest in established patterns of operation.

There emerged what Nollen, Abbey, and Newman (1997) call "sibling rivalry" between new and older units in their studies of contemporary FDI in Eastern Europe. In the extreme, Nollen, Abbey, and Newman find that the older units may use intrafirm connections and intrafirm economic transfers to limit or even ruin the prospects for the newcomers. The sectoral studies on the automotive, petrochemical, and electronics/computer sectors did not document sibling rivalry quite as poisonous as Nollen, Abbey, and Newman observe among Swedish-Swiss subsidiaries in the Czech Republic, but Shapiro's (1993, 1994) characterization of the disputes between GM headquarters in Detroit and GM do Brazil do not fall far short. The bureaucratic-politics phenomenon within large international firms in imperfectly competitive industries introduces the possibility of internal rent-seeking behavior into the FDI process. What appears to be a delay in investment intended to gain an optimum acquisition-of-information period along Dixit-Pindyck lines (1994) may instead be the result of efforts by large constituencies within firms to protect their interests.

Follow-the-Leader Behavior by Foreign Investors and Appropriability Problems

Quite apart from the stickiness in undertaking new investments, the rapid follow-the-leader behavior observed in these three sectoral studies, once a major firm has moved, raises new questions about market failure.

Here, the evidence from the sectoral studies falls into a well-researched pattern of "bunching" in FDI, first investigated in a systematic way by Knickerbocker (1973). Knickerbocker examined the FDI behavior of 187 major US manufacturing firms (the Harvard Business School Multinational Enterprise data base), over 20 years, to assess the extent to which they "bunched" the establishment of their subsidiaries together in 23 countries (15 developed countries, 8 developing countries). The firm sample included 54 industries, including food, paper, chemicals, petroleum, primary metals, fabricated metal products, machinery, electrical equipment, transportation equipment, and instruments.

Knickerbocker found that, of approximately 2,000 foreign subsidiaries, almost one-half were established within three-year clusters, and almost three-fourths were established in seven-year clusters. The results were similar industry by industry and country by country. This clustering was independent of other external events and differentiated from the overall trend of US investment abroad.

Knickerbocker (1973) found that this "bandwagon effect" on the part of the parent firms was, as a general rule, more prevalent in industries with high seller concentration than in industries with low seller concentration. There was, however, an exception to the rule: parent firms in industries with very high seller concentration and a paucity of new entrants were relatively more restrained.

Other investigators have discovered similar patterns for other nations and more recent time periods. Yu and Ito (1988) compared FDI behavior in the relatively concentrated tire industry with FDI in the much more competitively structured textile industry and found that the decision to set up a subsidiary in the former (275 observations for 55 developed and developing countries over 5 years) was clearly related to the prior behavior of rivals. Meanwhile, the decision to set up a subsidiary in the latter (240 observations for 20 developed and developing countries over the same time period) was not. Graham and others have found evidence of action-reaction dynamics in cross-investment among developed countries (Graham 1978, 1996b; Flowers 1976).

These follow-the-leader patterns could indicate appropriability problems for the investors: if making the investment is the only way to evaluate the principal uncertainties and risks involved in moving to a new site, then waiting, observing what happens to those who move first, and following after the ones who appear to make successful investments is a relatively costless way to eliminate risk and uncertainty. Alternatively, a firm could simply match the moves of the one that moves first, exposing the firm to exactly the same risks and uncertainties. The returns that first movers receive, consequently, might not be high enough or last long enough to compensate them for assuming the burden of going first.

An inability to "appropriate" sufficient returns to justify the initial investment means that FDI to new locales will be undersupplied, in comparison to what would be socially optimal on a global basis, and that public-sector support by individual hosts and the world at large would be needed to correct for the market failure.

In the sectoral studies undertaken in chapter 5 there is not sufficient detail about risk assessment, rates of return, and speed of response by rivals, in the aggregate data or even in the micro studies of FDI decisions, to assess whether the benefits that the first movers gained were sufficient to compensate them for the risks they bore. But there is scant support for the idea that successful first movers enjoyed long tranquil periods of supernormal rents. Instead, what evidence there is suggests that the rewards to parent profits and to managerial fates for risk taking are quite transitory, while the penalties for entrepreneurship gone sour are not.

Alternatively, the "clustering" of FDI could be indicative of strategic maneuvering within imperfectly competitive oligopolies, in which firms establish an implicit understanding to avoid an excessively intense rivalry. In the extreme, FDI might follow an exchange-of-threat rationale, and matching moves demonstrate that no first mover will be able to steal a march on other members of the oligopoly.

While this latter characterization of firm behavior has received its most direct confirmation by Graham (1978) (and others) with regard to cross-investment between the United States and Europe, it is possible that the dynamics are present in the sectoral studies presented above as well: no investor in the automotive, petrochemical, or electronics/computer industries is allowed to gain an advantage from global sourcing that enhances its position in developed-country markets without finding the other major participants rushing to duplicate such an advantage.

Whether there are appropriability problems or exchange-of-threat dynamics, the common conclusion is that left on its own FDI will be undersupplied Thus, there is a global public interest in facilitating and increasing FDI in full-scale manufacturing networks.

From the perspective of individual host governments in the developing countries and economies in transition, what is optimal for the foreign firms and for the host economy also diverges. There is a solid theoretical rationale for trying to attract the first investor and for trying to trigger follow-the-leader behavior. The benefits of success have been great—in particular in the automotive, petrochemical, and electronics/computer cases examined here—and the costs of sitting back and waiting for foreign investors to act on their own is substantial.

Second-Best Rationales for Host-Country Intervention

Distinct from the issue of whether there might be justification for host-country actions to compensate for market imperfections is a further question of whether there might be a rationale for intervention on second-best grounds, to offset interventions by authorities elsewhere.

The sectoral studies provide evidence of a growing effort by developed-country governments, beginning during the early period of globalization in the 1970s and extending to the present day, to use locational incentives to slow the exodus of manufacturing plants and attract new investments.

Interacting perversely with firms that are preoccupied with abandoning existing sites and making "irreversible investments" in new locales, home authorities have used what economic and political tools they could muster to fortify their own positions—with varying degrees of success. In the process, the home authorities have magnified exit costs, subsidized the continuation of existing production, and attracted new investors.[5]

Locational Incentives, Grants, and Subsidies

Between 1977 and 1982, there was a rapid expansion in the use of locational aids and subsidies in Europe and the United States. This process has escalated since then (OECD 1992, 1996a).

In a survey of nine regional incentive programs in Europe in 1981, Yuill and Allen (1981) found that all countries provided capital grants and interest-rate subsidies, four provided tax concessions, and four provided labor-related subsidies. The largest grants were equal to 60 percent of the cost of the project.

In the United States, between 1977 and 1984, the number of states offering a corporate income tax exemption to investors grew by one-third (from 21 to 28), the number of states offering incentives for establishing industrial plants in areas of high unemployment grew by 41 percent (from 17 to 24 states), and the number of states offering state financing aid for expansion of existing plants grew by 25 percent (from 29 to 37 states). Incentive programs "designed to attract new businesses or retain existing ones" grew to more than $20 billion annually (Council of State Governments 1989; Schweke, Risk, and Dabson 1994).

In 1986, concern about the competition in investment incentives within the developed countries prompted the OECD to launch an aggregate data-collection exercise. The overall level of support for industry (including research and development outlays) peaked in 1991 at $48 billion. However, the two components most directly involved in attracting or holding manufacturing firms—investment incentives and regional development incentives—have grown steadily, from 285 programs valued at $11 billion in 1989 to 362 programs valued at $18 billion in 1993 (the most recent year for which there are data). Grants have been the most widely used instruments: the share of grants in total industrial support from government exceeded 60 percent in 11 countries and 40 percent in 16 countries.

The focus of these programs, moreover, has expanded over time from a predominant concern with keeping companies and jobs in place to attracting new investments, in particular foreign investments. In the mid-1980s, OECD members worried that investment incentives and other industrial support would be confined to indigenously owned companies.

---

5. In addition to locational incentives, developed countries have used tariff escalation to protect domestic industries and discourage export-oriented investment in processing minerals or timber elsewhere.

Quite to the contrary, far from showing barriers to the participation of nonnationals in such programs, the OECD data record increasing efforts to use grants and tax concessions to attract foreign firms. The most recent OECD surveys show that fully 86 percent of all domestic support programs are available to foreign investors willing to establish domestic affiliates.

In the early 1990s, the OECD began to collect individual country reports from its members. Ireland, for example, reported to the OECD in 1994 that grants are the most commonly used incentive, with 80 percent of foreign start-ups receiving grant aid of up to 60 percent of fixed-asset costs (OECD 1994). New investors may be awarded additional grants that cover up to 100 percent of the costs of training employees; existing firms may receive up to 50 percent of the costs. The state provides office and building sites in industrial parks free of charge, along with capital grants or rent subsidies. Potential investors may be awarded "financial aid" of up to 50 percent of expenditures on feasibility studies. Ordinarily, grants need not be repaid.

Beyond these provisions, "special incentives may be negotiated for very large projects" in Ireland. In general, the corporate tax rate is 10 percent (in comparison to an OECD average of 30 to 35 percent). Boasting of what has been called the "Irish model," the country calculated that since 1977, these incentive programs have helped bring 1,100 foreign firms, employing 95,000 people, to Ireland, accounting for over half of the nation's industrial output and three-quarters of its manufactured exports.

Within the European Union, Ireland is considered a lagging region[6] and thus is allowed to provide greater incentive packages than are countries of the more developed core, such as France. France reported to the OECD in 1996 that the central government provided subsidies of up to 25 percent of a given investment (OECD 1996c). In addition, to foster job creation, it can provide total or partial exemption of an employer's social security contributions and reimbursement of training costs. Local authorities (regions, departments, and townships) can provide assistance by offering below-market prices for land, water, and electricity and by renting or selling commercial buildings under preferential conditions. They may also grant partial or temporary exemption from the business tax.

Since reunification, Germany has been allowed to provide subsidies to the former East Germany along lines of a "lagging region" and has offered the largest investment incentive packages within the European Union. Germany has not submitted a country study for OECD publication, but, according to the *Financial Times* (8 October 1996), "the amounts of aid Bonn has been prepared to sanction have far exceeded levels

---

6. Ireland, Portugal, and Greece, as well as large areas of Spain and Italy's Mezzogiorno, qualify as lagging regions and receive favorable treatment from EU authorities in approving subsidies for investors.

Table 6.1   Developed-country investment incentives

Site	Investor and date	Subsidy	Employment	Subsidy per employee
Automotive sector				
Kentucky, US	Toyota, 1985	$150 million	3,000	$50,000
Portugal	Ford, 1991	$484 million	1,900	$254,000
S. Carolina, US	BMW, 1992	$150 million	1,900	$ 79,000
Alabama, US	Mercedes Benz, 1996	$300 million	1,500-1,700	$200,000
Petrochemical sector				
Germany	Dow, 1996	$6.8 billion	2,000	$3,400,000
Louisiana, US	Shintech, 1997	$125 million	250	$500,000
Electronics/computer sector				
New Mexico, US	Intel, 1993	$289 million	2,400	$120,000
United Kingdom	Samsung, 1994	$ 89 million	3,000	$ 30,000
United Kingdom	Siemens, 1995	$ 77 million	1,500	$ 51,000
United Kingdom	Lucky Goldstar, 1996	$ 320 million	6,100	$ 48,000

Sources: UNCTAD (1996); *The New York Times* (9 November 1995, 1 September 1996); *Financial Times* (8 October 1996).

previously set by EU states, and forced other European governments to increase their own incentives."

Comparisons between the United States and other developed countries are extremely difficult because the United States uses tax expenditures at both the federal and the state level for industrial support far more than do other countries. The United States has reported to the OECD only on state-government development policies, indicating that 36 states devoted economic resources to attracting or retaining investments on a discretionary basis (OECD 1995). The report acknowledged that incentive packages in the range of $50 million to $70 million were "typical" for such purposes and that the value of such incentive packages had been escalating, "particularly for high-impact, high-visibility projects." For example, the report cited $300 million in incentives paid to attract a single automobile plant in 1993.

Thomas (forthcoming 1998) has suggested that local tax expenditures may be as high as state tax expenditures, given the near-universal use of property tax rate abatements by municipal governments. The earlier sectoral study of the automotive industry showed a sharp escalation of state and local investment-incentive packages in the United States: from $11,000 per job for Nissan in 1980; to $13,857 per job for Mazda in 1984; to $26,667 per job for Saturn in 1985; to $51,000 per job for Subaru/Isuzu in 1986; to $65,000 per job for BMW in 1992; and to $200,000 per job for Mercedes in 1996. For the three sectors examined earlier, investment incentive packages have been large, and rising, within the OECD (see table 6.1).

One would have to know the details of the proposed plants in each of these sectors, and the strategies of each of the parent firms, to judge to what extent there might be direct competition between developed countries and developing countries/economies in transition for any given particular investment. However, it is clear that the international companies are making their investment decisions in the context of a bidding war among alternative sites running to tens of thousands of dollars of subsidy, and sometimes hundreds of thousands of dollars of subsidy, per job created.

Impact of Locational Incentives on International Investment Decisions

While the extent to which developed- and developing-country production sites can substitute for each other surely varies by industry, large segments of the automotive, petrochemical, and electronics/computer industries turned out to be quite movable during this initial period of globalization. And the overlap among developed- and developing-country sources of inputs, components, and final products in these industries alone—especially in the automotive and petrochemical sectors—remains large. Still, on the basis of the evidence from these industries, it would be difficult to predict how "contestable" production sites within other manufacturing sectors might be.

But does the increase in locational incentives have any impact whatsoever on which investment sites multinational firms choose? One might wonder at the need to pose the question in such a way, as if such grants, subsidies, tax breaks, and other incentives might not affect the investment decision-making process at all.

But there is a long tradition of assertion that locational incentives offered by developed countries have little impact on firms' investment decisions (and are not, in any case, trade distorting) whereas export requirements (including incentives) offered by developing countries do have an impact (and are, in all cases, trade distorting).

What evidence has the debate over the impact of incentives on investment decisions produced? In the first extensive empirical survey on this issue, Reuber (1973) reported that 10 of 69 international firms in his sample indicated that incentives had little or no influence on the decision to undertake a particular project or not. The Reuber study noted (1973, 129), "It is evident that incentives are of some importance, particularly those provided via trade policy and tax measures. On the other hand, most firms are acutely aware of the difficulties posed by such incentives and frequently assert that they are reluctant to undertake projects that are heavily dependent for their success upon the incentives provided by the host country." The Reuber results have subsequently been interpreted

Table 6.2   Use of incentives to influence location

	Type of incentive that influenced location	
Market orientation of the project	Commodity (tariff protection)	Factor (tax holidays, grants, etc.)
Small domestic markets	23[a]	2
Large world-scale markets	1	15

a. Indicates that for 23 of the 41 projects examined, tariff protection was among the top 3 factors influencing the investment decision.
Source: Wells (1986).

to show that incentives are not, by themselves, significant determinants of where foreign investors choose to locate.

In the second principal empirical survey on this issue, Guisinger (1985) posed a counterfactual question to 30 international firms with regard to 74 investment decisions in some 20 developed and developing countries: if the host government were to offer you no incentives instead of the incentive package you received (or expect to receive for projects in process), would your investment decision have been different? In answer to this question, 50 of the 74 investors in the Guisinger sample reported that in the absence of the incentive package they would have abandoned the project, relocated it to another site, or served the market through exports.

Concurrent interviews with government officials demonstrated that they had considerable knowledge of investment packages offered elsewhere, and they believed that they could not reduce their packages to attract foreign firms without losing substantial FDI. Explicit performance requirements in return for incentive packages were more common in developing than in developed countries, but via careful structuring of such packages "developed countries achieve much the same result using implicit performance requirements " (Guisinger 1985, 1989)

Wells's (1986) recasting of the Guisinger (1985) data helps to reconcile the Reuber (1973)/Guisinger findings and clarify the role that incentives play. Wells divided the investment projects in the Guisinger sample into two groups: those whose output was destined exclusively for a small domestic market and whose size did not capture all the economies of scale in production and those whose output was destined for a large world-scale market and whose size did capture all relevant economies of scale. He then separated the locational inducements, following Guisinger's terminology, into "commodity incentives" (tariff protection) and "factor incentives" (fiscal benefits such as tax holidays and grants).

The results, summarized in table 6.2, show that, for projects oriented exclusively toward a small domestic market, investors consider tariff protection to be highly important but fiscal incentives less so. For projects oriented toward large world-scale markets, investors consider fiscal incentives (grants, tax holidays, or reduced tax rates) to be highly important, but not tariff protection. Wells argued that these findings are consistent with surveys showing that special tax treatment in Puerto Rico, for example, has had a significant impact on the locational decisions of international investors that want to supply the United States market. Encarnation and Velic (1998), too, argue that investment incentives play a larger role in the location of export-oriented operations than in the location of other kinds of activities.[7] Grants, tax holidays, and reduced tax rates do, in short, play a role in multinational corporate choice among locations for investment. (For a detailed examination of the corporate decision-making process at General Motors, for example, see box 6.1,[8] which provides a case study describing how the General Motors headquarters in Detroit instructed investment negotiators in Europe to compare the "long-term competitiveness" of alternative sites for EU-wide production in the United Kingdom, Belgium, Portugal, and then-East Germany and allow locational incentives and subsidies to be used as a tiebreaker.) The importance of relative tax burdens for the locational decisions of international firms has been demonstrated in recent econometric studies of the relationship between tax policy and the activities of multinational corporations. Hines (1996) has found that differential tax rates exert a "powerful effect on the location and magnitude of foreign direct investment." Outside the United States, countries with a 1 percent lower tax rate attract up to 3 percent more investment from the United States than they otherwise would; within the United States, states with low tax rates attract significantly greater FDI than high-tax states do. Policies that affect after-tax returns have a strong impact on investment decisions: a 1 percent increase in after-tax returns is associated with 1 percent greater investment (Hines 1996).[9]

---

7. Michalet (1997) argues that what zero-sum competition there is among alternative investment sites is confined primarily to particular regions, such as the European Union-Eastern Europe-Turkey, Asia, and the Western Hemisphere.

8. There is often a gap in perspective on the corporate decision-making process between business strategists and economists. Starting with assumptions of less than perfect competition, business strategists tend to consider major international corporate decisions to spring from competitive considerations that must endure for long periods of time—through changing economic circumstances, exchange rate relationships, and price fluctuations—with little attention to conditions at the margin at any particular moment in time. Locational grants, subsidies, and tax breaks are not likely, in their view, to play a large role in the choice of production sites. Starting (usually) with assumptions of near-perfect competition, economists consider firm decisions to spring more directly and rapidly from changes in market signals at the margin. Locational grants, subsidies, and tax breaks are likely, in their view, to have an impact in the choice of production sites. The case study in box 6.1 shows a blend of the two perspectives: competitive pressures drive corporate strategists to consider alternative ways to reinforce their long-term market position; locational grants, subsidies, and tax breaks then act as a tiebreaker among closely comparable sites.

9. Hines concludes that "governments compete with each other to offer firms ever-lower

Bond and Guisinger (1985; see also Guisinger 1989, forthcoming 1998) have been able to show, moreover, that changes in fiscal incentives do affect trade patterns, not unlike tariff protection. They found that the substitution of investment incentives for tariffs after Ireland's entry into the European Community left the effective rate of protection to manufacturers unchanged. Similarly, a study at the Federal Reserve Bank of St. Louis that focused on the relationship between fiscal incentives and export promotion has documented a positive correlation between the investment-promotion expenditures of individual states and subsequent exports from those states, even within a large country such as the United States (Coughlin 1988).

Overall, the most recent OECD assessment of locational incentives concludes, "the enormous amounts of support provided under such schemes, in the order of up to US$100,000 per job created by the investment, call for a policy discussion on their trade- and competition-distorting side-effects" (OECD 1996b, 6).

The escalation of locational subsidies in the developed countries over the past two decades has left the developing countries and economies in transition at a disadvantage along several fronts. With the exception of some oil-exporting states, the developing countries and economies in transition do not, as a rule, have the financial resources to offer grants along the lines of many OECD countries. Instead, the most frequently used investment incentives are tax holidays (in particular, "pioneer status" for firms that are just starting up), investment tax credits, and accelerated depreciation. But the complexities of deploying these tax incentives efficiently, combined with administrative weaknesses in the countries themselves, prevent these tools from being used effectively.

Detailed studies of the use of the tax system to promote investment in Brazil, Mexico, Pakistan, Turkey, Malaysia, and Thailand show, inter alia, that tax incentives lead to highly distorted decision making for domestic and foreign firms, because they discriminate between firms that show losses in early years and those that do not and between relatively capital-intensive activities and relatively labor-intensive activities. They also shift tax revenues abroad in cases where there are no tax-sparing agreements between home and host governments and often generate revenue losses for the government that exceed the value of the new activities stimulated (Shah 1995).

---

tax rates to attract activities that are believed to be beneficial to their economies." In a study of the behavior of 3,000 firms in 14 countries, Cummins, Hassett, and Hubbard (1996) found that tax treatment of corporate income had a significant effect on firms' investment decisions. In particular, when corporate income tax rates fell, the amount of investment increased. Other studies that have failed to find such an effect, they argue, did not examine corporate investment both before and after major changes in tax law. Cummins, Hassett, and Hubbard did not look at the investment behavior of foreign and domestic firms separately.

As a result, there is little support among fiscal experts for more aggressive use of tax breaks and tax incentives to try to stimulate foreign (or domestic) investment in the developing world or economies in transition. Instead, recommendations for fiscal reform highlight a need for greater simplicity in tax structure, adjustment of corporate tax rates so that they are similar to those of the capital exporting countries, nondiscrimination between foreign and domestic investors, and the avoidance of double taxation via tax treaties with capital exporting countries.

At the end of the day, therefore, the difficulties in designing effective incentive structures, the institutional drawbacks to implementing such incentive structures successfully, and the lack of resources to supply upfront grants put less-developed countries and economies in transition at a fundamental disadvantage in trying to compete with the developed countries for international investment.[10]

In this context, they are particularly vulnerable to adopting an illadvised path of least resistance, using rents generated via trade protection or other forms of market exclusivity as an off-budget way to match the locational incentive packages available elsewhere (see box 6.1).

In short, developing countries and economies in transition do not have the resources to compete with the developed countries in the struggle to attract international investment and often are driven to make poor policy choices in the effort to try. This not only results in economic inefficiencies but also generates a perverse political-economic dynamic as well: firms and workers with protected positions utilize what economic and political clout they have to slow down or prevent efforts to liberalize investment and trade flows.

Strategic-Trade Struggles and the Intersection between Trade Protection and Investment Diversion

There is a third rationale that might justify intervention by host governments that are trying to utilize FDI to penetrate international markets—namely, to strengthen or defend one's position in a strategic-trade battle over the distribution of rents.

On a theoretical level, FDI has all the underpinnings for just such a struggle: barriers to entry and imperfect competition are the necessary conditions for firms to deploy their "intangible assets" outside of the familiar home economy. These intangible assets generate rents, which may emerge in the form of supranormal profits for the investor; most often they are found in the higher wages and desirable activities (attractive "chunks" of inframarginal activities) conducted by the foreign corporation

---

10. For the self-defeating nature of competition for investment and the disadvantages of poorer countries in such a competition, see Graham (forthcoming 1998).

Box 6.1 Trade rents vs. grants and investment subsidies in the competition to attract automotive investors, 1990-96

Investment-incentive packages offered by the developed countries sometimes place direct pressure on developing countries and economies in transition to devise ways to present comparable offers. Less obvious are the cases where developing countries and economies in transition have had to compete indirectly, in the same environment of offer and counteroffer of incentives, often dealing with the same senior executives and the same negotiating teams reporting back to the same parent decision makers, but not necessarily having to "beat out" alternative developed country sites as head-to-head substitutes.

The negotiations in the early 1990s between General Motors and the German government to build an integrated auto assembly plant at Eisenach in the former East Germany and between General Motors and the Hungarian government to build an export-oriented engine plant at Szentgotthard show the impact of indirect competition of the latter kind.

The negotiations with German authorities came first. The General Motors business plan for Europe in 1990-93 included one new assembly plant for 150,000 vehicles (with possible expansion to 200,000), to meet volume projections. GM strategists took four alternative options under consideration: an extension of a Vauxhall plant at Ellsmere Port in the United Kingdom; the reactivation of a mothballed plant at Antwerp in Belgium; a greenfield plant in Axambuja, Portugal; and a quasi-greenfield plant at Eisenach in the former East Germany.

As background for the negotiating team, GM assembled the following internal data on government assistance for investments in the automobile industry: as of 1989, Ford had received 58 percent of a $200 million investment in Portugal; GM had received 45 percent of a $119 million investment in Portugal; GM had received 37 percent of a $124 million investment in Spain; and Chrysler had received 30 percent of a $599 million investment in Austria. Memos between GM headquarters in Detroit and the GM negotiating team in Germany contained instructions that "the most important thing that should influence the decision is the long-term competitiveness of the facility." Once the comparison was narrowed sufficiently to be a "wash," however, subsidies and other special locational advantages "might appropriately be used as a tie-breaker."

Armed with the incentive comparisons, the GM negotiating team made the pitch for government support at the highest level, to Chancellor Kohl on 5 October 1990. They argued that the German government had hitherto proposed investment subsidies for the Eisenach plant that were only two-thirds of those available elsewhere, that the GM request for an investment grant of $267 million would be repaid in personal tax, social security, and corporate tax payments within as little as three years of completion of the facility and that if GM's request were denied the company regretted that it would not be able to participate in the chancellor's grand plan to rebuild the east. Kohl approved the grant at very near the level requested by General Motors (the Harvard Business School case writers were sworn to secrecy as to the exact amount and required to promise to destroy their notes in case the documentation might subsequently be sought by Brussels).

(continued on next page)

Box 6.1 (*continued*)

At the same time, General Motors was negotiating with Hungary for a $300 million engine plant to produce 200,000 engines (1.6 and 1.4 liter) to be exported for use in cars assembled within the European Community. To launch this project, General Motors negotiated a 10-year tax holiday, a $76 million loan from the European Bank for Reconstruction and Development, and $37 million equity infusion from the Hungarian State Development Institute. Beyond this, however, the Hungarian government was able to mobilize an investment grant of no more than $25 million.

Searching for ways to supplement such a comparatively modest investment package, therefore, Hungary entered into agreement with General Motors for the construction of a boutique 15,000 vehicle assembly facility (alongside the full-scale engine plant) protected with a 22.5 percent import duty, plus offering GM the right to sell 2,000 additional vehicles duty free. The package, conveniently "off budget" for the Hungarian negotiators, would generate as much as $77 million per year in trade rents to be collected by General Motors. (What proportion of the trade rents accrues to GM as extra profits depends upon production costs in the boutique plant.)

The two-part General Motors facility has brought valuable benefits to Hungary: the engine plant capacity was approximately doubled in 1996 (to 460,000 units per year) and became even more firmly embedded in Opel's greater-European sourcing strategy. The determination of General Motors management to make it a success, combined with what turned out to be a highly motivated Hungarian workforce that was eager to be trained in western production methods, has resulted in the Szentgotthard engine plant winning quality awards in internal competition with GM engine plants in the United Kingdom and Germany. Suzuki has followed General Motors into Hungary, looking for an export platform into the European Union.

As for GM's boutique assembly plant, however, output peaked at 8 vehicles per hour in comparison to 90 vehicles per hour at GM's full scale assembly operations elsewhere in Europe. There are no plans to "grow" the plant out of protected infant-industry status. Hungarian authorities boast about the status conveyed by having a "Hungarian Opel." They have taken credit for the jobs created by the assembly plant (213 jobs in a single shift assembly operation in comparison to 890 workers in three shifts in the engine plant); however, they do not point out that the cost per job created has averaged approximately $300,000.

Hungarian trade negotiators fear that the labor/ministry/political constituencies, which now have an interest in preserving the "Hungarian Opel" with its 213 jobs, will exercise pressure to slow trade liberalization in the country's accession process into the European Union. Such protectionist coalitions, including protected foreign investors, have already had an impact on trade-and-accession policy in Poland (for details, see chapter 4).

Sources: Harvard Business School (1993); Klein (1995).

where it carries out production. In addition, they may generate externalities in the form of uncompensated spillovers of benefit to other sectors of the economy where the FDI is located.

Empirically, the studies of FDI in the automotive, petrochemical, and electronics/computer sectors bear this out. The direct operations of the foreign investors created tens of thousands of jobs (paying higher than average wages and training managers and workers who sometimes move elsewhere); produced billions of dollars of exports; introduced technology that was one-third newer than any other method of technology acquisition; produced a follow-the-leader effect on the investment behavior of rivals in the industry; and brought component companies with them as investors too.

At the same time, the foreign investors trained indigenous suppliers in management, quality control, and mastery of technical processes, and the founders of such indigenous suppliers often came from the ranks of their own managers. In the automotive and electronics/computer industries, they qualified hundreds of local firms to meet OEM and REM standards. They introduced domestic firms as suppliers to other subsidiaries of their parents abroad; many of those domestic firms began to export to arms-length buyers in international markets as well.

In this process of incorporating new host-country production sites into their global/regional/sourcing networks, they brought what this study has identified as an integration effect. That is, they linked the operations within hosts to the cutting edge of technology, best business practices, and quality control standards needed to maintain their competitive position around the globe. They introduced the subsidiary to the major leagues; they required the subsidiary to raise its state of play to championship levels and to maintain the quality of its contribution.

The strategic determination of the parent to tie the operations of the subsidiary to the parent's fate in international markets may constitute an FDI version of the phenomenon Richardson and Rindal (1996) and Richardson and Khripounova (1997) have found for companies that are "globally engaged." These authors discovered that a firm's commitment to link itself with international markets brings a set of challenges which, when met and mastered, sets it apart from firms that do not make such a commitment. The globally engaged firm shows better performance in terms of management, marketing, and technology; it is more flexible, agile, and responsive to threats and opportunities; it generates higher profits and pays higher wages and benefits than other firms; it grows faster and provides (surprisingly) greater stability for workers, managers, and suppliers.

Beyond the integration effect, the foreign investors' decision to establish full-scale export facilities in each of these sectors—automotive, petrochemical, and electronics/computer—frequently led to the clustering of related activities nearby, which themselves also carried economies of scale, economies of scope, opportunities for pooling and specialization, and probabilities of technological/human-resource spillovers.

To what extent do these clustered activities constitute "poles" of economic geography, replete with "thick externalities"? Specialists in the field of economic geography and strategic-trade theory will wish for more detailed studies of externalities and of agglomeration effects of scale, scope, and specialization, using case study analysis such as Borrus, Doner, Ernst, Rasiah, Linden, Peres Nuñez, Shapiro, etc. and using statistical analysis such as Aitken, Blomstrom, Haddad, Hanson, Harrison, etc. summarized in the previous chapter.

But just as Krugman (1991, 22) was impressed by Alfred Chandler's account of one or two great companies laying the basis for regional industrial centers with one or two great investment decisions in the United States (accompanied by follow-the-leader effects), so future economic geographers are likely to tie the establishment of industrial complexes around Sao Paulo, Minas Gerais, Monterrey, Matamoros, Surabaya, Jubail, and Penang to one or two investment decisions on the part of the multinational investment community (accompanied by follow-the-leader effects).

And practitioners in the construction of new economic geography in Russia, Ukraine, Romania, China, and Vietnam and in the reconfigured economic geography of India, Argentina, and the Philippines will want to understand the dynamics not just of the firms themselves but of the contending regions where the automotive, petrochemical, and electronics/computer industries (inter alia) of the future may come to be located.

As they do, they will note that there are two additional policy tools, besides locational incentives, that are increasingly being deployed in the struggle to attract international investment, capture rents, and fix the location of great industrial complexes.

These two additional policy tools are antidumping regulations and rules of origin. Each could be considered an important tool for hosts on the second-best grounds of the previous section. But they are even more appropriate to be considered here as an element of the strategic-trade struggle because of the central role they are likely to play as administrative protection turns trade wars into investment wars.

The analysis here adds a new dimension to the understanding of strategic-trade competition that is of special importance for developing countries and economies in transition. Strategic-trade theory, in general, draws on a stylized model in which all actors have comparable resources and comparable production sites and in which the public sector determines where investments become located. Rules of origin and antidumping regulations, however, are being deployed not simply to shift rents among comparable production sites but to cancel out and offset the structure of production that international comparative advantage would otherwise dictate. This has particularly ominous implications for countries that hope to use international investment to propel their growth along the path of comparative advantage.

Rules of Origin

Rules of origin determine which products enjoy the benefits of a preferential trading agreement as a function of how much domestic content is embodied in the product (Krueger 1992; Krishna and Krueger 1995). Their rationale is based in negotiating strategy: they prevent free riders from enjoying access to the liberalized internal market in a particular region without having to take comparable liberalizing measures themselves. They are also used as protectionist devices, to limit competition from sources outside the preferential trading area. Finally, they serve as investment-forcing measures, because they require companies that want to enjoy access to the preferential area to undertake production locally to meet the required domestic-content levels.

The simplest method that has traditionally been used to determine origin is a "change of tariff heading rule," which allows goods with local processing sufficient to move its classification from one Standard Industrial Trade Classification (SITC) code to another to qualify as a domestic product. The further rules of origin depart from this change of tariff heading standard and require greater levels of domestic content for a product to qualify as domestic, the more protectionist the impact and the greater the diversion of investment needed to meet the standard.

As the sectoral examination of the electronics/computer sector showed, the United States and European Union have imitated each other in utilizing rules of origin, along with other restrictive policies, to protect local industries and to shift FDI into member states (Skud 1996).

The use of rules of origin as protectionist devices first came to prominence, in fact, not in the electronics/computer sector, but in the automotive sector. After the United States-Canada Free Trade Agreement adopted a 50 percent local content requirement for automobiles, the United Kingdom and France proposed an 80 percent local content rule for the Nissan Bluebird to qualify as an EC product. In the end, they backed down in the face of Italian and German opposition and decided to rely on quantitative restrictions to protect against Japanese imports (Jensen-Moran 1996a, 1996b).

The use of rules of origin to divert investment soon came to focus on "high value added" activities associated with electronics/computers and other office equipment. As indicated earlier, in 1989, the European Union abruptly changed the rule of origin to require that "diffusion" (wafer fabrication) for semiconductors be done within Europe to avoid the high, 14 percent semiconductor tariff. Whereas US companies performed most of their diffusion operations in the United States prior to the decision, 7 of the largest 10 US producers built fabrication facilities in Europe following the rule change. Citing the need to comply with the new rule of origin, for example, Intel invested $400 million in Ireland for wafer fabrication and semiconductor assembly. The European Union has adopted high domestic-content rules of origin in other industries such as photocopiers, as well, and the European Union has also entertained proposals for even tighter requirements for printed circuit boards and telecom switching equipment.

A similar mix of protectionism and investment shifting was evident in the US effort in NAFTA to prevent "screwdriver" assembly operations from being set up within the borders of Canada, the United States, and Mexico that could utilize low-cost inputs from outside. For automobiles, electronic products (printers, copiers, television tubes), textiles, telecommunications, machine tools, forklift trucks, fabricated metals, household appliances, furniture, and tobacco products, NAFTA rules of origin require that a substantial portion of inputs originate in NAFTA countries.

In some sectors, the principal target for protection and/or investment shifting was another developed country. In automobiles, raising the domestic content rule from 50 percent in the United States-Canada Free Trade Agreement to 62.5 percent in NAFTA required Japanese and European firms to replace imports from their home countries. But the impact cannot be confined to developed countries: flows of parts and supplies from production sites in developing countries and economies in transition are certain to be affected as well.

As indicated in the section on electronics/computers, many of the domestic-content rules in NAFTA were aimed specifically at diverting imports and investment from developing-country sites and, in particular, at forcing investment in North America at the expense of Asian production locales. In telecommunications, the requirement that 9 out of 10 printed circuit boards be packaged in North America disadvantaged AT&T, Fujitsu, and Ericsson operations in Asia and led them to shift investment to North America. Similarly, in color television, the requirement that the major component in the set (the television tube) be of North American origin caused Hitachi, Mitsubishi, Zenith, Sony, and Samsung to initiate or to expand tube production within NAFTA borders. As for copying machines, the special rule of origin (equivalent to 80 percent value added) was instrumental in forcing Canon to build a $100 million-plus copier facility in the United States rather than in Malaysia or China, where the parent judged that costs would be lower.

As for regional trading restrictions elsewhere, in the EU association agreements with countries in Eastern and Central Europe, the relatively restrictive rules of origin have distorted trade and investment patterns in comparison to what international comparative advantage would dictate. The 60 percent domestic content in the automotive sector has forced the General Motors engine plant in Hungary to use high cost German steel as an input, preventing utilization of Hungarian or Polish steel instead, for example, let alone steel of Russian, Turkish, or other origin (Klein 1995). The near 100 percent domestic-content requirement in textiles and apparel has forced the German partner in the Brinkmann-Prochnik joint venture in Poland to load a truck with cotton fabrics, thread, buttons, and even labels in Germany; transport it to Lodz for stitching into trench coats; and reimport it for sale in the European Union—rather than allow the Polish partner to source from cheaper supplies locally or develop new suppliers in Belarus, Ukraine, Romania, or Bulgaria (Harvard Business School 1994).

Mercosur, likewise, has deployed a regime for rules of origin that has stimulated strong rates of internal investment. However, it has had a distortionary impact equivalent to relatively high tariff walls that has limited imports from nonmember countries in Latin America and elsewhere (Yeats 1997).

In the multilateral "harmonization exercise" for rules of origin within the WTO, as well as in regional negotiations to extend NAFTA into a Free Trade Area of the Americas, or to enlarge Mercosur, or to incorporate East and Central European states into the European Union, the central choice will be to maintain (or even deepen) the beggar-thy-neighbor thrust of current origin regimes or to reduce regional domestic-content provisions on a multilateral basis.

Host countries in the developing world and economies in transition not only have a high stake in an outcome dictated by others, but could themselves be instrumental in building higher or lower walls among regions. Their interest in widening the access for products incorporated in the global sourcing patterns of international investors along lines of comparative advantage should lead them to advocate the latter.

The thrust toward protecting local industries and diverting investment via rules of origin with high domestic-content reinforces, and interacts perversely with, a second tool that accomplishes the same objectives, namely, antidumping regulations. One might think that with an overall reduction in tariff levels, rules of origin might be of diminishing importance. But rules of origin ensure that only products that meet stringent domestic-content requirements will be exempted from the threat of antidumping prosecution, even as external tariffs decline.

Antidumping Regulations

Antidumping regulations do have a legitimate role in trade policy. That role is to prevent international price discrimination with a predatory objective of driving out competition and monopolizing foreign markets.

Selling abroad at a price lower than in domestic markets is prima facie evidence of the presence of trade restriction in the home market; otherwise, arbitrage and the reimport of domestic goods sold more cheaply abroad would force the price levels together. Such trade protection provides home-country producers with rents to use in trying to drive foreign producers out of business in a predatory manner.

In the past two decades, however, the legal test for dumping in the United States and the European Union has shifted from price discrimination to selling below "the fair cost of production," with the latter defined as average total cost plus a markup for overhead and profit. Because firms will be driven toward marginal cost (or average variable cost) in pricing their output under competitive conditions, this use of average cost to characterize "fairness" imposes an inefficient standard as the definition of dumping (Boltuck and Litan 1991; Deardorff 1989).

The standard based on average cost plus markup for overhead and profit also enshrines discrimination against external producers: local firms are allowed to respond to competitive conditions by pricing near marginal cost when market circumstances dictate. But foreign firms are not allowed to match this behavior without being found guilty of dumping. In short, two firms, one domestic and one foreign, can be pursuing exactly the same practices, pricing their output at exactly the same level, and the domestic firm can go about its business freely while the foreigner can be taken to court and found guilty because of the way that dumping is defined.

Antidumping actions are filled with a rhetoric about "unfair behavior" being perpetrated by foreigners. In contrast to such emotion-laden characterization, however, a review by the OECD of antidumping cases in Australia, Canada, the European Union, and the United States found that 90 percent of the import sales judged to be unfair according to contemporary antidumping standards would have been legal under corresponding domestic competition standards; that is, they would be considered perfectly fair if undertaken by a domestic firm making a domestic sale (Finger 1997).

The investment-diversion impact of antidumping regulations takes place in two ways: first, indirectly, by generating an obstacle or an uncertainty that retards a firm's investment in potential export operations and second, directly, by causing the redeployment of production to the market protected by antidumping regulations. The easiest way to avoid antidumping liability is to slip in under the umbrella of domestic competition law, establishing operations within the market where a firm hopes to sell its products rather than exporting to that market from abroad.

Overall, between 1985 and 1994 there were 450 antidumping investigations by the United States, 428 by Australia, 240 by the European Union, 203 by Canada, and 270 by all other countries together, with duties being levied in 70 to 80 percent of the cases for the United States and the European Union.

The inefficient, discriminatory, and investment-diverting nature of antidumping regulations is exacerbated when those regulations are applied against products from the economies in transition. The presumption for antidumping purposes is that prices are distorted in the former communist/socialist economies and that these economies do not have market forces strong enough to generate accurate information even on average costs of production. The developed countries, therefore, use "surrogate" countries to simulate "constructed costs" based on prices for inputs such as labor, raw materials, energy, and capital in the surrogate rather than the true exporting economy. Whatever comparative advantage the economy in transition might have from lower input costs and/or greater efficiency than in the surrogate is thereby lost.[11]

Producers in the countries chosen as surrogates are then petitioned to provide detailed information on their costs, which they often refuse to do (because such information is not infrequently used subsequently to prepare antidumping actions against them). The antidumping adjudication agencies then collect the best information available, much of which is supplied by lawyers for the petitioners, to make their determinations.

The choice of surrogate countries is both arbitrary and impossible to anticipate, leaving any firm (domestic or foreign) that wishes to consider investing in an export facility in a given economy in transition without any way to know how vulnerable such a facility might be to future antidumping actions. In two petrochemical cases (low-density polyethylene and polyvinyl chloride) Sweden was used as the surrogate country even though antitrust cases had shown cartel behavior to be particularly strong in Sweden and prices there were "the highest possible prices of reference" (Messerlin 1990a). Likewise, in a third petrochemical case (sodium carbonate), Austria was chosen despite its status as a highly protected market dominated by a single seller (a Belgium firm, Solvay), which was the main petitioner in the antidumping case, a drawback subsequently recognized by the EC Commission in its review of the case (Olechowski 1993).

Imputed costs of production of electric motors in Bulgaria, the Czech Republic, Hungary, Poland, and Romania have been calculated by the European Union by measuring the costs of production of electric motors in Sweden (Hindley 1993). The costs of steel plate from Romania have been derived by the US Commerce Department by reviewing the costs of production of steel plate in Finland (the Finnish producer's reward for cooperating was to find itself the subject of a subsequent antidumping review). The costs of manhole covers from China were first estimated on the basis of costs of production of manhole covers in Belgium, Canada, France, and Japan, with a resulting 11 percent antidumping duty. Three years later, the surrogate production site chosen to construct costs for the same Chinese manhole covers was redesignated as the Philippines (which does not export manhole covers to the United States), using imaginary raw materials from the United States, Britain, and Japan imported into the Philippines, then hypothetically exported back to the United States as manhole covers, with a resulting 97 percent antidumping duty (Down the Commerce Dept.'s Manhole, *The Washington Post*, 25 December 1990). With the arbitrary surrogate-country test,

---

11. Only a comparative advantage from using factors of production less intensively remains (Horlick and Shuman 1984).

an investor that wants to construct an export platform in an economy in transition cannot predict what liability the subsidiary may later encounter in prosecution for dumping.

Under such circumstances, the exports from the economies in transition have been easy targets. From 1980-90, the European Community imposed antidumping duties or negotiated "price undertakings" in 77 percent of the cases brought against exporters in Eastern Europe (Eymann and Schuknecht 1993).[12] From 1990-93, US antidumping actions brought against states of the former Soviet Union (Russia, Ukraine, Tajikistan, and Kazakhstan) were uniformly successful, with antidumping margins above 100 percent assessed in every case (Wagnon 1995; Michalopoulos and Tarr 1994).

Given the faulty microeconomics of the contemporary test for dumping, no investor in any sector can have confidence in its ability to engage in normal business practices in pricing products for export without ending up in court. Like rules of origin, antidumping regulations severely limit the possibility of using FDI (or indigenous investment, for that matter) to penetrate international markets.

In addition to the direct impact of antidumping regulations on trade flows, there are indirect, more subtle, effects. One might suppose that antidumping laws affect trade only when a petition is filed, dumping is proved, injury is demonstrated, and antidumping duties are imposed. But studies demonstrate that

- the mere existence of antidumping laws can stifle exports from countries that might be the target of such laws even in periods when no petitions are actually filed (Staiger and Wolak 1994);

- there are substantial "investigation effects" from antidumping petitions that prevent foreign exporters from aggressively pursuing market share;

- antidumping petitions withdrawn before a final determination can have as restrictive an impact on subsequent trade flows as would be the case if a "guilty" determination had been made and penalties imposed; and

- antidumping actions that are in fact rejected still have a substantial impact on exports from the named country (Prusa 1992, 1994, 1997).

The number of antidumping investigations initiated by industrialized countries rose precipitously during the late 1980s and early 1990s and

---

12. In the 1990s, the European Union has successfully initiated antidumping cases involving five commodities against Russia, Ukraine, Kazakhstan, and Belarus, although it is not known what percentage of all cases this represents (Michaloupolous and Tarr 1994).

Table 6.3 Antidumping investigations initiated, 1988-96

	1988-90	1991-93	1994-96
Industrial countries	289	539	310
Developing countries	31	118	246

Sources: GATT (1997); Finger (1997).

leveled off thereafter. Antidumping initiations by developing countries, in contrast, have surged (see table 6.3).

As in the case of rules of origin, the challenge for the developing countries and economies in transition that want to utilize FDI in penetrating international markets is to join ranks with multinational investors in unraveling these growing barriers to global sourcing along lines of comparative advantage. Their increase in use of antidumping regulations is a major step in the wrong direction.

Policy Implications for Using Foreign Investors to Penetrate International Markets: The Dilemmas of Passivism, Escalation, and Playing for a Draw

This chapter began by asking how well markets function in allocating production sites to serve international markets. It found indications of several possible kinds of market failure that suggest that FDI in world-scale export facilities is likely to be undersupplied. Furthermore, there is a role for would-be host governments to expend resources to trigger investor response on domestic welfare grounds and for multilateral policies to encourage and support the spread of such investment on global-welfare grounds. The stakes in attracting export-oriented investment, moreover, turn out to be much larger than conventional calculations suggest: the rewards are much greater, and the opportunity costs of waiting passively for such investment to arrive on its own are much higher.

Among the principal obstacles to effective market functioning, the imperfectly competitive nature of the industries and problems of information asymmetry and appropriability are not the only hindrances to optimal investment flows. The use of locational incentives by public authorities eager to maintain old production sites or attract investment to new ones provides a second-best justification for intervention to correct for distortions.

Finally, the competition for the particularly lucrative, externality-filled chunks of economic activity associated with FDI has all the characteristics of a strategic-trade battle to capture rents. In this context, the array of investment-shifting/rent-capturing devices deployed by the developed countries is more dangerous than commonly assumed. As this chapter shows, these devices cannot be excused as a mere nuisance. They are not simply a mild safety valve to be used to release economic and political pressure while the great processes of liberalization rolls ahead. Instead, they are highly disruptive to the proper functioning of markets and introduce serious distortions.

This leaves authorities in the developing countries and economies in transition with a dilemma of major proportions. On the one hand, there are multiple justifications for intervention, high rewards for success, and weighty penalties for passivity. On the other hand, joining in the struggle to attract investment with the policy tools already in play—locational subsidies (or trade rents from protected operations to substitute for grants), tight regional rules of origin, and antidumping actions—is quite unlikely to improve, and quite likely to harm, the ability of their countries to utilize FDI to penetrate international markets.

For developing countries and economies in transition to adopt a strategy of matching the interventions of the developed world would be to engage in a battle they cannot win, and whose outcome they may worsen.

The strategic-trade framework helps to identify the only effective way out of this dilemma. The internal dynamics of competition for rents is quite predictable. In particular, there is an endemic drive to search for advantage, with matching moves on the part of others and escalation the logical result, unless there is a common effort to establish a cease-fire and draw back.

The less-developed countries and economies in transition have a vital self-interest not to participate in the same myopic set of actions (expanding their own antidumping actions, tightening rules of origin in their own regions, engaging in the locational incentive race, etc.) that undermines the ability of all economies to develop along lines of international comparative advantage. Instead, their long-term self-interest requires that they support, participate in, and even lead such a cease-fire and drawback.

Host-Country Policies to Constrain Ownership on the Part of Foreign Direct Investors: Joint-Venture Mandates and Technology-Licensing Requirements

Introduction

Turning from host-country efforts to influence the activities of foreign investors to host-country efforts to limit foreign ownership, one of the most persistent, and ubiquitous, issues of the policy debate in the developing countries and economies in transition is whether to require foreign investors to take on local partners in joint ventures rather than operating with 100 percent ownership; or, further, whether to require foreign firms to enter the host economy only via licensing technology to local business firms (what has traditionally been called the "Korea model" or "Japan-Korea model") and not via direct investment at all.

What are the costs and benefits of each of these approaches to foreign investors? Here the analysis of policy options must move from purely economic considerations and begin to take in political and national-security implications as well.

7

FDI and Joint-Venture Requirements

The ostensible rationale for giving preference to or requiring joint ventures is to try to capture more of the benefits that foreign investors have to offer. In particular, host countries want to achieve greater "technology transfer," expanded access to external markets, and more robust backward linkages to the domestic economy than would take place without preferences/requirements for joint ventures. Broader issues—including building an indigenous business class, promoting self-reliance, and enhancing national defense—are treated in chapter 8.

How do preferences/requirements for joint ventures contribute to these objectives? For many kinds of operations, the joint-venture relationship offers benefits to all parties. Survey research shows that local partners can be particularly valuable in providing location-specific knowledge regarding host-country markets, local tastes, local business practices, local labor practices, local suppliers, and local business-government relations.

Beamish (1988) and Raveed and Renforth (1983) find that when choosing joint-venture partners, international investors look for help with entry into the local market, insights into local business practices, access to indigenous general managers, assistance with local financing, advice on board decisions, and provision of general knowledge of the local economy, politics, and culture. When these needs predominate, host authorities need not impose any kind of requirements or offer any kind of incentives to stimulate foreign investors to adopt the joint-venture form of operation.

At the same time, however, international firms weigh the revenue-enhancing and cost-reducing opportunities of using local partners against the strategic risks, principal-agent conflicts, and transaction costs they encounter when they enter into joint-venture arrangements.

For those activities for which parent firms consider dilution of control to be a primary concern, the parents are unlikely to form a joint venture at all, or, if they accept a requirement to do so, they record a high degree of dissatisfaction with the local partner and the joint ventures suffer a high rate of dissolution.

Parent firms place the highest value on "unambiguous control" (Stopford and Wells 1972) for those investor activities that involve rapid technological innovation, a large degree of brand recognition and product differentiation, and large economies of scale in production.

Drawing on the Harvard Business School database of 187 US multinationals, Stopford and Wells (1972) found that high research and development expenditures as a percentage of sales, high advertising as a percentage of sales, and an organizational proxy used to represent international rationalization of production were all clearly associated with a preference for wholly owned subsidiaries and an avoidance of the joint-venture format. Subsequent research by Fagre and Wells (1982) showed that the greater the technological intensity, advertising intensity, and export intensity of an investor's operations in the developing countries, the more likely the parent was to insist upon, and receive, wholly owned status for its affiliates. Reuber (1973) found that joint ventures had smaller scale, narrower product lines, and less input of parent technology than did wholly owned ventures.

Japanese firms demonstrated a greater propensity than did US or European firms to form joint ventures (Beamish and Delios 1997), but the data surveyed earlier from Encarnation (1992) shows that they are less likely to integrate offshore subsidiaries into global sourcing patterns, less likely to export in general, and more likely to focus on producing for the local market where the subsidiary is located.

Tsurumi (1976) has suggested that Japanese investors seek local expertise and political cover for historical and cultural reasons, but that after they had settled in, the Japanese parents often took full control of their subsidiaries. Makino and Delios (1996) record that as the Japanese parents of 558 joint ventures gained more than 10 years experience in East and Southeast Asian markets, the initially favorable impact of the local partner on the joint venture declined to the point where the presence of the partner was likely to be considered detrimental to the affiliate's performance.[1]

What happens when joint ventures are not a product of spontaneous choice, when international firms form joint ventures under host-country pressure, despite their preference for "unambiguous control"? This cat-

---

1. Makino and Delios (1996) did not control for the extent to which the subsidiary might be engaged in exports as opposed to purely domestic-oriented production. Beamish and Delios (1997) find that the propensity to form corporate alliances of all types has been declining since 1986.

egory of cases is not rare. In a survey of 66 joint ventures located in 27 less-developed countries, Beamish (1988) found that while 43 percent were created because the parent needed the local partner's skills, assets, or other attributes, a sizable majority (57 percent) resulted purely from host-government pressure or legislation. Dissatisfaction was widespread. While Beamish did not separate responses according to the voluntary or required nature of the union, 61 percent of the firms in this sample, overall, gave an "unsatisfactory" rating to the performance of the joint venture.

Within this same sample, there was an instability rate of 45 percent after three years of existence (in a separate study Reynolds [1984] found an instability rate of 50 percent). For joint ventures involving government partners, the instability rate was an even higher 56 to 58 percent.

What are the sources of conflict? Beamish (1988), like Rugman (1985) and Parry (1985), suggests that "opportunism" of the indigenous partner is at fault. In particular, he points to leakage of technology and appropriation of knowledge gained within the joint-venture arrangement as the primary reasons for dissatisfaction and failure (see also Miller et al. 1996).

Kogut (1988) finds that conflict among the partners and joint-venture termination increased as a function of the degree of coordination that the parents desire between the subsidiary and other corporate operations. Gomes-Casseres (1989) traces conflicts to differences of perspective between the foreign and domestic joint-venture partners on quality standards, exports, and the pricing of goods and services when either the parent or the local partner buys from or sells to the joint venture.

Overall, Caves (1982, 93) has observed that "joint ventures are shunned by the multinational enterprise that cherishes a secret intangible asset or extensively transfers components among its subsidiaries. Where a joint venture is forced on an unwilling multinational enterprise, the firm is likely to adapt by cutting back on the resources it commits to the business."

With this background, it is not surprising that the direct evidence is not promising on the use of joint ventures to try to enhance technology transfer, penetrate international markets, or even expand and strengthen backward linkages to the domestic economy.

Joint-Venture Requirements and Technology Transfer

Technology flows between nations are dominated by transfers among multinational corporate affiliates. From 1970-85, more than 80 percent of the payments made to the United States for the sale of technology came from external units of US firms (Grosse 1989). For Japan and Germany, between 60 and 90 percent of all technology payments from developing countries originated in the foreign affiliates of their own firms (United Nations Centre on Transnational Corporations 1988).

In measuring the speed of introduction of new technologies, Mansfield and Romero (1980) found that parent firms transferred technology to wholly owned subsidiaries in developing countries one-third faster, on average, than to joint ventures or licensees. In a sample of 31 firms and 65 technologies, they found that the mean age of the technology at the time of the first transfer to subsidiaries in developed countries was 5.8 years, to wholly owned subsidiaries in developing countries was 9.8 years, and to joint ventures and license holders was 13.1 years.

In the same vein, Vernon and Davidson (1979) traced the ownership pattern via which "innovations" in the US market came to be produced outside of the United States and measured the period between the first introduction of a new product in the United States by a US-based multinational firm and the first foreign production of that product. With regard to ownership pattern, over the first three decades of the post-World War II period 71.5 percent of the foreign production of goods that were recent innovations occurred within subsidiaries of the parent firm; 28.5 percent represented transfers via licensees. Even for "imitations" (products that closely resemble the innovations of other firms, although "new" for the introducing firm), the spread of overseas production via subsidiaries surpassed the spread via licensees by more than two to one. With regard to speed of technology transfer, more than 80 percent of the foreign production of new goods that occurred within three years of initial introduction in the home market were limited to subsidiaries; less than 20 percent took place via licensing. While licensing gained in importance for products that were more than 4 or 5 years old, it still accounted for less than a third of all production of new goods 10 years after the products had first been introduced in the home market. Although Vernon and Davidson did not subdivide their sample of subsidiaries into wholly owned, majority owned, and minority owned in their study, they were working with a data set in which research and development expenditures by the parents in the home market were highly correlated with the use of wholly owned subsidiaries abroad.

In a detailed case study of a single industry in a single country, Grieco (1984) found that as India moved away from mandatory shared ownership in the computer industry, abandoned attempts to create a national champion, and allowed international companies to engage in partnering and alliance relationships on their own, the country's technological lag (the difference in years between a system's introduction in the advanced countries and its adoption in India) decreased. The cost of technology acquisition—measured by Grieco as the price per bit of main memory—also declined.

In the automotive sector, China's joint ventures have utilized technology and manufacturing methods that have been a decade or more old when introduced (Uncertain Terrain: In China, GM Bets Billions on a Market Strewn With Casualties, *The Wall Street Journal*, 11 February 1998). Malaysia's effort to develop a "national champion" car firm, Proton, as a joint venture with Mitsubishi suffered from similar problems of technology lag, as documented in the case study in box 8.1 (Doner 1995b; Institute of Developing Economies 1995).

Reuber (1973) found fewer inputs of foreign-investor technology into joint ventures than into wholly owned subsidiaries.

Looking at technology performance requirements more generally, Kokko and Blomstrom (1995) found that the imposition of host-country mandates on the behavior of foreign affiliates was negatively associated with technology inflows into the host country. The strongest stimulus to increase technology imports to foreign affiliates, in contrast, came from increasing competitive pressures within the industries in which the multinational firms were located.[2] First documented in an examination of behavior in the Mexican manufacturing industry (Blomstrom, Kokko, and Zejan 1992), the power of local-market rivalry in forcing foreign affiliates to adopt more advanced technology was confirmed in a study of technology imports of US subsidiaries in 33 host countries, including 14 developing countries (Kokko and Blomstrom 1995).

Joint-Venture Requirements and Export Performance

Mandatory shared ownership does not brighten the prospects for penetrating international markets. Wholly owned affiliates are much more likely to be eligible to participate in the global/regional sourcing network of international firms. And, as a byproduct of such participation, there is evidence that they also better help suppliers to become exporters to other subsidiaries of the same parent and to independent external buyers.

Stopford and Wells (1972) found a negative correlation between subsidiaries' participation in the regional/global sourcing strategies of the parent and participation in joint ventures. Only 9 manufacturing firms of a sample of 55 that had regional/global patterns of production were jointly owned. And where joint ventures did exist, there were frequent reports of conflicts with partners over transfer prices, market allocation, and rationalization of production.

---

2. The performance requirements that Kokko and Blomstrom (1995) examined included mandates to use the most advanced technology available, perform research and development locally, have access to the parent's patents, or transfer skills to local personnel. The authors were not able to analyze the impact of joint-venture requirements directly.

Fagre and Wells (1982) found that of 54 foreign affiliates in Latin America that exported half or more of their output, 51 were wholly owned subsidiaries. In no instance was the parent corporation in one of the export-intensive operations a minority partner.

Overall, the evidence on joint ventures indicates that the requirement for a local partner weakens export performance in comparison to wholly owned foreign subsidiaries. As noted earlier, the technology employed is not as current as in the wholly owned foreign counterpart (to some extent out of fear of having the technology misappropriated), concerns about quality control inhibit integration of local production into the parent's global network, and the survivability of such joint ventures is quite precarious.

Once wholly owned subsidiaries undertake export operations, however, they often act as catalysts that stimulate the export performance of domestic firms. The sectoral studies in chapter 5 showed fully owned affiliates, under the "unambiguous control" of the parent (Stopford and Wells 1972), helping indigenous supplier firms to break into external markets, directly and indirectly.

In both the automotive and electronics/computer sectors, in both Latin America and Southeast Asia, foreign investors provided information, training, and network contacts that helped their suppliers to become exporters. Eight years after the parent auto firms began their own export drive from Mexico, six of the ten largest auto parts exporters (excluding engines) were wholly owned Mexican firms. All nine (of a sample of nine) local machine-tool firms that grew up serving foreign electronics investors in Malaysia became exporters, seven to affiliates of the subsidiaries they supplied at home and two to independent purchasers; the export composition of all local firms grew from less than 1 percent of output in 1984 to 32 percent of output in 1990.

Other research documents the same outcome, that the activities of foreign-owned exporters act as an export catalyst for local firms. The effect results from a spillover or externality from the mere presence of the former. Rhee and Belot (1989) offer 11 detailed case studies in which foreign investors opened export channels to local firms by providing inputs (contacts, quality control, management know-how, and knowledge about export markets) not available in the host country and not totally internalized by the foreign firms themselves.

Aitken, Hanson, and Harrison (1997) found, in a study of 2,104 Mexican manufacturing plants, that the probability that any given domestic-owned plant exported was positively correlated with proximity to foreign-owned plants. Their data contained the surprising discovery that the export activity of domestic-owned plants was uncorrelated with the local concentration of exporters overall. The link between exports on the part of domestic firms and proximity to foreign investors was robust when they controlled for overall industrial activity in a region, for proximity to the capital city, and for proximity to border regions. They concluded that the observed export spillover sprang directly from the presence of foreign investors.

The goal of enhancing the export potential of indigenous firms would best be served, therefore, by policies that maximize the presence of foreign plants engaged in exporting from the host country. This can be accomplished by encouraging wholly owned subsidiaries and eliminating joint-venture requirements.

Joint-Venture Requirements and Backward Linkages to the Domestic Industrial Base

With regard to backward linkages and the strengthening of domestic producers of goods and services, the survey evidence of Beamish (1988) introduced earlier indicates that foreign investors choose to enter into joint ventures so that they can utilize their partners' special managerial skills, local marketing skills, and access to local finance.

One would therefore expect to find that joint ventures have more extensive ties to the local economy and rely more on local suppliers than do wholly owned subsidiaries. Wholly owned subsidiaries, in contrast, are more likely to pull subsidiaries of other foreign companies into the local economy to act as suppliers to their own operations.[3]

Which of these patterns contributes more to the competitiveness of the local economy? More specifically, to what extent do foreign firms upgrade the capabilities and improve the productivity of local operations in which they are engaged as joint-venture partners in comparison to operations in which they are sole owners? And what is the likelihood of spillovers and externalities to the domestic economy from joint-venture operations in comparison to wholly owned operations?

There are detailed studies showing that foreign investors exhibit higher levels of total factor productivity than do their local counterparts (Haddad and Harrison 1993; Harrison 1996; see also Kokko and Blomstrom 1995), that sectors with a larger foreign presence exhibit higher levels of total factor productivity than do sectors with a lower foreign presence (Blomstrom and Persson 1983),[4] and that sectors with a higher foreign presence have a lower dispersion of productivity among all firms than do sectors with a lower foreign presence (suggesting a spillover from the foreign presence that moves domestic firms closer to the efficiency frontier)

---

3. Both contentions are consistent with observed differences in behavior between domestic and foreign firms (O'Brien 1993). O'Brien did not separate the behavior of wholly owned subsidiaries and joint ventures among the foreign firms.

4. Borenzstein, de Gregorio, and Lee (1995) find that FDI has a larger impact on growth than does domestic investment.

(Haddad and Harrison 1993).[5] However, there is remarkably little control in this research for differences between wholly owned and jointly owned ventures.[6]

A notable exception that attempted to establish a relationship between extent of ownership and productivity found a positive correlation. Using panel data following more than 4,000 firms in Venezuela from 1976 through 1989, Aitken and Harrison (1997) showed that a 10 percent increase in foreign ownership was associated with a 1.35 percent increase in output. Plants with 100 percent foreign ownership had output levels on average 13.6 percent higher than domestically owned plants. Because Aitken and Harrison controlled for differences in inputs, this increment in output represents a pure productivity gain.

Besides upgrading the productivity of the specific industries in which they are located, foreign wholly owned subsidiaries seem to exhibit dynamic patterns of backward integration to indigenous suppliers in the same or other industries.

The study of the automobile sector in chapter 5 showed that within 5 years of the foreign auto firms' decision to source from Mexico, there were more than 300 domestic producers of parts and accessories whose ranks included more than 100 Mexican firms with annual sales exceeding $1 million. Within 10 years of the foreign auto firms' decision to source from Thailand, there were 150 local firms qualified as OEM suppliers, and 250 qualified as REM suppliers.

In the electronics/computer sectoral studies in chapter 5, suppliers to semiconductor investors in Malaysia moved from simple machining and stamping to high precision tooling and sophisticated parts fabrication. O'Brien (1993) reports that domestic purchases of equipment and services by foreign investors in Malaysia's free trade zones have been on the increase. Lim and Fong (1977, 1982, 1991) trace an expansion of vertical linkages between multinational investors and local firms in the electronics industry over a five-year period in Singapore, Malaysia, and Thailand.

Combining the evidence here about backward linkages with the earlier indications of more rapid introduction of technology into the host economy and greater penetration of international markets from host production sites leads to the following point: the greater the activity of wholly owned subsidiaries in a given economy the more likely the prospects for spillovers and externalities to domestic firms.

---

5. Haddad and Harrison (1993) offer the caveat that this seems to represent a one-time increase in domestic firm efficiency and not an ongoing process.

6. Given, on the one hand, the strong relationship between speed and extent of transfer of technology and best management practices on the part of parent corporations and, on the other hand, their use of wholly owned subsidiaries abroad—as documented by several studies in this chapter—attempts to measure total factor productivity of foreign investors without controlling for ownership structure would appear to be seriously limited.

8
FDI and Technology-Licensing Requirements

Much of the literature on mandatory technology licensing as a substitute for FDI reaches well beyond the acquisition of technology per se and toward a broader goal of nurturing an indigenous business class, with a political as well as an economic rationale: to enhance national autonomy, national power, and national security.

In the analysis of whether technology-licensing requirements are the best method to meet these objectives, political and economic considerations need not necessarily be in conflict, because the (political) ability to influence events, resist external pressures, and, in the extreme, conduct military operations is a function of the (economic) resources a given country can devote to collective or individual efforts to affect outcomes upon the world stage. Thus, what enhances a country's economic prospects may also enhance its national power and autonomy.

But they are not always congruent, and sometimes require complicated trade-offs between how much independence and autonomy a country hopes to acquire in return for foregoing the creation of a certain amount of wealth.

The literature on replacing FDI with mandatory technology licensing draws inspiration from what has customarily been referred to as the "Korea model" (or the "Japan-Korea model") of development.

Despite the differences and idiosyncrasies in the historical evolution of Japan and South Korea, the key ingredients of this model are:

- import restraints combined with vigorous export promotion;

- fiscal subsidies and other preferences to create national-champion firms in particular sectors; and

- severe restrictions on FDI, combined with aggressive insistence upon licensing and other technology-sharing arrangements that leave control of firms in national hands (Westphal 1979; Amsden 1989; Haggard 1990; Wade 1990; Schive 1990).

In the aftermath of the Asian financial crisis of 1997-98, there is reason to ask whether a system of import restraint and export promotion that focuses on chosen sectors and preferred national firms can ever escape the political-economic corruption and crony capitalism that have figured so prominently in the history of many Asian economies. But to give as fair a hearing as possible to those who favor technology-licensing requirements, it might be appropriate to focus first on what has been the core appeal of the Korea model, namely, the alleged superiority of such requirements to a more liberal orientation toward FDI in four areas (two economic, two political):

- enhanced technological deepening, achieved by creating broader and more independent indigenous research and development capabilities;

- enhanced industrial deepening, achieved by transporting the country beyond mere screwdriver assembly;

- enhanced political autonomy, based on a greater ability to control the actions of national champion firms; and

- enhanced national security, based on greater self-reliance and less dependence upon outsiders.

How well do mandatory technology-licensing requirements accomplish these objectives in comparison to a more liberal approach to trade and FDI?

Mandatory Technology Licensing and Technological Deepening

Perhaps the strongest argument on behalf of the model comes from comparing the levels of indigenous research and development in South Korea and elsewhere. Evans (1995), for example, highlights the different levels of internal research and development in South Korea and Mexico: the two countries have roughly equal amounts of local manufacturing value added, but South Korea has indigenous research and development expenditures of approximately 2 percent of GDP whereas Mexico has indigenous expenditures of only about 0.02 percent of GDP.

This is an impressive contrast. It is important, however, to look more closely at how the superior South Korean performance came about. A large part of this vigorous internal effort is accounted for by a relatively small number of firms in a single industry. The electronics industry, led by three firms—Samsung, Lucky Goldstar, and Hyundai—accounted for more than 40 percent of all research and development personnel in South Korean industry in 1992 (Ernst 1994).

And this intensity in research and development is a recent phenomenon. It did not emerge during the heyday of the Japan-Korea model (from the promulgation of the law for electronics industry promotion in November 1969 until the basic guidelines of policy for liberalization of technology imports of February 1978), when a combination of import protection, FDI restriction, and mandatory technology licensing helped to found the *chaebols* (South Korean industrial conglomerates).

As Westphal (1979, 252) has noted, even the electronics industry had a thin layer of research and development activity as late as 1979. "Electronics production," he observed, "is largely an assembly operation, and little infusion of the basic technological know-how has taken place."

Instead, the drive to deepen the technological capabilities of the *chaebols* grew out of exposure to competitive pressures as labor costs rose in South Korea, and the South Korean firms had to match the prices and quality of their rivals when those rivals spread their operations through Southeast Asia in the 1980s.

Between 1980 and 1984 the number of industry-managed research and development institutes grew four-fold, from 8 to 32. Between 1985 and 1991, the number of research and development personnel in the electronics industry grew from roughly 5,000 (32 percent of all researchers in South Korean industry) to about 16,000 (41 percent of all researchers in South Korean industry). Research and development spending climbed to 4 percent of turnover (Ernst 1994).

Throughout this period, the *chaebols* benefited from a highly favorable business environment. Sound macroeconomic policies and a high savings rate not only provided fiscal incentives for research and development but also funded a strong educational infrastructure to back it up (World Bank 1993; Fishlow et al. 1994).

To be sure, South Korean authorities targeted specific levels of research and development expenditures (six key technologies in the Sixth Five-Year Economic and Social Development Plan). But the public-sector share of research and development expenditure fell steadily, from 68 percent in 1978 to 16 percent in 1990. And, while the centrally directed public intervention did mobilize resources within highly concentrated industries to help them to master reverse engineering and efficient mass-production techniques, the targeting effort, in the view of a close observer, has had a seriously detrimental by-product, namely, a dearth of independent and innovative small and medium-sized supplier firms that has "substantially constrained" the prospects for on-going technological expansion (Ernst 1994, 56).

In the aftermath of the financial upheavals in Asia, what must South Korea do now to ensure that the country once again becomes a model of economic growth and development? Ironically, according to Ernst and others, the best approach to ensure that South Korea regains its position as a developmental model for other countries is to abandon the Japan-Korean model of development. These observers recommend turning the public and private sectors away from industrial targeting and toward policies that focus more on diffusing technology, in particular, on expanding "the future role of inward FDI as a vehicle for technology diffusion" (Ernst 1994, 118).[1]

The evidence introduced in chapters 5 and 7 by Mansfield and Romero (1980), Vernon and Davidson (1979), Blomstrom, Kokko, and Zejan (1992), Haddad and Harrison (1993), and others—showing that wholly owned subsidiaries within highly competitive industries provide the most rapid vehicle for the transfer of technology into a given economy, with potentially significant spillovers to indigenous firms—supports this recommendation. Products and processes that are less than three years old are more likely to be introduced for local production via the subsidiaries of foreign investors than via licensing, by a ratio of 4 to 1. Products and processes that are 10 years old are still more likely to be introduced for local production via the subsidiaries of foreign investors than via licensing, by a ratio of 3 to 1.

Why should this recommendation for contemporary South Korea not be the preferred strategy for other hosts from the beginning, if the policy is supported by fiscal, educational, and competition policies of a kind that will reward research and development activity in general?

The answer, according to Evans (1995), for example, is that a particular historical sequence is required: (1) the erection of a "greenhouse" of tariffs to protect infant sectors from external competition and (2) "midwifery" of fiscal support and preferred procurement. Only after this preparation can indigenous firms be ready to participate successfully in international markets (see also Evans and Tigre 1989).

It is difficult to judge such a contention because there is no calculation of the opportunity cost to the economy of following the steps recommended by Evans (1995) compared with a sequence featuring greater openness to trade and investment. Furthermore, the subsequent developmental contribution of national firms generated via such midwifery has not been compared to that of the national firms Peres Nuñez (1990) found growing to international status in the midst of the Mexican automotive industry or that of the national firms Borrus (1994), Ernst (1994), Rasiah, and Linden (1996) found growing to international status in the midst of the Malaysian electronics/computer industry. And there is no calibration

---

1. Ernst argues that the challenge for South Korea now lies in trying to use inward FDI and alliance relationships with foreign companies to acquire "best practice" management, production, and marketing techniques, as well as product and process technology. In both areas, "outdated policy instruments that focus on excessive restrictions continue to be an important constraint" (1994, 119).

of how difficult and costly it is to ensure that there are institutional prerequisites for successful midwifery, including relentless exposure of greenhouse-grown national firms to international competition at the right moment, ruthless cutoff of greenhouse life support to apparent losers, and independent and noncorruptible public authorities who can navigate such a rent-seeking-filled environment with minimal blemish.

Until such calculations, comparisons, and calibrations can be investigated more thoroughly—however optimistic the investigators are willing to be that political-economic payoffs and other manifestations of crony capitalism can be kept under control—it would seem that the burden of proof that this constitutes a superior path for development should fall on those who might still advocate pursuit of the Korea model.

Technology-Licensing Requirements and Industrial Deepening

From the outset, any assessment of the Korea model of industrial self-sufficiency has to be modified to note that, in the South Korean case, US companies actually played a central role in the creation and subsequent development of the electronics industry.

As Ernst (1994) points out, four American firms—Motorola, Signetics, Fairchild Semiconductor, and a joint venture called Komy Semiconductor—dominated the creation of South Korea's chip assembly industry from its inception in the late 1960s through the end of the 1970s. These foreign investors opened up export channels for chips and for consumer electronics assembled in South Korea: their share of exports did not drop below 40 percent until 1980. They also, in Ernst's estimation (1994), exposed South Korean workers and managers to organizational techniques that helped to curb the rigidities and inefficiencies of the highly authoritarian South Korean business practices.

Then, even after the South Korean *chaebols* began to dominate in the industry, these *chaebols* relied on OEM relations with major US firms to penetrate external markets: Samsung selling videocassette recorders and microwave ovens via General Electric; Daewoo selling televisions for Zenith and Emerson; and Goldstar selling videocassette recorders via Zenith and Philips and microwave ovens via Whirlpool. In 1986, OEM contracts accounted for 33 to 81 percent of all consumer electronics exports from South Korea, depending upon the product; by 1992, the overall OEM share of South Korean consumer electronics exports was 69 percent.

Thus, the stylized view of the emergence of South Korean firms as self-sufficient except for licensed technology has to be modified to take into account a rather large direct and indirect contribution from FDI and foreign corporate alliances.

While the appeal of the Japan-Korea model comes from the dynamic growth that has taken place in leading sectors, such as electronics and automobiles, the appeal dims in examining the situation in lagging sectors. Here, the relatively weak performance of South Korea in some industries, such as chemicals/petrochemicals, can be traced in large part to the regulations and controls (joint-venture requirements, technology-transfer requirements, etc.) that host authorities placed upon foreign investors such as Dow Chemical (Schwendiman 1984).

The Korea model thus contains notable cases of unsuccessful deepening and poor industrial performance. Proponents of the Korea model have not systematically compared the list of successes in building national champions with counter examples plagued by large expenditure of resources and far less successful results.

Moving beyond South Korea, there is impressive evidence of a growing number of national champions and Third World multinational corporations emerging from among the ranks of local firms in the developing countries and the economies in transition (Evans 1993; Evans and Tigre 1989; Encarnation 1989; Lall et al. 1983; Wells 1983). And, once such national champions achieve a certain level of size, experience, and self-confidence, they hold their own in negotiating technology transfer, product development, and marketing arrangements with foreign firms. They use international business ties, including the acquisition of foreign companies, to enhance their competitive position in international markets.

But the studies of the automotive, petrochemical, and electronics/computer industries in chapter 5 showed multiple examples of such firms growing up in industries filled with foreign investors, often beginning as suppliers to foreigners.

In light of this, the contention that countries that adopt a more liberal approach to FDI will be caught in the trap of mere final assembly is not supported by the data. The automotive industry in South Korea should be compared with the automotive industry in Brazil and Mexico, and the electronics/computer industry in South Korea should be compared with the electronics/computer industry in Malaysia and Thailand.

Such comparisons would have to consider the nontrivial issue of diversification. In the automotive industry, for example, the prospects for the countries examined earlier—Mexico, Brazil, and Thailand—are linked to the performance of almost all the major international companies from the United States, Japan, and Europe, whereas the prospects for South Korea are much more directly dependent upon the fate of a single national champion, Hyundai, backed at some distance by Daewoo. As for electronics/computers, the dependence is less stark for South Korea, with three principal national champions, Samsung, Lucky Goldstar, and Hyundai. However, there is still nowhere near the robust diversification that Malaysia or Thailand enjoy in this sector.

Technology-Licensing Requirements and Enhanced Control over National Champions

Placed in comparative historical perspective, the ability to control national champions in ways that meet internal developmental needs better than FDI turns out to be a somewhat elusive undertaking.

The sectoral studies in chapter 5 showed evidence of some of the European frustrations with their own national-champion strategies. The Italian government provided subsidies and preferences to Fiat in the hope that the Italian national champion would then serve as an agent of regional development. Fiat did become such an agent of regional development, but in Minas Gerais, not the Mezzogiorno. Volkswagen faced similar conflicting loyalties, between the demands of the government that had helped launch it and the demands of an increasingly independent senior management that saw the future of the company as requiring a thoroughly global strategy. Even France, the strongest proponent of national-champion industrial targeting, had to watch as Michelin built plants abroad at a rate twice that of the rate at home (Vernon 1974).

Overall, the idea that national champions would better serve domestic developmental goals than would other firms soon ran into the dilemma that to remain competitive such champions preferred to, and had to, match the behavior of their rivals elsewhere. If they did not, they increasingly became wards of the state and a burden on indigenous development.[2]

The "Who-Is-Us?" debate—questioning whether firms of own-country nationality can be counted on to behave systematically differently from firms of other-country nationality—is likely to grow more intense, not less, for national planners in the developing world and economies in transition. To maintain their competitive position in international markets, South Korean firms have positioned their research and development and higher-value-added activities in developed-country markets, not at home. And developed-country hosts are not making this choice any less agonizing: as recorded previously, the United Kingdom set a new record for attracting investment in the electronics/computer sector with its $320 million, $48,000 per job bid for Lucky Goldstar.

The case study in box 8.1 records the costly and comparatively ineffective effort of Malaysia to establish Proton, a national-champion automobile company. Now, after great domestic sacrifice for Malaysia in launching the national champion, Proton is repaying the favors bestowed upon it by moving production offshore to Vietnam and the Philippines (Institute of Developing Economies 1995).

Finally, wherever national-champion companies ultimately decide to

---

2. Well before the "Who-Is-Us?" debate became popular, this dilemma was explored in Bergsten, Horst, and Moran (1978, chapter 11).

Box 8.1 **The problematic experience of creating a**
national-champion car company in Malaysia

Malaysia's decision to develop a national-champion automotive company, Proton, via technology licensing from a minority Japanese partner, provides a marked contrast to its more successful strategy with multiple foreign investors and multiple ownership patterns in the electronics sector. Like other countries in Southeast Asia, Malaysia's early approach to auto-sector development centered on local-content requirements. Like them, it struggled to break into export markets in the face of export prohibitions on the part of Japanese investors.

Instead of offering trade liberalization on imports in exchange for higher export performance, however, as Thailand, Mexico, and Brazil did, Malaysia demanded increasingly higher levels of domestic content, from 42 percent to 80 percent, supplied by firms that had to meet "bumiputera"—quotas of Malay ownership. Instead of letting foreign investors choose where comparative advantage might dictate an opening for international market penetration (e.g., engines or wiring harnesses), Malaysia insisted upon production and export of a particular product, a national car, built by Proton. Instead of playing rival investors off against one another, Malaysia relied on a single joint venture between Mitsubishi and the Heavy Industry Corporation of Malaysia (HICOM), the government's principal development agency from 1983 to 1993.

In an effort to achieve economies of scale, Malaysian authorities gave Proton's passenger car substantial preferences and advantages in the Malaysian market. Reductions in or exemptions from tariffs on imported components were made only to Proton. Exemptions of sales tax were made only to Proton. Civil servants were able to receive special low-interest loans only when they purchased automobiles from Proton.

"Consumer choice has been restricted by (Malaysian) policy, as buyers have little option but to purchase relatively expensive Proton products," concluded a study by the Institute of Developing Economies in Tokyo. "It cannot be denied that one critical key to the success of the Proton lies in the transfer of economic rents from other sectors."

With this help, Proton's market share in Malaysia grew to almost 50 percent in the mid-1980s. But output remained around 80,000 units per year. It became evident that the key to achieving full economies of scale lay in penetrating international markets.

(*continued on next page*)

position their highest-value-added and most rapidly growing divisions, the adoption of a national-champion development strategy opens the door, inevitably, to pleading for special preferences on the part of powerful rent-seeking constituencies that may well not be able to distinguish their own self-interest from their interpretation of the national interest.

Technology-Licensing Requirements and National Security

In much of the literature about the Korea model, national security appears to be in the eye of the beholder; that is, the phrase "national

Box 8.1 (continued)

Its joint venture partner, Mitsubishi, however, did not want to introduce competition among the products the parent sold in the English market and continued to use its Australian facility for exports to Great Britain rather than expanding production in Malaysia.

Searching for ways to break out into international markets, Malaysian authorities decided to sidestep Mitsubishi's established sales channels. In 1984, Proton contracted with an independent British importer, Mainland Investment, which had franchise rights for eleven automobile models in Great Britain, to serve as an outlet for Proton cars. It simultaneously arranged with a second independent agent, Bricklin, which marketed Yugos in the United States, to act as distributor in the Western Hemisphere. This strategy, of exporting Mitsubishi-produced cars via non-Mitsubishi distribution networks, did not prove viable.

Malaysia was left in 1988 with having to reverse direction, turning greater control over the direction of its national champion to the joint-venture partner, Mitsubishi, in return for an expansion of capacity and a promise of exports. Despite ongoing complaints about the slow pace of incorporating the newest product and process technology, Proton attained a domestic market share of 81 percent by 1993 and boasted of exports approaching 20,000 vehicles. Considered a success by Malaysian authorities in comparison to previous low export levels, this accomplishment still amounted to less than one-fifth the value of Thai automotive exports or one-thirtieth the value of Mexican automotive exports in the same period.

Proton automobiles cost approximately 15 to 20 percent more in Malaysia than in Europe. "Why are the cars so expensive?" asked the Economist Intelligence Unit. "The labour costs are low, demand is high and the tax rates for locally made cars are not outrageous. The answer, it seems, is that local buyers are having to pay high prices to subsidise the growth in exports."

The Proton-Mitsubishi alliance announced plans in 1995 to internationalize its own operations, producing small buses in Vietnam and manufacturing automotive components in the Philippines, eventually leading to the production of passenger cars there.

Sources: Doner (1991, 1995b); Lim and Fong (1991); Institute of Developing Economies (1995); Economist Intelligence Unit, 1996.

---

security" can be evoked to justify practically any set of policy interventions without measurement of cost, effectiveness, or alternatives.

In the debate about national security and industrial policy (or strategic-trade policy) in the developed countries, in contrast, the national-security rationale for public-sector intervention has come to assume a much more rigorous and even measurable form. The threat that requires genuine national-security attention is the possibility of denial, delay, manipulation, or the placing of conditions upon the provision of some good or service to domestic users for whom the cost of moving to the next best available alternative is quite high (Moran 1990, 1993; Graham and Ebert 1991; Graham and Krugman 1995).

The necessary condition for such a genuine national-security threat to exist is a high degree of concentration among external suppliers. While there is learned debate about exactly how to measure the necessary degree of concentration, one rule of thumb suggests that if more than four suppliers from four countries control more than 50 percent of the market, translated into an appropriate Hirschman-Herfindahl index, there is little likelihood of effective collusion to enable suppliers to engage in denial, delay, manipulation, or the placing of conditions upon the provision of the good or service.

Absent such concentration, there is no genuine national-security threat. Absent such concentration, there is no well-justified reason to protect nationally owned suppliers, or to prevent FDI from competing with nationally owned suppliers, or to block foreign acquisition of nationally owned suppliers.[3]

This attempt to define with rigor a legitimate national-security rationale for public intervention substantially narrows the sphere where this justification applies. It helps to separate out instances in which there may be a real threat to national security from the variety of other rent-seeking behaviors parading under the national-security label.

The number of industries, or subindustries, with such a high degree of concentration is quite small, even in the sphere of military and dual-use technologies and equipment High performance jet engines, space launch vehicles, satellite equipment, advanced materials, avionics, displays, and associated high-speed computer processing are some goods for which there is tight supplier concentration, and even here the availability of slightly second-best suppliers of these goods is growing.

Countries with a robust indigenous business sector have more options to maintain such crucial products or technologies in national hands on national soil or to diversify suppliers. But, for better or for worse, the realm in which host countries in the developing world and the economies in transition can claim a genuine national-security justification for creating and supporting exclusive national suppliers is becoming quite narrow, and the cost and performance penalties for choosing to rely on exclusive national suppliers is rising steeply (Moran 1990).

At the same time, the possibility of establishing commonly defined, commonly measured national-security exceptions to predominantly liberal treatment of trade and investment appears more likely than it has in the past, at least in theory. This approach should be acceptable to developed and developing countries alike, without any need to appeal for broader restrictions of FDI as contained in the Japan-Korea model.

---

3. For the subtle (but not analytically distinct) case of foreign acquisition of nationally owned military suppliers, see Moran (1993).

IV

Host-Country Policies toward Natural-Resource and Private-Infrastructure Investment

Introduction

Of all the tensions aroused by FDI in the developing countries and the economies in transition, perhaps none are more deep-seated, or more widespread, than those surrounding petroleum, mineral, and private-infrastructure projects.

Will these tensions disappear in the contemporary period? Are there problems that are inherent in these sectors that may require special multilateral measures to ensure that foreign firms can continue to play an appropriate role in their development?

Foreign investment in natural-resource and private-infrastructure projects merits a special section of its own because of a distinctive vulnerability to changes in the terms of the initial contractual arrangements—a distinctive kind of market failure in the "credibility of commitments" on the part of host authorities—that overshadows other kinds of policy concerns.

9

Structural Vulnerability, Imperfect Contracts, and "Political Risk" in Natural-Resource and Private-Infrastructure Projects

Natural-resource and private-infrastructure investments have always aroused unusually strong reactions. Fears about loss of sovereignty, exploitation, gunboat diplomacy, and foreign intervention go back to the 19th century and before. There are sensitive questions about foreign ownership of subsoil rights and about loss of control over exhaustible resources.

For all of these reasons, foreign investors in these sectors have been particular targets of nationalistic actions on the part of host authorities. From the 1950s through the late 1970s, there was no other sector where there were more demands for host-government ownership, and prominent nationalizations took place in mining, petroleum, and foreign-owned utilities (Lipson 1985; Rodman 1988; McKern 1993; Minor 1994).

With greater overall acceptance of FDI in the developing countries and economies in transition today and privatization replacing public-sector ownership at a rapid pace around the globe, one might think that foreign investors in natural-resource and private-infrastructure projects could come to be treated just like FDI in any other sector. But this is not likely to be so. Besides the political sensitivity of investment in minerals, petroleum, pipelines, and other infrastructure, there are structural characteristics associated with such projects that endow them with special vulnerability in their relations with host authorities, special exposure to what Vernon (1971) first identified as the "obsolescing bargain"—adverse changes in the terms of the investment after the project is successfully launched—that will not automatically disappear, and could even be exacerbated, within a climate of greater openness and eagerness toward FDI.

Structural Vulnerability and the Obsolescing Bargain

The obsolescing-bargain model grew out of early efforts by Penrose (1959, 1968) and Kindleberger (1965) to understand the negotiations between foreign investors and host countries within the framework of bilateral monopoly, with the firm controlling sector-specific capabilities and the host government controlling the conditions of access.

Within this bilateral monopoly, Penrose argued, the host should aim to offer no more than the bare minimum to attract FDI. Quite to the contrary, countered Kindleberger, foreign investors should expect to receive returns at least equal to the scarcity value of their services. According to him, hosts should consider how much worse off they would be if they had to move to the next-best alternative for the exploitation of their resources and be prepared to offer anything above that to the potential investor.

Two conclusions emerged from the Penrose/Kindleberger debate: first, the outcome of negotiations between foreign investors and host authorities about the terms of entry was indeterminate. Second, the range among plausible solutions was quite broad.

But Vernon (1971) believed that the bilateral monopoly framework of Penrose and Kindleberger was too static (see also Moran 1974; Smith and Wells 1975). What adds dynamism to the foreign-investor/host-country relationship is the evolution of risk and uncertainty over the life of an investment project.

Before the investment is sunk, risk and uncertainty are high and the potential investor should be able to extract quite favorable terms to compensate for both. These terms are enhanced by the investor's quasi-monopolistic position. But as risk and uncertainty dissipate after the project proves successful and as other potential investors emerge to erode the quasi-monopolistic position, the host finds itself in a position to renegotiate the initial terms rather than keep paying the opening risk premium forever.

This dialectic in investor-host relations produced abundant evidence of the obsolescing bargain from the mid-1960s to the mid-1980s. Even in cases where no host ownership or nationalization took place, the typical time interval between negotiation and renegotiation of investment contracts shortened and the swing in tax rates alone grew by 30 to 40 percentage points.

While the dynamics of the obsolescing bargain were frequently surrounded by heavy emotion in individual cases, Vernon's insight underscored a "rational" thrust of self-interest that lay beneath the terms demanded by both sides, by the foreigner in the terms sought at the beginning and by the host in the terms sought in subsequent periods.

The thrust of self-interest sprang from political as well as economic origins: initial host authorities would award terms attractive enough to entice the first investment; successor host authorities would claim that those terms were overly generous and constituted an affront to national needs. But this political dialectic was itself suprapolitical: left-wing governments engaged in it and so did right-wing governments; democratically elected governments engaged in it and so did authoritarian governments; civilian governments engaged in it and so did military governments.

Even when FDI remained welcome and nationalization and expropriation were never threatened, this political dialectic has tended to overshoot. Rival political aspirants could not resist demanding renegotiation of contracts in these sectors, even if the process retarded reinvestment by the original investor or scared off new investment by other companies in the same sectors.

In one of the most detailed analyses of this phenomenon, Mikesell (1975, xx) examined the internal rate of return on the investment for two large "successful" mining projects, one in Latin America and one in Southeast Asia. His study covered lengthy project life cycles, and he concluded that there was a common pattern of undercompensation for the investors that created the prospect for suboptimal patterns of investment even when there was no overt threat of nationalization. He concluded that if the changes in the regulatory environment "had been anticipated by the foreign investors, it is doubtful whether either of these mines would have been constructed."

The inability of host authorities to keep promises hurt themselves, hurt the investors, and hurt the world at large. FDI in natural-resource projects (and, by inference, private-infrastructure projects) are more exposed to this "structural vulnerability" than are investors in other sectors. They must make large lump-sum investments that require payment of a high risk premium long after the initial risk and uncertainty have dissipated. Furthermore, the parent firms must require that winners in a particular country not only pay for themselves but also pay for losers elsewhere.

And, while the success of their investments is particularly sensitive to stability in the host regulatory environment, they do not have the tools that other investors have to deflect the obsolescing bargain. They suffer from the "hostage effect" associated with large sunk capital, and unlike small investors, they cannot easily threaten to withdraw. They do not as a rule have rapidly changing technology, proprietary processes, or brand-name recognition to withhold in resisting renegotiation of their contracts.[1]

---

1. While there is a great deal of sophisticated technology in the exploration and construction phases of natural-resource and infrastructure projects, the ability to withhold these intangible assets is largely expended, so to speak, once the project is launched. Unlike rapidly changing product and process technology in many manufacturing investments, control over provision of the technology cannot be used effectively to offset the vulnerability of an operating project to renegotation of the initial contractual terms. For a survey of techniques and strategies used by international firms to manage political risk, see Moran (1993, 1998).

This structural vulnerability that petroleum, mining, pipeline, and infrastructure projects continue to be exposed to constitutes "the new face of political risk" in the contemporary era (Wells 1998; Moran 1998).

Such structural vulnerability represents a classic case of market failure due to imperfect contracts. Credibility in honoring commitments is a valuable asset in strategic negotiations. Lack of credibility is so costly that strategic negotiators will search for ways to demonstrate that they have bound their own hands (and the hands of their successors) to enforce their own promises (Schelling 1966; Williamson 1985). Absent such credibility, the strategic agreements fall short of what is socially optimal.

Conventional financially oriented approaches to political risk illustrate the shortcomings of private investors acting on their own (Tilton 1992). One corporate response has been to raise the hurdle rate for approving new investments. But the challenge of dealing with structural vulnerability does not spring from the stinginess of the entry conditions; rather, it comes from the likelihood that the terms of the contract will be altered by political leaders once the project is successfully underway.

A second corporate response has been to limit approval to projects that could be successfully front loaded, with a payback period of no more than three or four years. Except for a handful of petroleum cases, this condition would eliminate from consideration a vast array of commercially promising projects.

A third corporate response has been to self-insure by diversifying the investor's exposure among many projects. But if all the projects in a parent firm's portfolio suffer from the same structural vulnerability, the investor exposes itself to potential systemic risk.

A final corporate response has been to alleviate risk by buying private political-risk insurance. But the traditional coverage of private political-risk insurers—expropriation, war, and civil disturbance—has not included exposure to the obsolescing bargain.

What was needed were mechanisms that would allow natural-resource and private-infrastructure projects that had favorable basic cost characteristics under foreign developers to move forward despite the fact that the regulatory commitments of initially enthusiastic and compliant host authorities were quite suspect.

Over the course of the 1980s, therefore, international investors began to develop strategies to address the problems of credible commitments directly. Some investors turned to nonrecourse project financing, which lowered their own equity exposure and replaced it with more highly leveraged syndicates of financial intermediaries that loaned funds directly to the project and could not seek compensation from the parent if conditions went awry in the host country (see table 9.1).

More important, these investors began to organize such syndicates into a network of interested parties (including export-financing agencies

Table 9.1 Project financing via loan syndications for infrastructure development in developing countries and economies in transition, 1986-95 (millions of dollars)

	1986	1987	1988	1989	1990	1991	1992	1993	1994	1995
Private sector	100	165	137	917	2,002	3,509	5,756	12,267	15,734	15,607
Loans	100	165	137	767	1,380	126	1,536	6,271	6,007	11,086
Bonds	0	0	0	150	500	740	1,155	3,867	5,810	3,262
Equity	0	0	0	0	121	2,643	3,065	2,130	3,918	1,259

Note: Amounts are those covered by closed transactions, not necessarily disbursements.
Source: Euromoney Loanware and Bondware and World Bank staff estimates.

from multiple home governments) to try to create deterrence structures against major changes in investment agreements, deterrence structures that extended to the actions of future authorities meddling with agreements that they had not personally approved.

Multilateral Mechanisms to Enhance the Stability of Investment Agreements

Increasingly, deterrence structures have exhibited a multilateral dimension, in which three institutions within the World Bank Group—the World Bank itself (i.e., the International Bank for Reconstruction and Development [IBRD]), the International Finance Corporation (IFC), and the Multilateral Guarantee Agency (MIGA)—have figured prominently (Benoit 1996; World Bank 1995; Spiller 1994).

First, the IBRD launched a program of guarantees for investors, both direct guarantees that help to protect the investors themselves and indirect guarantees via loans to host governments to fund their own guarantees to investors.

In the direct guarantee program, the IBRD covers lenders to a project against certain specified risks (partial-risk guarantee), or it covers specified payments to lenders against all risks (partial-credit guarantee). By specifying the actions on the part of the host that might prevent the investor from fulfilling its obligations to the lenders, the guarantee extends protection to the investor. When the IBRD issues its guarantee, it requires a counter-guarantee from the host country and holds the country financially responsible for any payments that the IBRD is forced to make.

The partial-risk guarantees cover risks arising from nonperformance of sovereign contractual obligations or from force majeure events that affect a project. Sovereign contractual obligations can include "maintaining the agreed-upon regulatory framework, including tariff formulas."

Force majeure events can include "changes in law." In the 1994 Hub River Power project in Pakistan, for example, the IBRD provided a partial risk guarantee covering $240 million of the $680 million in internationally syndicated commercial bank loans to the project company. The government of Pakistan simultaneously signed an indemnity agreement to reimburse the World Bank for any amounts distributed under the IBRD guarantee.

The partial credit guarantees cover all events of nonpayment for a designated part of the financing, usually the later maturities (such as the 10th to 15th year). The Yangzhou Thermal Power Project in China in 1994 included commercial loans of $120 million the out-year payments of which were guaranteed by the IBRD, with an indemnity agreement similar to that of the Hub River project. The involvement of the IBRD in the later maturities, in general, can be particularly comforting for investors concerned about a long-term swing in the obsolescing bargain.

In addition, the IBRD has supported host-government guarantees to investors by providing loans to the host to finance them. In 1995 the IBRD provided $30 million to Moldova to cover foreign-supplier credits provided to exporters from Moldova against a variety of political and force majeure risks.

Because the World Bank guarantee programs always entail a corresponding obligation from the host government, there is a financial disincentive for whatever government is in office (whether the government that signed the counterguarantee or a successor government) to take actions that would trigger payments to the investors. More broadly, however, because "developing countries often rely on continued financial support from the World Bank to support their development strategies," the World Bank occupies "a relatively strong position to address and resolve with host governments disputes regarding government actions which might adversely affect the project" (Benoit 1996, 48).

Second, the IFC has taken an increasingly aggressive role in participating in these sectors. The IFC is the only institution within the World Bank Group that takes an equity position in projects. The IFC characterizes itself as a passive rather than an active investor and is prohibited from assuming responsibility for the management of any enterprise in which it has invested, but it frequently positions itself as the swing vote to which both foreigner and host authorities must appeal on major management decisions.

In a proposal for the development of the Amantayau goldfield in Uzbekistan in 1996, for example, the IFC considered contributing $13 million out of a total of $70 million in equity and shareholder subordinated loans. For this it would receive 8 percent of the shares, with Lonrho (the principal foreign investor) gaining 35 percent and two Uzbek partner companies each holding 28.5 percent (giving the Uzbeks the majority holdings). The Supervisory Board that determines all of Amantayau's major operational decisions, however, would consist of nine members: four from Lonrho, two from each of the Uzbek partner companies, and one from IFC. The IFC vote, therefore, would likely be decisive in any dispute between the foreign investor and the Uzbek partners (Ubaidullaev 1996).[2]

Besides small amounts of equity capital, the IFC also provides loans from its own resources (known as "A-loans") and has an extensive loan syndication program (known as "B-loans"). Under the latter, IFC remains the lender-of-record for the borrower; this practice not only secures commercial financing for many borrowers that would not otherwise have access to long-term project funds on reasonable terms but mitigates currency transfer and other political risks for the lenders.

As both an equity investor and a lender/syndicator, the IFC is directly affected by any dramatic changes in the regulatory environment. Because the IFC reports to the World Bank Group on the health of the projects in which it has invested, IFC participation in any particular project opens a path to scrutiny by World Bank agencies, "which in turn often can exercise considerable influence over countries in support of sound investment policies" (Benoit 1996, 71) (see box 9.1).

Finally, MIGA provides political-risk insurance via contracts of guarantee for foreign-equity and related debt investments. In addition to covering losses from currency inconvertibility, expropriation, and war and civil disturbance, it can insure investors against host-country breach of contract if the investor is denied access to an appropriate forum to adjudicate its claim within a reasonable period or denied the right to enforce a favorable judgment regarding the breach. In addition, it can extend coverage to other specific noncommercial risks if requested by the investor and the host country and approved by the MIGA Board.

Beyond this, MIGA and the IBRD have been exploring an initiative in which the latter would offer a loan to the host to provide designated investors with coverage against specified political risks, while the former would evaluate and process any investor claims. MIGA would then pay investor claims from the proceeds of the IBRD loan, and the host would be obligated to repay all amounts withdrawn from the loan to the IBRD.

The use of political-risk insurance—including coverage provided by private, national, and multilateral agencies—has been growing rapidly. The Berne Union, comprising 24 national investment insurers and MIGA, reported a sixfold increase in coverage, from $2.3 billion in 1989 to over $15 billion in 1997. Private insurers have extended their periods of cover for expropriation and contract frustration from 3 to 10 years and have added a new category of coverage for "breach of undertaking" (Brownlees 1997). Their activities complement those of multilateral and national insurance agencies: in a metaphor introduced by West (1996), "if both

---

2. With the slump in gold prices in 1997-98, the project did not move forward.

Box 9.1   Escondida copper in Chile and the IFC/World Bank Group umbrella against political risk

The $1.1 billion investment by Broken Hill Proprietary in the Escondida copper mine in Chile, launched in 1991, was a pioneer in using the IFC to provide an umbrella against political risk.

Broken Hill asked the IFC to help with the syndication of the $680 million loan package and to take a 2.5 percent equity position itself. In the Australian firm's estimation, the inclusion of the IFC would help to ensure the stability of the investment agreement. A change in the tax rate (negotiated at 49.5 percent for the 20-year duration of the investment contract) would materially affect the IFC. An act of expropriation would constitute a breach of the broader IFC-Chilean operating agreement, which proscribes any form of seizure by executive or legislative action. While neither a tax change nor a nationalization would legally require the World Bank Group to take action with regard to its entire portfolio of loans to Chile, it "could not help but take note of such an abrogation of contract as it considered new Chilean loan applications."

The financing for Escondida was executed on a nonrecourse basis, with the Chilean subsidiary, Minera Escondida Limitada, as borrower, not parent equity holders (BHP 57.5 percent, RioTinto-Zinc 30 percent, and a Japanese consortium headed by Mitsubishi 10 percent). The Industrial Bank of Japan was appointed trustee for the lenders, with the proceeds of all sales paid into an offshore account. The Industrial Bank of Japan has responsibility for disbursing the monies generated by sales according to the terms of the 20-year investment agreement.

The buyers and export-credit financing agencies provided further support for the stability of BHP's investment agreement. Three-quarters of the output through 2002 was committed under a 12-year sales contract to smelters in Japan, Germany, and Finland, giving them a stake in a steady flow of copper. The long-term contracts were then used to generate export financing from the Export-Import Bank of Japan ($350 million), the Kreditanstalt fuer Wiederaufbau of Germany ($140 million), and the Kansallis-Osake-Pankki of Finland ($47 million) for the full 12-year period. An interruption in production, in the assessment of BHP, "would have the Export-Import Bank of Japan banging on the door of the Chilean government."

Sources: Moran (1993); Broken Hill Proprietary Company Limited, Form 20-F, submitted to the US Securities and Exchange Commission (various years).

---

groups were property insurers, it could be said that one group (private insurers) installs lightning rods (i.e., provides service to mitigate the effects of a loss) and the other (national and multilateral insurers) both installs lightning rods and seeks to influence the weather (i.e., to reduce the frequency of lightning strikes on the building)." Private investors need both kinds of service—compensation for loss and deterrence against the prospect of suffering loss.

Beyond offering these services, however, political-risk insurers indicate that they have a potentially even more important role to play—as negotiator and facilitator when investment disputes arise. One national insurer has reported, for example, that out of four recent notifications of a potential claim by insured investors, only one actually led to a claims payment. The other three were resolved, informally and quietly, before they resulted in a loss (West 1996).

A Balance between Stability and Flexibility

The growing efforts to reinforce the stability of investment contracts in natural-resource and private-infrastructure projects poses a public-policy challenge for developing countries and economies in transition.

On the one hand, the magnitude of possible investments is staggering. Even after discounting the slowdown from the Asian financial crisis, infrastructure projects alone may total more than $1 trillion over the next 10 years. To bring them to fruition requires successful intermediation between the structural vulnerability of the investors and the imperfections in contract markets.

As in other forms of strategic bargaining, mechanisms that enhance the credibility of commitments—mechanisms that "bind the hands" of particular players—can actually strengthen the bargaining position of those players and magnify the payoffs they receive from successful negotiations (while at the same time raising global welfare) (Schelling 1966). Somewhat paradoxically, therefore, it is in the hosts' own interest to participate in and support some measures of self-denial. In so doing, host states are absorbing risk; they are doing no more than providing the equivalent of an extended warranty that covers extra-commercial breakdowns to potential investors.

On the other hand, such mechanisms are undeniably intended to limit the sovereignty of host-country actions, including the sovereignty of democratically elected representatives. Beyond the political issue of sovereignty, there is a genuine economic question of how long investors should deserve to be rewarded for initial risks and uncertainties after those risks and uncertainties have dissipated. Finally, there is a fundamental divergence between investor and host perceptions of what constitutes adequate returns, with the investors wanting successful projects in any given host country to pay for unsuccessful projects elsewhere—hardly an appealing reward for a host with favorable sites and self-disciplined behavior.

While supporting multilateral restraint mechanisms in general, therefore, authorities in the developing world and economies in transition will nonetheless want some flexibility in how long international investors can enforce the initial terms of their investment agreements; however, they will seek to avoid impeding the initial investment decision. One possible approach to compromise is contained in the Elaboration on Foreign Investment Principles in the OECD's Commonwealth of Independent States (CIS) Expert Group, in which the horizon of stability for investment agreements is set at 10 years. At that time, a reasonable standard for any potential adjustment of terms of investment might be "national treatment"—that is, tax and tariff (input-price) levels no different from those available to companies in the economy at large.

V

Findings, Conclusions, and Policy Implications

Introduction

The challenge of utilizing FDI as part of the development process is much more complicated than conventional wisdom suggests. The direct and indirect benefits from well-constructed FDI projects are substantially greater than commonly assumed, but they do not come easily. To capture the full advantages that international investors have to offer requires a much broader and more energetic action agenda than developing countries and economies in transition have been accustomed to pursue. This concluding section tries to delineate that agenda and sketch out alternative strategies to pursue it.

10

Incorporating FDI into the Development Process: From Traditional Concerns to a New Agenda for Action

This book has addressed three broad sets of questions: First, what are the benefits and opportunities of trying to use FDI to encourage development, and what are the lingering risks and dangers? When are the benefits and opportunities likely to outweigh the risks and dangers?

Second, how well do international markets function in supplying FDI to the development process, and what have been the principal obstacles preventing those markets from functioning more effectively? What is the role of market failure and market distortion in allocating FDI among developed countries, developing countries, and economies in transition?

Finally, beyond getting micro and macroeconomic fundamentals right, do hosts and would-be hosts in the developing world and the economies in transition need a distinctive policy toward FDI? Or, after concentrating on the large array of microeconomic, macroeconomic, and institutional fundamentals, can they be confident that international markets will offer them appropriate amounts of FDI? If, instead, they need a distinctive policy, how should it be fashioned?

This book has provided novel and somewhat surprising answers to all three. Looking first at the dangers and opportunities offered by foreign investors, both are substantially greater than conventional calculations would indicate. On the negative side, foreign firms with subscale operations and protection from competition generate the usual list of inefficiencies and misallocation of resources in the host economy. In many cases, they leave the recipient country worse off than if it had never received the investment in the first place. More than this, however, small protected FDI creates a vicious dynamic of adverse signals and perverse incentives (both economic and political) for all parties. Instead of providing a path for growth, dynamic learning, and development, this FDI tends to produce stasis and conflict, generating constituents that are likely to use their influence to maintain their privileged position and undermine the impetus to economic reform.

Compared to foreign firms with no constraints on ownership, those with constraints exhibit older technology and business practices and lag in introducing upgrades in technology and business practices. Constrained firms are less likely to export, and their backward linkages into the local economy are less sophisticated and dynamic.

On the positive side, foreign investors with full-scale operations under reasonably competitive conditions with no restrictions on ownership offer the usual list of capital, technology, and management benefits to the host economy. In addition, their local subsidiaries exhibit an integration effect when they become part of the parents' strategy to maintain a competitive position in world markets that provides more rapid upgrading of management, technology, and quality control than any other form of transfer. Thus, they create a dynamic link to the global frontier of best practices, most advanced technologies, and most sophisticated operational techniques in an industry. Simultaneously, they generate direct and indirect spillovers and externalities for domestic suppliers. FDI that creates a proprietary network of suppliers introduces a powerful interaction between parents and subsidiaries and between subsidiaries and host economies.

The payoff from success in attracting internationally competitive FDI in manufacturing, and in natural resources and private infrastructure, is often not limited to one plant or one project. In manufacturing and natural resources, the data exhibit a frequent follow-the-leader response of rival firms moving to the same country or region after the first movers in a given industry decide to undertake major rearrangements in their patterns of international production. Supplier firms, too, follow the prime companies. The clusters of resulting economic activity show further evidence of rents and externalities. In the industries examined most closely here—automotive, petrochemical, and electronics/computer—they exhibit agglomeration properties as well, including economies of scope, scale, and specialization. Even after the Asian economic crisis, FDI in infrastructure projects, in part linked to such clusters, still may accumulate to more than one trillion dollars in little more than a decade.

The rewards for success in attracting investors in well-structured projects, therefore, are large. So are the penalties and opportunity costs of failure. But how much, and what kind of, host-country intervention is needed to ensure success? Do international markets function well enough for hosts and would-be hosts in the developing countries and economies in transition simply to sit back passively and wait for FDI to appear?

Market Failures, Market Interventions, and the Struggle for International Corporate Operations

Turning next, therefore, to the second focus of inquiry in this study—how well the markets in which foreign investors are located allocate investment—there is evidence of major obstacles to the spread of international investment along lines that comparative advantage would otherwise dictate.

Some of the obstacles spring from various kinds of market failure. The launching of export-oriented manufacturing operations from new locations in the developing countries and the economies in transition often involves acquiring information (about work ethic and culture, labor practices, ability of the surrounding economy to provide inputs, resilience of legal institutions, and credibility of public-sector commitments about taxes and other regulatory issues) that can only be generated through learning by doing, that is, by making the investment. This creates a conundrum, particularly severe for new world-scale-size indivisible projects: investors cannot obtain the information they need to invest without having already "tried out" the project. For firms caught in this bind and having to make irreversible investments under uncertainty, learning takes place at a socially suboptimal pace from the point of view of global welfare.

Then, once a first mover in an industry establishes a new site successfully, rivals move in a rapid follow-the-leader sequence that may undercompensate the initial investor for bearing the initial risk. Taken together, the catch-22 properties of learning and the appropriability problems for early movers are likely to lead to investment in new world-scale integrated manufacturing operations that is suboptimal for world growth. Thus, there is a rationale, at least in theory, for both multilateral and host-country efforts to subsidize the creation of externality-laden international production networks by multinational firms.

The analysis of natural-resource and private-infrastructure projects introduces a different kind of market failure, failure in long-term contracts. Natural-resource and private-infrastructure projects often require payment of a high risk premium long after the initial risk has dissipated, but (unlike most manufacturing investors) the parent corporations cannot use control over technology, advertising, and marketing (as the former can) to ensure that host countries honor the investment agreements that incorporate the high risk premium. They suffer greater structural vulnerability to the obsolescing bargain, as host authorities (often the successors to those who signed the original investment agreement) are tempted to tighten the favorable initial terms.

Without external efforts to strengthen the credibility of the initial-investment agreements, this can also lead to underinvestment in comparison to what would be socially optimal for would-be hosts and for the world at large.

Beyond the problems associated with market failures, hosts and would-be hosts in the developing countries and the economies in transition face the need to correct for market interventions by others on second-best grounds. In particular, national and subnational authorities in the developed countries have launched a counteroffensive of interventions to hinder or prevent the realignment of production along lines that global efficiency would suggest. This counteroffensive has grown in magnitude as the process of globalization has proceeded.

One might interpret this counteroffensive as simply old-fashioned protectionism attempting to slow down the ever-greater liberalization of trade and investment. But the characteristics of the industries in which FDI is found—imperfect competition, high wages, high benefits, high product differentiation, high research and development, large economies of scale—suggest a more serious, genuinely zero-sum struggle that is embedded with strategic-trade properties.

The same rent-generating, spillover-producing, externality-rich operations of international companies—often with agglomeration features of scope, scale, and specialization (at least in the automotive, petrochemical, and electronics/computer sectors examined here)—have become prominent targets for capture, or recapture, by developed countries as well. The international corporate activities that helped to create the industrial complexes of Minas Gerais, Sao Paulo, Monterrey, Matamoros, Surabaya, Jubail, and Penang, and could generate thick economic clusters of similar dimensions within new hosts like China, Russia, Romania, and Vietnam or within old hosts like India, Argentina, and the Philippines, have become prime objects for diversion back to locations in Europe, North America, and North Asia.

The central components of the counteroffensive—locational incentives, rules of origin, and antidumping regulations—are not just being used to protect inefficient industries but rather to recast the shape of economic geography, often along paths contrary to what comparative advantage would otherwise dictate.

The use of the strategic-trade framework to analyze this struggle is not just a theoretical embellishment. In contrast to conventional trade analysis, the strategic-trade framework suggests that the competition for international corporate investment will not necessarily be moderated by more thoughtful leaders and more careful analyses showing that protection and promotion hurt the country that engages in them. Instead, those thoughtful leaders are likely to be able to find justification in the data for energetic protection and promotion, just as their less thoughtful counterparts will. Only common agreement to limit the competition for FDI can control the escalatory dynamics of strategic-trade warfare.

What specific policies toward FDI—beyond improvement in the micro and macroeconomic fundamentals and in institutional structures—should hosts and would-be hosts in the developing countries and the economies in transition adopt? And what policy approach, individually and collectively, will best serve them as they try to incorporate FDI into their development strategies?

A New Policy Agenda toward FDI

Turning to the final question—the fashioning of a distinctive policy to incorporate FDI most effectively into the development process—what is striking is not only what should be included in the new agenda for action but what should be excluded.

High at the top of the list of what should be included in the new agenda are policies aimed at integrating world-scale manufacturing subsidiaries into the global/regional sourcing network of the parent and policies aimed at reinforcing the longer-term stability of investment agreements in natural-resource and private-infrastructure projects.

Both are more difficult and more contentious than conventional wisdom suggests. To accomplish these priorities requires three efforts on the part of authorities in the developing countries and economies in transition:

- *First,* support for extending and toughening the exercise (begun in the OECD) to make transparent, and then to limit, locational subsidies and locational incentives of all sorts;

- *Second,* mobilization of a campaign to halt, and roll back, the use of rules of origin and antidumping regulations to protect producers and divert investment flows from one region to another; and

- *Third,* participation in initiatives within the multilateral financial institutions to enhance the reliability of natural-resource and private-infrastructure agreements, with some flexibility for adjustment to national-treatment levels over long-term project life cycles.

Of equal importance is what is missing from this action agenda after evaluating the balance of costs and benefits of various popular policies toward FDI in relation to the economic and political/national security goals that those policies are intended to advance. Most resolutely dismissed is the use of domestic-content requirements to promote backward linkages, industrial deepening, or mere job creation.

FDI projects with high domestic-content mandates exhibit all of the negative characteristics listed earlier in this chapter, and more. They have high costs, show a lag in both technology and management practices, and offer slim hope of maturing from infant status to internationally competitive operations. They incorporate a political-economic logic of self-protection that frequently extends, in the cases examined here, to retarding host efforts at liberalizing trade and investment more generally. The contemporary effort of some developing countries and economies in transition to prolong the use of domestic-content requirements, or to make them less visible, or to craft the language of the requirement to be ostensibly consistent with WTO obligations is ill-advised as a development strategy.

Next-most confidently discarded is the use of joint-venture requirements to enhance development objectives such as technology transfer, international market penetration, or development of a robust supplier base.

FDI projects launched with joint-venture requirements show a high degree of conflict among the partners, suffer from a high degree of instability, and exhibit older technology, slower rates of technology transfer to the venture, fewer prospects for exports, and less sophistication in backward linkages to suppliers than do FDI projects without the mandate for joint ownership.

Finally, rejected with a considerable degree of skepticism is the so-called Korea model of insisting upon technology licensing agreements in place of FDI, with the hope of building an indigenous business class that might be more vibrant, or more effective in avoiding threats to national security, than one generated as a byproduct of less-intrusive policies.

The use of technology-sharing agreements as a substitute for FDI exhibits the same kind of large economic costs as do joint-venture requirements: lags in technology acquisition, in management practices, in external-market penetration, and in generation of an advanced supplier network. A path of development via the creation of national-champion firms and industries is fraught, in the evidence collected here, with traps and dangers for the country that adopts such an approach.

As for possibly offsetting political benefits, the breadth of instances in which maintaining ownership in national hands for genuine national-security reasons may be justified—to avoid dependence on monopolistic external suppliers—is quite narrow. Furthermore, the penalties in cost and performance associated with self-sufficiency in such instances is quite large.

Thus, domestic-content requirements, joint-venture mandates, and technology-licensing requirements as a substitute for FDI—however popular they continue to be—are decidedly absent from the list of policy recommendations for hosts and would-be hosts in the developing world and the economies in transition.

How can reformers in the developing countries and economies in transition who wish to pursue this new agenda of policy initiatives and policy rejections weave together the components to enhance their prospects for success? Should they undertake reform unilaterally and piecemeal or as part of a grand bargain with reformers in the developed countries that is incorporated into a specially designed Multilateral Agreement on Investment (MAI)? What allies might be mobilized to help create such a structure?

Tactics for Pursuing the New FDI Agenda: Following a Path of Unilateral Restraint

Host countries must initiate many of the most important actions to attract and utilize FDI in their development programs on their own—in particular, improving the micro and macroeconomic functioning of their economies and strengthening commercial and judicial institutions that provide stability and dependability to all domestic as well as foreign investors.

At the same time, the most important FDI policy improvements recommended here—abandoning the use of domestic-content, joint-venture, and technology-licensing requirements and strengthening the credibility of long-term public-sector commitments—could also be adopted unilaterally, to the benefit of host authorities in the developing world and economies in transition.

The analysis undertaken earlier shows, for example, that

- the imposition of domestic-content requirements in protected local markets leads to less efficient production and provides less valuable backward linkages than does allowing foreign firms to set up operations oriented toward global or regional markets;

- the demand for joint ventures with local partners retards the introduction of latest technologies into the local economy; and

- the award of market exclusivity reduces the pressure for continual upgrading of inputs and best practices on the part of foreign investors.

Armed with these insights, Chinese development planners might want to reconsider the efficacy of bestowing sole right of establishment upon individual foreign investors or foreign investor groups for each segment of a given industrial sector, while insisting upon partnerships with indigenous firms. These joint operations utilize demonstrably older technology and have a poor record of adopting cutting-edge management methods. In the automotive sector—to give one example—this approach has already set in place an array of undersized plants more than ten years behind the competitive frontier of new products, processes, and management practices.

Similarly, the analysis introduced here shows that multilateral investment guarantees—sponsored by the Inter-American Development Bank, the World Bank Group, or other lending agencies—provide an umbrella of political-risk protection over large infrastructure projects. Projects such as multicountry regional power plants, whose underlying economics are quite favorable but whose prospects for contract stability are otherwise questionable, can rely on such guarantees to convince foreign investors to proceed. Armed with this insight, Central American development planners, or their counterparts in other regions, might want to reconsider the appeal of participating in such credit-guarantee programs, even though the latter deliberately constrain the flexibility of successor authorities to renegotiate the initial terms of such projects (Powers 1998).

There is no underestimating, however, how painful the decision will be for hosts and potential hosts in the developing world and economies in transition to give up the imposition of domestic-content requirements and to forego the use of joint-venture and technology-licensing mandates. Rules governing local content, ownership structure, and technology acquisition represent a vast pool of favors to bestow upon rent-seeking constituencies, and the abandonment of public-sector regulation in these areas is sure to generate powerful opposition. As evidence of such resistance, there is considerable uncertainty already about whether and how rapidly many countries will actually phase out domestic-content restrictions, despite the ostensible commitment to do so, as part of the Uruguay Round agreements, under WTO auspices.

Moreover, unilateral self-abstention from the use of domestic-content, joint-venture, and technology-licensing requirements—however beneficial the outcome will be to those countries that follow this route—leaves host authorities in the developing countries and the economies in transition tactically disarmed, so to speak, in the face of the counteroffensive against the globalization of industry launched by developed countries, and tactically disarmed against the escalation in the use of locational subsidies, rules of origin, and antidumping actions, which are hindering economic activity from moving along lines of comparative advantage in a North-South direction.

Host authorities in the developing countries and the economies in transition might want to think more broadly, therefore, about how they could work collectively to shape the treatment of international corporate activity around the world, seeking support in such an endeavor from among their own counterparts as well as among developed-country governments. The elements of the new agenda toward FDI outlined here are, in fact, well suited to the negotiation of a "grand bargain" that would incorporate trade-offs among the most objectionable investment-related policies of all parties, North and South.

Leaders from the developing countries and the economies in transition might well conclude that they should seize the initiative and propose their own structure for an MAI configured substantially differently from the undertaking that has been pursued under OECD auspices.

Rather than making the challenge of trade and investment liberalization doubly difficult, mixing together the concerns of both developed and developing countries might, paradoxically, enhance the prospects for success.

Tactics for Pursuing the New Agenda toward FDI: Negotiating a Grand Bargain within a Broadened and Revised MAI

How would an MAI structured to serve the interests of host authorities in the developing countries and economies in transition, as well as to advance global economic welfare, be similar to and differ from the MAI under negotiation within the OECD? What forces might be mobilized to move a reconfigured MAI forward? What forum would be most appropriate to sponsor such an exercise?

Several of the central issues in the MAI discussions within the OECD—in particular, national treatment, right of establishment, sector-specific reservations, and national security exceptions—might well reappear in an MAI that had been recast to suit the particular interests of developing countries and economies in transition. The analysis introduced here should help to loosen their resistance to compromise

National Treatment

The national-treatment principle allows foreign affiliates in a country to be subject to laws and policies no less favorable than those applied to domestically owned firms operating in the same sectors. An abandonment of domestic-content, joint-venture, and technology-licensing requirements would eliminate the three largest areas in which developing countries and economies in transition have been inclined to insist upon the right to impose special conditions on the operations of foreign firms. The foregoing of export-performance requirements in return for discipline on all locational incentives and reform in rules of origin and antidumping (the key element in the negotiation of the grand bargain, as indicated below) would end discriminatory practice in a fourth area. The incorporation of a multilateral standard in natural-resource and private-infrastructure agreements to limit renegotiations after 10 years to economywide tax levels disposes of the final area.

Right of Establishment

Right of establishment refers to the principle that FDI be allowed in all sectors of a domestic economy, with any exceptions being completely transparent (see sector-specific reservations and national-security exceptions, below). The dynamic that most effectively triggers investment flows of the kind and magnitude that contribute most to host development comes from attracting investors to engage in operations that may improve their competitive position worldwide. This upsets the equilibrium in the industry and all firms have to adjust. In the process, various externality-laden operations are relocated to the benefit of developing countries and economies in transition. This is antithetical to one of the principal ways in which hosts have tried to control right of establishment, namely, to divide a domestic industry into segments and award investment rights within each segment to a single foreign investor (often with a designated domestic partner). Opening domestic industries up to competition for entry among foreign investors, while letting the latter choose whether or not they prefer local partners, both enhances the benefits generated for the host economy and sweeps away a principal use for controls over right of establishment.

Sector-Specific Reservations and National-Security Exceptions

In light of the analysis offered here, sector-specific reservations to national treatment and right of establishment merit sharp reduction or elimination. The practice of limiting foreign ownership by insisting upon joint ventures or technology-sharing agreements carries severe disadvantages as a development strategy. So does the attempt to build industries of international competitive status via special cultivation of national-champion firms. Legitimate exceptions to safeguard national security, moreover, fall within a relatively narrow and objectively defined band that is likely to preclude extensive appeal on these grounds.

As indicated earlier, genuine national-security threats arise only when external suppliers of a vital good or service are sufficiently concentrated that those suppliers could collude to delay, deny, or place onerous conditions on the provision of the good or service. Foreign firms in industries that do not exhibit the twin characteristics of vitalness and extreme concentration should be free to enjoy national treatment and right of establishment, including right of establishment via acquisition. The national-security needs of developed countries, developing countries, and economies in transition can be met with a common attempt to agree on how to measure such worrisome degrees of concentration, with transparent debate about whether specific cases fall therein.

Thus, a careful reassessment of the costs and benefits of some of the most-objected-to practices on the part of developing countries and economies in transition, as developed here, should assist in convincing those who defend these practices to limit or constraint their use. But if host authorities in the developing countries and economies in transition are going to shift their policies to meet many of the conditions that developed countries have been demanding of them, why not exact some concessions on issues of extreme importance to themselves in the process?

As part of a grand bargain, therefore, host authorities from the developing countries and economies in transition will want to halt the counteroffensive against the spread of FDI along lines of comparative advantage by ensuring that the reconstituted MAI incorporates limits on the award of investment incentives, including investment incentives by subnational entities, and includes substantial reform of rules of origin and antidumping regulations.

Within the context of the grand bargain, host authorities in the developing countries and economies in transition should probably be willing to give up their right to use export-performance requirements as well, however useful and justified such requirements might have been in the past. World welfare would probably be enhanced by creating a playing field for international investment that sloped slightly in favor of developing countries and economies in transition because, as demonstrated earlier, such a slope would facilitate experimentation and learning on the part of international investors. However, the best outcome that representatives from these areas can aim for is a relatively level playing field in place of the adverse tilt that antidumping regulations, rules of origin, and locational subsidies on the part of developed countries now generate.

This suggests that the WTO, and not the OECD, is the appropriate forum in which to seek such a grand bargain, because in the WTO the concerns of most vital interest to the developing countries and economies in transition can adequately be addressed.

To be successful in extracting concessions from the developed countries under the auspices of the WTO, however, the developing countries and economies in transition will have to ensure that blocking coalitions do not emerge from within their own ranks. Latin American countries such as Argentina, Chile, and Mexico, for example, may have to lure India, China, and several of the Southeast Asian nations away from the lingering desire to avoid national treatment or to maintain domestic-content requirements. Similarly, the members of regional groupings such as ASEAN or Mercosur will have to sublimate their urge to deploy investment incentives against each other into global limitations on locational subsidies.

In short, a potent negotiating strategy within the WTO will depend upon the ability of leaders from the developing countries and economies in transition to weave together agreement on sensitive investment-policy issues among their own members.

Within both richer and poorer countries around the globe, the pursuit of a grand bargain is certain, to be sure, to generate considerable opposition among the more entrenched and less-competitive economic groups. But if reformers in the developing countries and economies in transition do manage to muster support internally for changes in the use of domestic-content, export, joint-venture, and technology-licensing requirements, they would then be able to reach out to reformers in the developed countries to mobilize support for changes in the use of locational incentives, rules of origin, and antidumping regulations. The task ahead for liberalizers in the South and North remains, nonetheless, daunting.

Especially difficult will be the challenge of imposing discipline over developed-country authorities in awarding large packages of locational incentives to investors. For the very reasons that developing countries value world-scale operations by international companies—high wages and benefits, associated research and development, possible externalities and agglomeration effects—national and subnational governments in the developed world are continuously being tempted to "race to the top" in offering grants and subsidies.[1] Within the developing world, regional rivalries—such as those among Singapore, Malaysia, and Indonesia—generate the same competitive dynamic.

At the same time, however, the OECD has achieved slow and steady progress in bringing transparency and public concern to the incentive race. In the European Union, Thomas (1998) argues that the European Commission's Directorate General IV, which is responsible for competition policy, has been relatively successful in implementing notification requirements for investment subsidies and limiting (sometimes lowering) their dimensions. In Canada, the creation of a Code of Conduct on Incentives, with complaints referred to the Internal Trade Secretariat for consultations, has had some impact on moderating incentive competition, despite the considerable autonomy of the provinces from the federal government. Even in the United States, there have been "no raiding" agreements in the Midwest and the Northeast, accompanied by a rise of nongovernment organizations dedicated to educating public officials and the public at large about the pernicious impact of subsidy races—although the United States remains the outlier in terms of lack of self-discipline. While locational grants are advertised as creating jobs, they constitute subsidies to capital and make income distribution less equal. Taxpayer coalitions have objected to large investment incentives as corporate welfare.[2]

---

1. For the futility of such a race, and the disadvantages for poorer contestants, see Graham (1998).

2. On campaigns against corporate welfare that include the call to limit locational incentives for international companies, see Thomas (1997); A Circle of Spiraling Payments, *Financial Times*, 8 October 1996; O Governor, Won't You Buy Me a Mercedes Plant? A Bidding War's Bite in Alabama, *The New York Times*, 1 September 1996.

The attempt to constrain subsidy races with multilateral disciplines may offer better prospects for success than the competition between leading and lagging areas within a nation or regional grouping would allow. Like the European Union, Canada, or the United States, developing countries that have trouble controlling competition for investment within their own regional organizations—such as ASEAN, where relatively rich Singapore is prone to veto the call for prohibitions on investment subsidies—may discover that the extra benefits that would accompany the establishment of global limitations offer a channel for self-restraint that is otherwise unavailable.

But, despite some progress in transparency and acknowledgment of the mutually destructive nature of subsidy races, much work remains to be done in controlling the use of investment incentives.

Perhaps less difficult may be the job of harmonizing and restraining the use of rules of origin to divert investment to particular regional trading associations. In part this is due to the fact that the next rounds of regional negotiations—NAFTA-enlargement, Free Trade Area of the Americas, EU-Eastern Europe accession agreements, EU-Mercosur expansion—will both highlight the contradictions among rules and necessitate some kind of harmonization under WTO auspices. In part, this is because international firms are realizing, from experience, that the special-interest-driven process that pervaded earlier EU and NAFTA policy formation is damaging their own prospects for global sourcing and is incompatible with their own longer-term self-interest.

More arduous will be the attempt to redefine the basis for antidumping actions in line with the original objectives of prohibiting international price discrimination and predatory business practices. The task is especially difficult because the new structure of protectionist and distortionary antidumping regulations is now incorporated in the WTO. In this ostensibly arcane but extremely important area, the international corporate community missed an important opportunity for reform in the Uruguay Round (Cumby and Moran 1997).

But the costliness of the error has been registered in remarkably rapid fashion: the United States has become one of the largest targets of antidumping actions in the world, launched not only by other developed countries but increasingly by authorities in the developing countries and economies in transition as well. Finger (1997) has detected the beginnings of possible pressures from the business communities of both the United States and the European Union for modification of antidumping procedures.

There is no doubt that achieving the changes and reforms in the most objectionable investment-related policies of all parties, North and South alike, will be a long, hard, uphill battle. But at least it is possible to see more clearly now what kinds of trade-offs are essential and what kind of outcome would be most beneficial to all parties.

Leadership, Vision, and a New North-South Dialogue

To have a chance at success, leadership and vision will play a crucial role. Because the process will be politically painful for authorities in the developing world and the economies in transition, and for authorities in the developed world as well, the former may be tempted to pursue the new agenda slowly, half-heartedly, and with reluctance and hesitation. The result would be a grudging, reactive participation of developing countries and economies in transition in the liberalization of trade and investment, with a prolonged and slow phaseout of domestic-content, joint-venture, and technology-licensing requirements. The complementary demand for developed countries to end the distortionary practices that prevent investment from moving more freely from the capital-rich countries would likely be met with an equally grudging response on the part of the latter.

How it would turn history on its head if the reverse were true, that is, if instead of reluctance and hesitation, reformers in the South were to provide the impetus to launch the next great round of liberalization. For that to occur, a group of visionary, assertive, and even indignant new leaders must emerge, eager to transform the WTO into an institution that meets their needs on trade and investment issues, preaching liberalization and equal treatment rather than protection and special treatment. They could define the issues and dominate the terms of debate for the next decade, leading both North and South toward the common goal of bringing investment-forcing interventions around the world under multilateral discipline.

To have this truly global initiative for reform originate in the developing countries would mark a watershed in international governance.

This could ignite a new convergence of effort between liberalizers in the North and liberalizers in the South to improve the competitive workings of markets in the international arena, as well as in their own domestic economies.

References

Aitken, Brian, Gordon H. Hanson, and Ann E. Harrison. 1997. Spillovers, Foreign Investment, and Export Behavior. *Journal of International Economics* 43, no. 1-2 (August): 103-32.

Aitken, Brian, and Ann Harrison. 1997. Do Domestic Firms Benefit from Foreign Direct Investment? Evidence from panel data. International Monetary Fund and Columbia Business School. Photocopy.

Aitken, Brian, Ann Harrison, and Robert E. Lipsey. 1996. Wages and Foreign Ownership: A Comparative Study of Mexico, Venezuela, and the United States. *Journal of International Economics* 40, no. 3-4 (May): 345-71.

Akerlof, George. 1970. The Market for "Lemons": Quality Uncertainty and the Market Mechanism. *Quarterly Journal of Economics* 84, no. 3 (August): 488-500.

Amsden, Alice. 1989. *Asia's Next Giant: South Korea and Late Industrialization*. New York: Oxford University Press.

Bale, Harvey E., Jr., and David Walters. 1986. Investment Policy Aspects of U.S. and Global Trade Interests. *Looking Ahead*. NPA Pamphlet No. 9. Washington: National Planning Association.

Beamish, Paul W. 1988. *Multinational Joint Ventures in Developing Countries*. London: Routledge.

Beamish, Paul W., and Andres Delios. 1997. Incidence and Propensity of Alliance Formation by U.S., Japanese, and European MNEs. In *Cooperative Strategies: Asian-Pacific Perspectives*, ed. by Paul W. Beamish and J. Peter Killing. San Francisco: The New Lexington Press.

Bennett, Douglas C., and Kenneth E. Sharpe. 1985. *Transnational Corporations versus the State: The Political Economy of the Mexican Auto Industry*. Princeton, NJ: Princeton University Press.

Benoit, Philippe. 1996. *Project Finance at the World Bank: An Overview of Policies and Instruments*. Technical Paper No. 312. Washington: World Bank.

Bergsten, C. Fred. 1974. Coming Investment Wars? *Foreign Affairs* 53, no. 1 (October): 135-52.

Bergsten, C. Fred, Thomas Horst, and Theodore H. Moran. 1978. *American Multinationals and American Interests*. Washington: Brookings Institution.

Bergsten, C. Fred, and Marcus Noland. 1993. *Reconcilable Differences? United States-Japan Economic Conflict*. Washington: Institute for International Economics.

Blomstrom, Magnus. 1986. Multinationals and Market Structure in Mexico. *World Development* 14, no. 4 (April): 523-30.

Blomstrom, Magnus. 1990. *Transnational Corporations and Manufacturing Exports from Developing Countries*. New York: United Nations.

Blomstrom, Magnus, and Ari Kokko. 1997. *How Foreign Investment Affects Host Countries*. Policy Research Working Paper No. 1745. Washington: World Bank, International Economics Department, International Trade Division.

Blomstrom, Magnus, Ari Kokko, and Mario Zejan. 1992. *Host Country Competition and Technology Transfer by Multinationals*. National Bureau of Economic Research Working Paper No. 4131. Cambridge, MA: National Bureau of Economic Research.

Blomstrom, Magnus, Robert Lipsey, and Mario Zejan. 1995. *What Explains Developing Country Growth?* National Bureau of Economic Research Working Paper No. 5057. Cambridge, MA: National Bureau of Economic Research.

Blomstrom, Magnus, and Hakan Persson. 1983. Foreign Investment and Spillover Efficiency in an Underdeveloped Economy: Evidence from the Mexican Manufacturing Industry. *World Development* 11, no. 6 (June): 493-501.

Boltuck, Richard, and Robert E. Litan. 1991. *Down in the Dumps: Administration of the Unfair Trade Laws*. Washington: Brookings Institution.

Bond, Eric W., and Stephen E. Guisinger. 1985. Investment Incentives as Tariff Substitutes: A Comprehensive Measure of Protection. *The Review of Economics and Statistics* 67, no. 1 (February): 91-97.

Bond, Eric W., and Larry Samuelson. 1986. Tax Holidays as Signals. *American Economic Review* 76, no. 4 (September): 820-26.

Bond, Eric W., and Larry Samuelson. 1989. Bargaining with Commitment, Choice of Techniques, and Direct Foreign Investment. *Journal of International Economics* 26, no. 1-2 (February): 77-97.

Borenzstein, Eduardo, Jose de Gregorio, and Jong Wha Lee. 1995. *How Does Foreign Direct Investment Affect Growth?* National Bureau of Economic Research Working Paper No. 5057. Cambridge, MA: National Bureau of Economic Research.

Borrus, Michael. 1994. Left for Dead: Asian Production Networks and the Revival of U.S. Electronics. In *Japanese Investment in Asia: International Production Strategies in a Rapidly Changing World*, ed. by Eileen M. Doherty. San Francisco: The Asia Foundation and Berkeley Roundtable on International Economics.

Bower, Joseph L. 1986. *When Markets Quake: The Management Challenge of Restructuring Industry*. Boston, MA: Harvard Business School Press.

Brander, James A., and Barbara J. Spencer. 1983. International R&D Rivalry and Industrial Strategy. *Review of Economic Studies* 50, no. 4 (October): 707-22.

Brecher, Richard A., and Carlos F. Diaz Alejandro. 1977. Tariffs, Foreign Capital and Immiserizing Growth. *Journal of International Economics* 7, no. 4 (November): 317-22.

Brownlees, Kit. 1997. A Private Market Comes of Age. *Reinsurance* (June): 30-31.

Buckley, Peter J., and Mark C. Casson. 1976. *The Future of the Multinational Enterprise*. London: MacMillan.

Campa, Jose, and Linda Goldberg. 1997. *The Evolving External Orientation of Manufacturing Industries: Evidence from Four Countries*. National Bureau of Economic Research Working Paper No. 5919. Cambridge, MA: National Bureau of Economic Research.

Cardoso, Eliana A., and Rudiger Dornbusch. 1989. Foreign Private Capital Flows. In *Handbook of Development Economics*, vol. 2, ed. by Hollis Chenery and T. N. Srinivasan. London: Elsevier Science Publishing Company.

Caves, Richard E. 1982. *Multinational Enterprise and Economic Analysis*. Cambridge, UK: Cambridge University Press.

Caves, Richard E. 1996. *Multinational Enterprise and Economic Analysis*, 2d ed. Cambridge, UK: Cambridge University Press.

Chandler, Alfred. 1990. *Scale and Scope: The Dynamics of Industrial Capitalism.* Cambridge, MA: Harvard University Press.

Chapman, Keith. 1991. *The International Petrochemical Industry: Evolution and Location.* Cambridge, MA: Blackwell.

Chen, Edward K. Y. 1983. *Multinational Corporations, Technology and Employment.* New York: MacMillan.

Cline, William. 1987. *Informatics and Development: Trade and Industrial Policy in Argentina, Brazil, and Mexico.* Washington: Economics International.

Connor, John M. 1977. *The Market Power of Multinationals.* New York: Praeger.

Coughlin, Cletus C. 1988. The Competitive Nature of State Spending on the Promotion of Manufacturing Exports. *Federal Reserve Bank of St. Louis Review* 70, no. 3 (May/June): 34-42.

Council of State Governments. 1989. *Economic Development in the States: State Business Incentives and Economic Growth: Are They Effective? A Review of the Literature.* Washington: Council of State Governments.

Cumby, Robert E., and Theodore H. Moran. 1997. Testing Models of the Trade Policy Process: Antidumping and the 'New Issues.'" In *The Effects of U.S. Trade Protection and Promotion Policies,* ed. by Robert C. Feenstra. Cambridge, MA: National Bureau of Economic Research.

Cummins, Jason, Kevin Hassett, and Glenn Hubbard. 1996. *Tax Reforms and Investment: A Cross-Country Comparison.* National Bureau of Economic Research Working Paper No. 5232. Cambridge, MA: National Bureau of Economic Research.

David, P., and J. Rosenblum. 1990. Marshallian Factor Market Externalities and the Dynamics of Industrial Location. *Journal of Urban Economics* 28, no. 3 (November): 349-70.

Davidson, Carl, Steven J. Matusz, and Mordechai E. Kreinin. 1985. Analysis of Performance Standards for Direct Foreign Investments. *Canadian Journal of Economics* 18, no. 4 (November): 876-90.

Deardorff, Alan V. 1989. Economic Perspectives on Antidumping Law. In *Antidumping Law and Practice: A Comparative Study,* ed. by John H. Jackson and Edwin A. Vermulst. Ann Arbor: University of Michigan Press.

Dixit, Avinash K., and Robert S. Pindyck. 1994. *Investment under Uncertainty.* Princeton, NJ: Princeton University Press.

Doner, Richard F. 1991. *Driving a Bargain: Automobile Industrialization and Japanese Firms in Southeast Asia.* Berkeley: University of California Press.

Doner, Richard F. 1995a. Notes on the Automotive Sector in Thailand. Emory University. Photocopy.

Doner, Richard F. 1995b. Notes on the Automotive Sector in Malaysia. Emory University. Photocopy.

Dunning, John H. 1988. The Eclectic Paradigm of International Production; A Restatement and Some Possible Extensions. *Journal of International Business Studies* 19, no. 1 (Spring): 1-31.

Dunning, John H. 1993a. *Multinational Enterprises and the Global Economy.* Reading, MA: Addison-Wesley Publishing Company.

Dunning, John H. 1993b. *The Theory of Transnational Corporations.* London and New York: Routledge.

Eastman, H., and S. Stykolt. 1970. A Model for the Study of Protected Oligopolies. *Economic Journal* 70: 336-47.

Encarnation, Dennis J. 1989. *Dislodging Multinationals: India's Strategy in Comparative Perspective.* Ithaca, NY: Cornell University Press.

Encarnation, Dennis J. 1992. *Rivals Beyond Trade.* Ithaca, NY: Cornell University Press.

Encarnation, Dennis J. 1994. Bringing East Asia into the U.S.-Japan Rivalry: The Regional Evolution of American and Japanese Multinationals. In *Japanese Investment in Asia; International Production Strategies in a Rapidly Changing World,* ed. by Eileen M. Doherty. San Francisco: The Asia Foundation and the Berkeley Roundtable on International Economics.

Encarnation, Dennis J., and Boris Velic. 1998. *Competing for Foreign Direct Investment: Government Policy and Corporate Strategy in Asia*. New York: Oxford University Press. Forthcoming.

Encarnation, Dennis J., and Louis T. Wells Jr. 1986. In *Investing in Development: New Roles for Private Capital?* ed. by Theodore H. Moran. Washington: Overseas Development Council.

Ernst, Dieter. 1983. *The Global Race in Microelectronics: Innovation and Corporate Strategy in a Period of Crisis*. New York and Frankfurt: Campus.

Ernst, Dieter. 1994. What Are the Limits to the Korean Model? The Korean Electronics Industry Under Pressure. *Berkeley Roundtable on the International Economy (BRIE) Research Paper*. Berkeley: University of California at Berkeley.

Ernst, Dieter. 1998. Globalization, Convergence and Diversity: The Asian Production Networks of Japanese Electronics Firms. In *Rivalry or Riches: International Production Networks in Asia*, ed. by Michael Borrus, Dieter Ernst, and Stephan Haggard. Cornell, NY: Cornell University Press. Forthcoming.

Ernst, Dieter, and David O'Connor. 1992. *Competing in the Electronics Industry: The Experience of the Newly Industrializing Economies*. Paris: Organization for Economic Cooperation and Development.

Evans, Carol. 1993. Defence Industrialisation in the NICs: Case Studies from Brazil and India. PhD. diss., London School of Economics and Political Science.

Evans, Peter. 1995. *Embedded Autonomy: States & Industrial Transformation*. Princeton, NJ: Princeton University Press.

Evans, Peter, and Paulo Tigre. 1989. Going Beyond Clones in Brazil and Korea: A Comparative Analysis of NIC Strategies in the Computer Industry. *World Development* 17, no. 11 (November): 1751-68.

Eymann, Angelika, and Ludger Schuknecht. 1993. Antidumping Enforcement in the European Community. In *Antidumping: How It Works and Who Gets Hurt*, ed. by J. Michael Finger. Ann Arbor: University of Michigan Press.

Fagre, Nathan, and Louis T. Wells Jr. 1982. Bargaining Power of Multinationals and Host Governments. *Journal of International Business Studies* 13, no. 2 (Fall): 9-23.

Fayad, Marwan, and Homa Motamen. 1986. *The Economics of the Petrochemical Industry*. London: Frances Pinter.

Feenstra, Robert C., and Gordon H. Hanson. 1995a. *Foreign Investment, Outsourcing and Relative Wages*. National Bureau of Economic Research Working Paper No. 5121. Cambridge, MA: National Bureau of Economic Research.

Feenstra, Robert C., and Gordon H. Hanson. 1995b. *Foreign Direct Investment and Relative Wages: Evidence from Mexico's Maquiladoras*. National Bureau of Economic Research Working Paper No. 5122. Cambridge, MA: National Bureau of Economic Research.

Finger, J. Michael. 1993. *Antidumping: How It Works and Who Gets Hurt*. Ann Arbor: University of Michigan Press.

Finger, J. Michael. 1997. GATT Experience with Safeguards: Making Economic and Political Sense of the Possibilities that GATT Allows to Restrict Imports. Washington: World Bank. Photocopy.

Fishlow, Albert, Catherine Gwin, Stephan Haggard, Dani Rodrik, and Robert Wade. 1994. *Miracle or Design? Lessons from the East Asian Experience*. Washington: Overseas Development Council.

Flowers, Edward B. 1976. Oligopolistic Reactions in European and Canadian Direct Investment in the United States. *Journal of International Business Studies* 7, no. 2 (Fall/Winter): 43-55.

Frank, Isaiah. 1980. *Foreign Enterprise in Developing Countries*. Baltimore, MD: Johns Hopkins University Press.

Frischtak, Claudio. 1986. Brazil. In *National Policies for Developing High Tech Industries: International Comparisons*, ed. by Francis W. Rushing and Carole Ganz Brown. Boulder, CO: Westview Press.

Frischtak, Claudio, and Richard S. Newfarmer. 1994. *Transnational Corporations: Market Structure and Industrial Performance.* New York and London: Routledge.

Gillis, Malcolm, Dwight H. Perkins, Michael Roemer, and Donald R. Snodgrass. 1996. *Economics of Development,* 4th ed. New York: W. W. Norton.

Gomes-Casseres, Benjamin. 1989. Ownership Structures of Foreign Subsidiaries; Theory and Evidence. *Journal of Economic Behavior and Organization* 11, no 1 (January): 1-25.

Graham, Edward M. 1978. Transatlantic Investment by Multinational Firms: A Rivalistic Phenomenon? *Journal of Post Keynesian Economics* 1, no. 1 (Fall): 82-99.

Graham, Edward M. 1996a. *Global Corporations and National Governments.* Washington: Institute for International Economics.

Graham, Edward M. 1996b. The (Not Wholly Satisfactory) State of the Theory of Foreign Direct Investment and the Multinational Enterprise. *Economic Systems* merged with *Journal of International and Comparative Economics* 20: 183-206.

Graham, Edward M. 1998. The Economic Effects of Investment Incentives on Host Economies. In *Competing for Foreign Direct Investment: Government Policy and Corporate Strategy in Asia,* ed. by Dennis J. Encarnation and Boris Velic. New York: Oxford University Press. Forthcoming.

Graham, Edward M., and Michael Ebert. 1991. Foreign Direct Investment and National Security: Fixing the Exon-Florio Process. *The World Economy* 14, no. 3 (September): 245-68.

Graham, Edward M., and Paul R. Krugman. 1995. *Foreign Direct Investment in the United States,* 3rd ed. Washington: Institute for International Economics.

Gray, H. Peter, and Ingo Walter. 1984. Investment-Related Trade Distortions in Petrochemicals. *Journal of World Trade Law* 17, no. 4 (July-August): 283-307.

Grieco, Joseph M. 1984. *Between Dependency and Autonomy: India's Experience with the International Computer Industry.* Berkeley: University of California Press.

Grieco, Joseph M. 1986. Foreign Investment and Development: Theories and Evidence. In *Investing In Development: New Roles for Private Capital?* ed. by Theodore H. Moran. Washington: Overseas Development Council.

Grosse, R. 1989. *Multinationals in Latin America.* London: Routledge.

Grossman, Gene. 1981. The Theory of Domestic Content Protection and Content Preferences. *The Quarterly Journal of Economics* 96, no. 4 (November): 583-603.

Grossman, Gene, and Elhanan Helpman. 1991a. Quality Ladders and Product Cycles. *Quarterly Journal of Economics* 106, no. 2 (May): 557-86.

Grossman, Gene, and Elhanan Helpman. 1991b. *Innovation and Growth in the Global Economy.* Cambridge, MA: MIT Press.

Guisinger, Stephen. 1985. A Comparative Study of Country Policies. In *Investment Incentives and Performance Requirements,* ed. by Stephen Guisinger and Associates. New York: Praeger.

Guisinger, Stephen. 1989. Total Protection: A New Measure of the Impact of Government Interventions on Investments Profitability. *Journal of International Business Studies* 20, no. 2 (Summer): 280-95.

Guisinger, Stephen. 1998. Investment Incentives and the Internal Operations of Multinationals. In *Competing for Foreign Direct Investment: Government Policy and Corporate Strategy in Asia,* ed. by Dennis J. Encarnation and Boris Velic. New York: Oxford University Press. Forthcoming.

Guyton, Lynne. 1996. Japanese Investments and Technology Transfer to Malaysia. In *Capital, the State, and Late Industrialization,* ed. by John Borrego. Boulder, CO: Westview Press.

Haddad, Mona, and Ann Harrison. 1993. Are There Positive Spillovers from Direct Foreign Investment? Evidence from Panel Data for Morocco. *Journal of Development Economics* 42, no. 1 (October): 51-74.

Haggard, Stephan. 1990. *Pathways from the Periphery: The Politics of Growth in the Newly Industrializing Countries.* Ithaca, NY: Cornell University Press.

Harrison, Ann. 1996. Determinants and Effects of Direct Foreign Investment in Côte d'Ivoire, Morocco, and Venezuela. In *Industrial Evolution in Developing Countries: Micro Patterns of Turnover, productivity, and Market Structure*, ed. by Mark J. Roberts and James R. Tybout. New York: Oxford University Press.

Harvard Business School. 1990. *Mexico and the Microcomputers*. Case 9-390-093. Cambridge, MA: Harvard Business School.

Harvard Business School. 1993. *Adam Opel AG*. Case 9-392-100, 101, 127. Cambridge, MA: Harvard Business School.

Harvard Business School. 1994. *Prochnik: Privatization of a Polish Clothing Manufacturer*. Case 9-394-038. Cambridge, MA: Harvard Business School.

Helleiner, Gerald K. 1981. *Intra-Firm Trade and the Developing Countries*. New York: St. Martin's Press.

Helpman, Elhanan, and Paul Krugman. 1985. *Market Structure and Foreign Trade*. Cambridge, MA: MIT Press.

Herander, Mark G., and Christopher R. Thomas. 1986. Export Performance and Export-Import Linkage Requirements. *The Quarterly Journal of Economics* 101, no. 3 (August): 591-607.

Hindley, Brian. 1988. Dumping and the Far East Trade of the European Community. *The World Economy* 11, no. 4 (December): 445-63.

Hindley, Brian. 1993. *Helping Transition through Trade? EU and US Policy towards Exports from Eastern and Central Europe*. European Bank for Reconstruction and Development Working Paper No. 4. London: European Bank for Reconstruction and Development

Hines, James. 1996. *Tax Policy and the Activities of Multinational Corporations*. National Bureau of Economic Research Working Paper No. 5589. Cambridge, MA: National Bureau of Economic Research.

Horlick, Gary N., and Shannon S. Shuman. 1984. Nonmarket Economy Trade and U.S. Antidumping/Countervailing Duty Laws. *International Lawyer* 18, no. 4 (Fall): 307-40.

Hymer, Stephen H. 1976. The International Operations of National Firms. 1959 PhD. diss. Cambridge, MA: MIT Press.

Institute of Developing Economies. 1995. *The Automotive Industry in Asia: The Great Leap Forward?* Tokyo: Institute of Developing Economies.

International Council of Chemical Associations. 1996. Statement on the World Trade Organization Singapore Ministerial Meeting (5 October).

Jensen-Moran, Jeri. 1996a. Trade Battles as Investment Wars: The Coming Rules of Origin Debate. *The Washington Quarterly*. 19, no. 1 (Winter): 239-53.

Jensen-Moran, Jeri. 1996b. Choice at the Crossroads: Regionalism and Rules of Origin. *Law and Policy in International Business* 27, no. 4 (Summer): 981-89.

Katz, Jorge M., ed. 1987. *Technology Generation in Latin American Manufacturing Industries*. New York: St. Martin's Press.

Katz, Lawrence F., and Lawrence H. Summers. 1989. Industry Rents: Evidence and Implications. *Brookings Papers on Economic Activity: Microeconomics* (special issue): 209-75.

Keesing, Donald B., and Sanjaya Lall. 1992. Marketing Manufactured Exports from Developing Countries: Learning Sequences and Public Support. In *Trade Policy, Industrialization, and Development: New Perspectives*, ed. by Gerald K. Helleiner. Oxford: Clarendon Press; New York: Oxford University Press.

Kindleberger, Charles P. 1965. *Economic Development*. New York: McGraw-Hill.

Kindleberger, Charles P. 1969. *American Business Abroad*. New Haven, CT, and London, UK: Yale University Press.

Klein, Karen. 1995. *General Motors in Hungary: The Corporate Strategy Behind Szentgotthard*. Washington: Georgetown University, Pew Economic Freedom Fellows Program.

Knickerbocker, Frederick T. 1973. *Oligopolistic Reaction and Multinational Enterprise*. Boston, MA: Harvard University Graduate School of Business Administration.

Kogut, Bruce. 1988. Joint Ventures: Theoretical and Empirical Perspectives. *Strategic Management Journal* 9, no. 4 (July/August): 319-32.

Kokko, Ari, and Magnus Blomstrom. 1995. Policies to Encourage Inflows of Technology through Foreign Multinationals. *World Development* 23, no. 3 (March): 459-68.

Kokko, Ari, R. Tansini, and M. Lejan. 1996. Local Technological Capability and Spillovers from FDI in the Uruguayan Manufacturing Sector. *Journal of Development Studies* 34: 602-11.

Krause, Allen Sangines. 1985. The Cost of Overprotection in the Mexican Computer Industry. Cambridge, MA: Harvard University. Photocopy.

Krishna, Kala, and Anne O. Krueger. 1995. *Implementing Free Trade Areas: Rules of Origin and Hidden Protection.* National Bureau of Economic Research Working Paper No. 4983. Cambridge, MA: National Bureau of Economic Research.

Krueger, Anne O. 1975. *The Benefits and Costs of Import Substitution in India: A Microeconomic Study.* Minneapolis: University of Minnesota Press.

Krueger, Anne O. 1992. Free Trade Agreements as Protectionist Devices: Rules of Origin. Stanford University. Photocopy.

Krugman, Paul R. 1986. *Strategic Trade Policy and the New International Economics.* Cambridge, MA: The MIT Press.

Krugman, Paul R. 1991. *Geography and Trade.* Cambridge, MA: MIT Press.

Lall, Sanjaya. 1978. Transnationals, Domestic Enterprises and Industrial Structure in LDCs: A Survey. *Oxford Economic Papers* 30, no. 2 (July): 217-48.

Lall, Sanjaya. 1980. Vertical Interfirm Linkages in LDCs: An Empirical Study. *Oxford Bulletin of Economics and Statistics* 42, no. 3 (August): 203-26.

Lall, Sanjaya, and Paul Streeten. 1977. *Foreign Investment, Transnationals and Developing Countries.* Boulder, CO: Westview Press.

Lall, Sanjaya, in collaboration with Edward K. Y. Chen, Jorge M. Katz, Bernardo Kosacoff, and Annibal Villela. 1983. *The New Multinationals: The Spread of Third World Enterprises.* Chichester: John Wiley & Sons.

Lawrence, Robert Z. 1994. *Trade, Multinationals and Labor.* National Bureau of Economic Research Working Paper No. 4836. Cambridge, MA: National Bureau of Economic Research.

Lim, Linda Y. C., and Pang Eng Fong. 1977. *The Electronics Industry in Singapore: Structure, Technology, and Linkages.* Monograph Series No. 7. Singapore: National University of Singapore Economic Research Press.

Lim, Linda Y. C., and Pang Eng Fong. 1982. Vertical Linkages and Multinational Enterprises in Developing Countries. *World Development* 10, no. 7 (July): 585-95.

Lim, Linda Y. C., and Pang Eng Fong. 1991. *Foreign Direct Investment and Industrialization in Malaysia, Singapore, Taiwan and Thailand.* Paris: Organization for Economic Cooperation and Development.

Linden, Greg. 1996. Japan and the United States in the Malaysian Electronics Sector. Berkeley, CA: Berkeley Roundtable on International Economics. Photocopy.

Lipson, Charles. 1985. *Standing Guard: Protecting Foreign Capital in the Nineteenth and Twentieth Centuries.* Berkeley: University of California Press.

Lucas, Robert E. 1993. Making a Miracle. *Econometrica* 61, no. 2 (March): 251-72.

Makino, Shige, and Andres Delios. 1996. Local Knowledge Transfer and Performance: Implications for Alliance Formation in Asia. *Journal of International Business Studies* 27, no. 5 (special issue): 905-27.

Mansfield, Edwin, and Anthony Romero. 1980. Technology Transfer to Overseas Subsidiaries by US-based Firms. *Quarterly Journal of Economics* 95, no. 4 (December): 737-50.

Marshall, Alfred. 1920. *Principles of Economics: An Introductory Volume.* London: MacMillan.

McKenna, C. J. 1986. *The Economics of Uncertainty.* New York: Oxford University Press.

McKern, Bruce. 1993. *Transnational Corporations and the Exploitation of Natural Resources.* London: Routledge.

Messerlin, Patrick A. 1990a. Anti-dumping Regulations or Pro-Cartel Law? The EC Chemical Cases. *The World Economy* 13, no. 4 (December): 465-92.

Messerlin, Patrick A. 1990b. Antidumping. In *Completing the Uruguay Round: A Results-Oriented Approach to the GATT Trade Negotiations*, ed. by Jeffrey J. Schott. Washington: Institute for International Economics.

Michalet, Charles-Albert. 1997. *Investment Strategies of Multinational Corporations and the Attractiveness of Host Countries: The Impact of the Opening of Central and Eastern Europe on the Location of Foreign Direct Investment*. Foreign Investment Advisory Service, Occasional Paper No. 10. Washington: World Bank and International Finance Corporation.

Michalopoulos, Constantine, and David G. Tarr. 1994. *Trade in the New Independent States*. Washington: The World Bank/UNDP.

Mikesell, Raymond F. 1975. *Foreign Investment in Copper Mining: Case Studies of Mines in Peru and Papua New Guinea*. Baltimore: Johns Hopkins University Press for Resources for the Future.

Miller, Robert R., Jack D. Glen, Frederick Z. Jaspersen, and Yannis Karmokolias. 1996. International Joint Ventures in Developing Countries: Happy Marriages? *International Finance Corporation, Discussion Paper No. 29*. Washington: International Finance Corporation.

Minor, Michael S. 1994. The Demise of Expropriation as an Instrument of LDC Policy 1980-1992. *Journal of International Business Studies* 25, no. 1 (First Quarter).

Moran, Theodore H. 1974. *Multinational Corporations and the Politics of Dependence: Copper in Chile*. Princeton, NJ: Princeton University Press.

Moran, Theodore H. 1990. The Globalization of America's Defense Industries: Managing the Threat of Foreign Dependence. *International Security* 15 (Summer): 57-99.

Moran, Theodore H. 1993. *American Economic Policy and National Security*. New York: Council on Foreign Relations Press.

Moran, Theodore H., ed. 1998. *Managing International Political Risk: New Tools, Strategies and Techniques for Investors and Financial Institutions*. New York: Blackwell.

Nelson, Douglas R. 1996. The Political Economy of U.S. Automobile Protection. In *The Political Economy of American Trade Policy*, ed. by Anne O. Krueger. Chicago: University of Chicago Press for the National Bureau of Economic Research.

Newfarmer, Richard, and Linda Marsh. 1992. Industrial Structure, Market Power, and Profitability. *Industry Series Paper No. 63*. Washington: World Bank (August).

Nezu, M. Risaburo. 1996. *Trends and Patterns of Public Support to Industry in the OECD Area*. Speech (15 October). Paris: Organization for Economic Cooperation and Development.

Nollen, Stanley D., Jacqueline M. Abbey, and Karen L. Newman. 1997. *ABB PBS I and II*. Washington: Georgetown University, case study prepared for the Pew Economic Freedom Fellows.

O'Brien, Leslie. 1993. Malaysian Manufacturing Sector Linkages. In *Industrializing Malaysia: Policy, Performance, Prospects*, ed. by K. S. Jomo. London: Routledge.

Olechowski, Andrej. 1993. Chemicals from Poland: A Tempest in a Teacup. In *Antidumping: How It Works and Who Gets Hurt*, ed. by Michael Finger. Ann Arbor: University of Michigan Press.

Organization for Economic Cooperation and Development (OECD). 1992. *Industrial Support Policies in OECD Countries: 1986-1989*. Paris: Organization for Economic Cooperation and Development.

Organization for Economic Cooperation and Development. 1994. *OECD Reviews of Foreign Direct Investment: Ireland*. Paris: Organization for Economic Cooperation and Development.

Organization for Economic Cooperation and Development. 1995. *OECD Reviews of Foreign Direct Investment: United States*. Paris: Organization for Economic Cooperation and Development.

Organization for Economic Cooperation and Development. 1996a. *Public Support to Industry; Report by the Industry Committee to the Council at Ministerial Level*. Paris: Organization for Economic Cooperation and Development.

Organization for Economic Cooperation and Development. 1996b. *OECD Reviews of Foreign Direct Investment: France*. Paris: Organization for Economic Cooperation and Development.

Organization for Economic Cooperation and Development. 1996c. *Trade and Competition: Frictions after the Uruguay Round*. Paris: Organization for Economic Cooperation and Development.

Parry, Thomas G. 1985. Internalization as a General Theory of Foreign Direct Investment: A Critique. *Weltwirtschaftliches Archiv* 121, no. 3 (Summer): 564-69.

Penrose, Edith T. 1959. Profit Sharing between Producing Countries and Oil Companies in the Middle East. *Economic Journal* 69 (June): 238-54.

Penrose, Edith T. 1968. *The Large International Firm in Developing Countries: The International Petroleum Industry*. London: Allen and Unwin.

Peres Nuñez, Wilson. 1990. *Foreign Direct Investment and Industrial Development in Mexico*. Paris: Organization for Economic Cooperation and Development.

Pirnia, Neda. 1998. The Relative Impact of Investment Incentives on FDI: A Literature Review. In *Competing for Foreign Direct Investment: Government Policy and Corporate Strategy in Asia*, ed. by Dennis J. Encarnation and Boris Velic. New York: Oxford University Press. Forthcoming.

Powers, Linda F. 1998. New Forms of Protection for International Infrastructure Investors. In *Managing International Political Risk: New Tools, Strategies and Techniques for Investors and Financial Institutions*, ed. by Theodore H. Moran. New York: Blackwell. Forthcoming.

Prodi, Romano. 1974. Italy. In *Big Business and the State: Changing Relations in Western Europe*, ed. by Raymond Vernon. Cambridge, MA: Harvard University Press.

Prusa, Thomas J. 1992. Why Are So Many Antidumping Petitions Withdrawn? *Journal of International Economics* 33, no. 1-2 (August): 1-20.

Prusa, Thomas J. 1994. Pricing Behavior in the Presence of Antidumping Law. *Journal of Economic Integration* 9, no. 2 (June): 260-89.

Prusa, Thomas J. 1997. The Trade Effects of U.S. Antidumping Actions. In *The Effects of U.S. Trade Protection and Promotion Policies*, ed. by Robert C. Feenstra. Cambridge, MA: National Bureau of Economic Research.

Rasiah, Rajah. 1993. Free Trade Zones and Industrial Development in Malaysia. In *Industrializing Malaysia: Policy, Performance, Prospects*, ed. by K. S. Jomo. London: Routledge.

Rasiah, Rajah. 1994. Flexible Production Systems and Local Machine-Tool Subcontracting: Electronics Components Transnationals in Malaysia. *Cambridge Journal of Economics* 18, no. 3 (June): 279-98.

Rasiah, Rajah. 1995. *Foreign Capital and Industrialization in Malaysia*. New York: St. Martin's Press.

Raveed, S. R., and W. Renforth. 1983. State Enterprise - Multinational Corporation Joint Ventures: How Well Do They Meet Both Partners' Needs? *Management International Review* 23, no. 1: 47-57.

Reuber, Grant L. 1973. *Private Foreign Investment in Development*. Oxford, UK: Clarendon Press.

Reynolds, John I. 1984. The Pinched-Shoe Effect of International Joint Ventures. *Columbia Journal of World Business* 19, no. 2 (Summer): 23-29.

Rhee, Y. W., and T. Belot. 1989. *Export Catalysts in Low-Income Countries*. Industry Series Paper No. 5. Washington: World Bank.

Richardson, J. David. 1989. Empirical Research on Trade Liberalization with Imperfect Competition: A Survey. *OECD Economic Studies*, no. 12 (Spring): 8-50.

Richardson, J. David, and Elena B. Khripounova. 1997. U.S. Labor Market Power and Linkages to International Trade: Identifying Suspects and Measures. Institute for International Economics. Photocopy.

Richardson, J. David, and Karin Rindal. 1996. *Why Exports Matter: More!* Washington: Institute for International Economics and National Association of Manufacturers.

Richardson, Martin. 1993. Content Protection with Foreign Capital. *Oxford Economic Papers* 45, no. 1 (January): 103-17.

Roberts, Mark J., and James R. Tybout. 1997. *What Makes Exports Boom?* Washington: World Bank.

Rodman, Kenneth A. 1988. *Sanctity vs. Sovereignty: The United States and the Nationalization of Natural Resource Investments.* New York: Columbia University Press.

Rodrik, Dani. 1987. The Economics of Export-Performance Requirements. *The Quarterly Journal of Economics* 102, no. 3 (August) 633-50.

Rodrik, Dani. 1988. Imperfect Competition, Scale Economies and Trade Policy in Developing Countries. In *Trade Policy Issues and Empirical Analysis*, ed. by Robert E. Baldwin. Chicago: University of Chicago Press.

Rogers, Allan. 1979. *Economic Development in Retrospect: The Italian Model and Its Significance for Regional Planning in Market-Oriented Economies.* New York: John Wiley & Sons.

Rugman, Alan M. 1985. Internalization Is Still a General Theory of Foreign Direct Investment. *Weltwirtschaftliches Archiv* 121, no. 3 (Summer): 564-69.

Samuels, Barbara C. 1990. *Managing Risk in Developing Countries: National Demands and Multinational Response.* Princeton, NJ: Princeton University Press.

Schelling, Thomas. 1966. *Arms and Influence.* New Haven, CT: Yale University Press.

Schive, Chi. 1990. The Next Stage of Industrialization in Taiwan and South Korea. In *Manufacturing Miracles: Paths of Industrialization in Latin America and East Asia*, ed. by Gary Gereffi and Donald L. Wyman. Princeton, NJ: Princeton University Press.

Schweke, William, Carl Risk, and Brian Dabson. 1994. *Bidding for Business: Are Cities and States Selling Themselves Short?* Washington: Corporation for Enterprise Development.

Schwendiman, John S. 1984. Managing Environmental Risk: Cases and Lessons for Corporate Strategy. In *International Political Risk Management: New Dimensions*, ed. by Fariborz Ghadar and Theodore H. Moran. Washington: Georgetown School of Foreign Service.

Sedgewick, M. W. 1995. Does Japanese Management Travel in Asia? Managerial Technology Transfer and Japanese Multinationals. MIT-Japan Program. Photocopy.

Shah, Anwar, ed. 1995. *Fiscal Incentives for Investment and Innovation.* New York: Oxford University Press for the World Bank.

Shapiro, Helen. 1993. Automobiles: From Import Substitution to Export Promotion in Brazil and Mexico. In *Beyond Free Trade: Firms, Governments and Global Competition*, ed. by David Yoffie. Boston, MA: Harvard Business School Press.

Shapiro, Helen. 1994. *Engines of Growth.* New York: Cambridge University Press.

Skud, Timothy. 1996. Customs Procedures as the Residual Barriers to Trade. *Law and Policy in International Business* 27, no. 4 (Summer): 969-79.

Smith, David N., and Louis T. Wells Jr. 1975. *Negotiating Third World Mineral Agreements: Promises as Prologue.* Cambridge, MA: Ballinger.

Spiller, Pablo T. 1994. *The Policy Environment for Foreign Direct Investment in Infrastructure.* Washington: Foreign Investment Advisory Service of the World Bank and the International Finance Corporation.

Spitz, Peter H. 1988. *Petrochemicals: The Rise of an Industry.* New York: John Wiley & Sons.

Staiger, Robert W., and Frank A. Wolak. 1994. The Trade Effects of Antidumping Investigations: Theory and Evidence. In *Analytical and Negotiating Issues in the Global Trading System*, ed. by Alan V. Deardorff and Robert M. Stern. Ann Arbor: University of Michigan Press.

Stobaugh, Robert. 1988. *Innovation and Competition: The Global Management of Petrochemical Products.* Boston, MA: Harvard Business School Press.

Stopford, John M., and Louis T. Wells Jr. 1972. *Managing the Multinational Enterprise.* New York: Basic Books.

Tachiki, D., and A. Aoki. 1991. The Globalization of Japanese Business Activities. *RIM Pacific Business and Industries.* Tokyo: Sakura Institute of Research

The, Alfred E. L. 1989. Ancillary Firms Serving the Electronics Industry: The Case of Penang. In *Changing Dimensions of the Electronics Industry in Malaysia*, ed. by Narayanan et al. London: Routledge.

Thomas, Kenneth P. 1997. *Capital Beyond Borders: States and Firms in the Auto Industry, 1960-1994*. New York: St. Martin's Press.

Thomas, Kenneth P. 1998. *Competing for Capital: European and North American Responses.* Washington: Georgetown University Press. Forthcoming.

Tilton, John E. 1992. *Mineral Wealth and Economic Development* Washington: Resources for the Future.

Trade Promotion Coordinating Committee. 1996. *Fourth Annual Report to Congress.* Washington: Department of Commerce.

Tsurumi, Y. 1976. *The Japanese Are Coming: A Multinational Interaction of Firms and Politics.* Cambridge, MA: Ballinger.

Ubaidullaev, Alisher. 1996. *Proposed Investment in Amantayau Goldfields (AGF)*. Washington: Georgetown University, Case Study of the Pew Economic Freedom Fellows Program.

United Nations Centre on Transnational Corporations (UNCTC). 1988. *Transnational Corporations in World Development: Trends and Prospects.* New York: United Nations.

United Nations Centre on Transnational Corporations (UNCTC). 1991. *The Impact of Trade-Related Investment Measures on Trade and Development.* New York: United Nations.

United Nations Conference on Trade and Development (UNCTAD). 1996. *Incentives and Foreign Direct Investment.* Geneva: UNCTAD.

United Nations Conference on Trade and Development, Division on Transnational Corporations and Investment. 1995. *World Investment Report 1995: Transnational Corporations and Competitiveness.* New York: United Nations.

United Nations Conference on Trade and Development, Division on Transnational Corporations and Investment. 1996. *World Investment Report 1996: Investment, Trade and International Policy Arrangements.* New York: United Nations.

United Nations Conference on Trade and Development, Division on Transnational Corporations and Investment. 1997. *World Investment Report 1997: Transnational Corporations, Market Structure and Competition Policy.* New York: United Nations.

United States International Trade Commission. 1983. *The Probable Impact on the U.S. Petrochemical Industry of the Expanding Petrochemical Industries in the Conventional-Energy-Rich Nations.* Washington: Government Printing Office.

Urata, Shujiro. 1995. Emerging Patterns of Production and Foreign Trade in Electronics Products in East Asia: An Examination of a Role Played by Foreign Direct Investment. San Francisco, CA: The Asia Foundation. Photocopy.

Vernon, Raymond. 1966. International Trade and International Investment in the Product Cycle. *Quarterly Journal of Economics* 83, no. 1: 190-207.

Vernon, Raymond. 1971. *Sovereignty at Bay.* New York: Basic Books.

Vernon, Raymond, ed. 1974. *Big Business and the State: Changing Relations in Western Europe.* Cambridge, MA: Harvard University Press.

Vernon, Raymond, and W. H. Davidson. 1979. Foreign Production of Technology-Intensive Products by U.S.-Based Multinational Enterprises. National Science Foundation. Photocopy.

Wade, Robert. 1990. Industrial Policy in East Asia: Does It Lead or Follow the Market? In *Manufacturing Miracles: Paths of Industrialization in Latin America and East Asia*, ed. by Gary Gereffi and Donald L. Wyman. Princeton, NJ: Princeton University Press.

Wagnon, Todd. 1995. *US Antidumping Laws and Procedures: The Treatment of Exports from Economies in Transition.* Washington: Georgetown University, Pew Economic Freedom Fellows Case Study.

Wells, Louis T. Jr. Automobiles. 1974. In *Big Business and the State: Changing Relations in Western Europe*, ed. by Raymond Vernon. Cambridge, MA: Harvard University Press.

Wells, Louis T. Jr. 1983. *Third World Multinationals.* Cambridge, MA: MIT Press.

Wells, Louis T. Jr. 1986. Investment Incentives: An Unnecessary Debate. *The CTC Reporter* 22 (Autumn): 51-62.

Wells, Louis T. Jr. 1998. Good and Fair Competition: Does the Foreign Direct Investor Face Still Other Risks in Emerging Markets? In *Managing International Political Risk: New Tools, Strategies and Techniques for Investors and Financial Institutions*, ed. by Theodore H. Moran. New York: Blackwell. Forthcoming.

Wells, Louis T. Jr., and Alvin G. Wint. 1990. *Marketing a Country: Promotion as a Tool for Attracting Foreign Investment.* Foreign Investment Advisory Service Occasional Paper No. 1. Washington: International Finance Corporation and the Multilateral Investment Guarantee Agency of the World Bank Group.

West, Gerald. 1996. Managing Project Political Risk: The Role of Investment Insurance. *The Journal of Project Finance* 2, no. 4 (Winter): 5-11.

Westphal, Larry. 1979. Manufacturing. In *Korean Policy Issues for Long-Term Development*, ed. by P. Hasan and D. C. Rao. Baltimore, MD: Johns Hopkins University Press for the World Bank.

Williamson, Oliver E. 1985. *The Economic Institutions of Capitalism.* New York: The Free Press.

Willmore, Larry N. 1976. Direct Foreign Investment in Central American Manufacturing. *World Development* 4, no. 6 (June): 499-519.

World Bank. 1993. *The East Asian Miracle: Economic Growth and Public Policy.* New York: Oxford University Press for the World Bank.

World Bank. 1995. *The World Bank Guarantee: Catalyst for Private Capital Flows.* Washington: World Bank.

World Bank. 1997. Global Development Finance. Washington: World Bank.

Yanarella, Ernest J., and William C. Green. 1989. *The Politics of Industrial Recruitment: Japanese Automobile Investment and Economic Development in the American States.* New York: Greenwood Press.

Yarbrough, Beth V. 1988. Comment. In *Trade Policy Issues and Empirical Analysis*, ed. by Robert E. Baldwin. Chicago: University of Chicago Press.

Yeats, Alexander. 1997. *Does Mercosur's Trade Performance Raise Concerns about the Effects of Regional Trade Arrangements?* Policy Research Working Paper No. 1729. Washington: World Bank, International Economics Department, International Trade Division.

Yu, Chwo-Ming, and Kiyohiko Ito. 1988. Oligopolistic Reaction and Foreign Direct Investment: The Case of US Tire and Textile Industries. *Journal of International Business Studies* 19, no. 3 (Fall): 449-60.

Yuill, Douglas, and Kevin Allen. 1981. *European Regional Incentive Programs 1981.* Glasgow, Scotland: University of Strathclyde.

Index

advertising. *See also* investment promotion
  by host country
    costs and benefits of, 3-4, 120
    personal vs. impersonal, 39
aerospace, Boeing-Airbus competition, 8-9, 83
agglomeration
  foreign/indigenous firms and, 6, 166
  petrochemical industry and, 66
Algeria, petrochemical export facilities
  development, 65, 68
antidumping regulations. *See also* Rules of
  origin
  electronics/computer industry, 79
  enforcement of by developing/developed
    countries, 8, 11, 63, 83, 158
  petrochemical industry, 64, 69, 71
  restriction of use of, 159, 167
  strategic-trade conditions and, 109-113
Apple and HP vs. IBM in Mexico, 5, 47-48b,
  86. *See also* electronics/computer
  industry
appropriability problems, follow-the-leader
  behavior and, 92-94
Argentina. *See also* Latin America
  FDI distribution in, 15
  Uruguay Round participation, 68
Asia. *See* Southeast Asia
Association of Southeast Asian Nations
  (ASEAN). *See also* Southeast Asia
  automotive firms participation in, 61
Atlan Industries, 78
automotive industry. *See also specific
  corporations*
  benefits to host economy, 5-6

compared to petrochemical industry, 67, 70-
  71
diversification issues and, 10
domestic-content requirements, 42, 46
economies of scale requirements, 43, 44
export-performance requirements
  assessment, 61-63
  Brazil global/regional sourcing, 57-59
  globalization issues, 50, 81-84
  Mexico and Brazil, 51-53
  Mexico global/regional sourcing, 53-56
  Thailand global/regional sourcing, 59-61
Azerbaijan, FDI distribution in, 17

backward linkages. *See also* indigenous
  suppliers; technology transfer
  domestic-content requirements and, 41, 159-
    160, 161
  infant industries and, 5
  joint-venture requirements and, 125-126
  Mexican automotive industry, 55-56
  in parent/subsidiary firm arrangements, 6,
    62
  Thailand automotive industry, 60-61
Bakti Comintel, 77-78
balance of payments, government strategies to
  enhance, 32
"Bandwagon effect." *See* clustering; follow-the-
  leader behavior
barriers to entry. *See also* protected markets;
  trade barriers
  FDI effectiveness and, 2, 20, 21
  parent-firm strategies for, 22

Fiat. *See also* Automotive industry
  Latin America operations, 52, 57, 58, 86, 133
  operations in Poland, 5, 46
Flour Corporation, 65
follow-the-leader behavior
  appropriability problems and, 92-94
  new investment strategy and, 7, 86-87, 106, 157
force majeure events. *See also* Multilateral risk-guarantee program
  risk guarantees against, 145-149
Ford. *See also* Automotive industry
  Latin American operations, 45, 52, 54, 58, 86
foreign direct investment (FDI)
  benefits and dangers, 1, 153, 155
  benign model of FDI and development, 19-20
  development process and
    in general, 155-156
  domestic-content requirements and, 41-48
    adverse impact of, 43-45
    adverse political economy of, 45-48
    evidence about, 41-43
  market failures and interventions, 157-159
  new policy agenda, 159-160
  new policy agenda tactics, 161-167
  market imperfections and, 23
  net assessments of impact, 3, 24-25
foreign firms. *See also* parent firm
  advantages of, compared to indigenous firms, 21-22
  assumed advantages of, 21
  developed-countries efforts for attracting, 96
  domestic-content requirements and, 45-48
  export-oriented investment policies, 7
  host country investment promotion and, 37-40
  relations with indigenous firms, 75-76
  response to political/economic risk, 144-145
  as satisficers rather than profit maximizers, 33
France
  concentration ratios and outward investment, 23
  Michelin tire plants, 133

General Electric (GE), Asian operations, 73, 86, 131
General Motors (GM)
  Eisenach plant incentives, 8, 103-104*b*
  grants and incentives for plant locations, 8, 100
  Hungarian Szentgotthard plant, 8, 43, 103-104*b*, 108
  Latin America operations, 52, 54, 56, 58-59, 86
  geology, natural resources development and, 22

General Motors do Brasil. *See also* automotive industry; Brazil
  disputes with GM Detroit, 92
  global sourcing strategies and, 58
Germany
  concentration ratios and outward investment, 23
  incentives for GM Eisenach plant, 8, 103-104*b*
  locational incentives use by, 8, 96-97
  opposition to off-shore plant relocation, 52
  petrochemical industry, 69
  technology transfer profits, 121-122
global welfare. *See also* National welfare
  beneficial impacts on, 6, 66
  export-performance requirements and, 50
  optimal investment patterns for, 88, 90-91, 165
globalization of manufacturing industries. *See also* Liberalization
  in general, 85
  market failure rationales for host-country intervention, 86-94
    follow-the-leader behavior and appropriability problems, 92-94
    stickiness and "irreversible investments under uncertainty," 87-92
  policy implications of passivism, escalation, playing for draw, 113-114
  second-best rationales for host-country intervention, 94-102, 162
    locational incentives, grants, subsidies, 95-98
    locational incentives impact on international investment decisions, 98-102
  strategic-trade struggles/protectionism and trade diversion, 102-113
"good citizenship" standards, for international development, 2
Grand bargain. *See also* Multilateral risk-guarantee program
  negotiation of, 162, 163-167
    national treatment and, 163
    right of establishment, 163-164
    sector-specific reservations and national-security exceptions, 164-167
grants. *See also* Investment promotion; Locational incentives
  rationales for using, 95-98, 99-100
Greece, EU favorable investment treatment, 96*n*
greenfield investment, investment incentives and, 70

Hewlett-Packard (HP). *See also* Electronics/computer industry
  Apple and HP vs. IBM in Mexico, 5, 47-48*b*, 86
  Asian operations, 75, 78

investment promotion. *See also* advertising
  costs and benefits of, 3-4, 31
  foreign firms and, 37-40, 120
  host country intervention in, 31-35, 37
    market failure rationales for, 86-94
    pros and cons of, 3, 7-8, 37-38, 85
    second-best rationales for, 94-102
Investment Promotion Network (IPAnet), 39
IPAnet. *See* Investment Promotion Network
  (IPAnet)
Iran, petrochemical export facilities development, 65
Ireland
  electronics/computer industry, 79, 107
  locational incentives use by, 8
Irish model
  characteristics of, 96
  Mexican automotive industry subsidies
    compared to, 53
  "irreversible investments under uncertainty"
    home authority response to, 94-95
    welfare effects of, 87-92
Isuzu
  Latin American operations, 86
  Southeast Asian facilities, 59
Italy
  Mezzogiorno development, 52, 57, 96n, 133
  opposition to off-shore plant relocation, 52
  petrochemical industry, 69

Japan. *See also* East Asia
  concentration ratios and outward
    investment, 23
  petrochemical tariffs, 68
  technology transfer profits, 121-122
Japanese firms. *See also* foreign firms
  competition with US firms, 72-73
  East Asian domestic-content requirements
    satisfaction, 44, 46, 59
  electronics/computer industry
    compared to United States developments, 73-78
    "fish" behavior, 73, 83, 87
    Southeast Asian plant development, 59,
      60, 61, 78
  intra-*keiretsu* behavior, 74, 78, 81
  joint-venture participation, 9, 120
jobs. *See also* Labor; Wages
  Irish model for development of, 53, 96
  locational incentives costs for, 8, 63, 69, 97,
    101, 104b, 133
  Mexican automotive industry, 55
  in research and development, 129
joint-venture requirements
  analysis of, 11, 160
  backward linkages and, 125-126
  compared to technology licensing, 117, 161
  export performance and, 123-125
  foreign firms participation in, 9, 74, 119-121

Mexican automotive industry, 55-56
technology transfer and, 9, 119, 121-123, 161

Kazakhstan, FDI distribution in, 17
Kia, industrial development and, 10
Komy Semiconductor, 131
Korea model (Japan-Korea model). *See also*
  South Korea
  discussed, 10, 117, 127, 128, 130, 131-132, 160

labor. *See also* jobs
  opposition to off-shore plant relocation, 52,
    61-62, 89
  subsidies for, 95
labor pooling, foreign/indigenous firms and, 6
Latin America. *See also specific countries*
  automotive industry, 45
  computer industry, 45
  cultural issues effecting investment, 51
  electronics/computer industry, 72, 77n
  FDI distribution in, 15, 17
  relations with Southeast Asian countries,
    165
  sourcing networks, 6
legal issues, effect on investment decisions, 89
lemons problem. *See also* information gaps
  new investment strategy and, 7, 90, 157
liberalization. *See also* globalization
  North-South dialogue for, 168
local markets. *See also* domestic economy
  foreign firm exploitation of, 22, 23
local suppliers. *See* indigenous suppliers
locational incentives. *See also* economic
  incentives
  developed countries use of, 8, 61-62, 63, 72,
    83, 94-95, 158, 166-167
  "commodity" and "factor," 99-100
  impact on international investment
    decisions, 98-102, 99t
  rationales for using, 95-98
  developing countries use of, 11
  for electronics/computer industry, 78-79, 81
  for petrochemical industry, 69-70, 71
  transparency and limits for, 159
Lonrho, 146-147
Lopez Portillo, Pres., 54
Lucky Goldstar, South Korea venture, 129,
  131, 133
Lucy, Patrick, 54

machine-tool firms. *See also* indigenous
  suppliers
  Malaysia, 10, 76-77
MAI. *See* Multilateral Agreement on
  Investment
Malaysia. *See also* Southeast Asia
  automotive industry, 10-11, 45, 59, 89

electronics/computer industry, 72, 73-78, 87, 91, 126, 130, 132
export capacity development of machine-tool firms, 10
foreign firms concentration in local markets, 23
locational incentives offered by, 101
machine-tool firms and foreign firms, 76-77
national champion Proton joint venture, 10-11, 76n, 123, 134-135b
regional rivalries, 166
managerial development. *See also* best practices; coaching; dynamic-learning effects
domestic-content requirements and, 45
in electronics/computer industry, 75, 76, 77, 81
FDI effect on, 20, 156
foreign plant effect on, 6, 82
in Japanese subsidiary firms, 59
parent/subsidiary firms and, 54n, 92, 125
managerial incentives, infant industries and, 5
market concentration, competition level and, 20-21
market failure
automotive industry globalization and, 62
development process and, 157-159
in natural resources/infrastructure development, 11
new investment strategy and, 7, 114
rationales for host-country intervention, 86-94
stickiness and "irreversible investments under uncertainty," 87-92
market function, domestic-content requirements effect on, 43
market imperfections, relation to foreign direct investment, 23
market intervention. *See also specific interventions*
development process and, 157-159
market structure, relation to FDI impact on development, 21-24
marketing theory, host-country promotional efforts and, 4
Mazda. *See also* Automotive industry
Latin American operations, 86
Southeast Asian facilities, 59
US operations, 97
Mercedes-Benz, US operations, 97
Mercosur, rules of origin, 109, 167
Methane. *See also* Petrochemical industry
shipment and costs, 64, 66-67, 86
Methanol. *See* Methane
Mexico. *See also* Latin America
Apple and HP vs. IBM in Mexico, 5, 47-48b
automotive industry, 10, 11, 46, 63, 86, 91, 124, 132
export-performance requirements, 51-53
global/regional sourcing, 53-56

joint-venture requirements, 55-56
Trade-Related Investment Measures (TRIM), 53
electronics/computer industry, 45, 79-80, 108
export performance of firms, 123, 124
foreign firms ownership of productive capacity in local market, 23
locational incentives offered by, 101
peso crisis, FDI flows and, 15
petrochemical export facilities development, 65, 66
technology transfers, 123
Mezzogiorno. *See* Italy
MIGA. *See* Multilateral Guarantee Agency
mining, 143. *See also* natural resources development
Amantayau goldfield project, 146
Escondida copper mine project, 11, 148b
regulatory changes effect on, 143
Mitsubishi
Latin American operations, 86
Proton/Malaysia joint-venture, 10-11, 76n, 123, 134-135b
Southeast Asian facilities, 59
Moldova, risk-guarantee program, 146
Montedison, 69n
Moody's, 39
Motorola, Asian operations, 73, 75, 77-78, 87, 131
Multilateral Agreement on Investment (MAI), 12, 161-162, 163, 165
Multilateral Guarantee Agency (MIGA), multilateral risk-guarantee program, 145-149
multilateral institutions, role in credibility assurance, 11, 157
Multilateral Investment Guarantee Agency of the World Bank Group, Investment Promotion Network (IPAnet), 39
multilateral risk-guarantee program. *See also* grand bargain
agencies involved in, 11, 12, 39, 145-149, 157, 161

NAFTA. *See* North American Free Trade Agreement
National champions
"crony capitalism" and, 10
Hyundai/South Korea, 10
Malaysia, Proton, 10-11, 76n, 123, 134-135b
South Korea, 132, 133
technology licensing and, 132, 133-135, 160
national security
grand bargain negotiation and, 164-167
technology licensing and, 135-136, 160
National Semiconductor, Asian operations, 73, 87
national treatment. *See also* foreign firms
grand bargain negotiation and, 163

Other Publications from the
Institute for International Economics

POLICY ANALYSES IN INTERNATIONAL ECONOMICS Series

Latin American Adjustment: How Much Has Happened?
John Williamson, editor/*April 1990*
ISBN paper 0-88132-125-7   470 pp.

The Future of World Trade in Textiles and Apparel
William R. Cline/*1987, 2d ed. June 1990*
ISBN paper 0-88132-110-9   432 pp.

**Completing the Uruguay Round: A Results-Oriented Approach
to the GATT Trade Negotiations**
Jeffrey J. Schott, editor/*September 1990*
ISBN paper 0-88132-130-3   252 pp.

Economic Sanctions Reconsidered (in two volumes)
Economic Sanctions Reconsidered: Supplemental Case Histories
Gary Clyde Hufbauer, Jeffrey J. Schott, and
Kimberly Ann Elliott/*1985, 2d ed. December 1990*
ISBN cloth 0-88132-115-X   928 pp.
ISBN paper 0-88132-105-2   928 pp.

Economic Sanctions Reconsidered: History and Current Policy
Gary Clyde Hufbauer, Jeffrey J. Schott, and Kimberly Ann Elliott/*December 1990*
ISBN cloth 0-88132-140-0   288 pp.
ISBN paper 0-88132-136-2   288 pp.

Pacific Basin Developing Countries: Prospects for the Future
Marcus Noland/*January 1991*
ISBN   cloth 0-88132-141-9   254 pp.
(out of print)   ISBN paper 0-88132-081-1   254 pp.

Currency Convertibility in Eastern Europe
John Williamson, editor/*October 1991*
ISBN paper 0-88132-128-1   480 pp.

International Adjustment and Financing: The Lessons of 1985-1991
C. Fred Bergsten, editor/*January 1992*
ISBN paper 0-88132-112-5   358 pp.

North American Free Trade: Issues and Recommendations
Gary Clyde Hufbauer and Jeffrey J. Schott/*April 1992*
ISBN paper 0-88132-120-6   392 pp.

Narrowing the U.S. Current Account Deficit
Allen J. Lenz/*June 1992*
(out of print)   ISBN paper 0-88132-103-6   640 pp.

The Economics of Global Warming
William R. Cline/*June 1992*   ISBN paper 0-88132-132-X   416 pp.

U.S. Taxation of International Income: Blueprint for Reform
Gary Clyde Hufbauer, assisted by Joanna M. van Rooij/*October 1992*
ISBN cloth 0-88132-178-8   300 pp.
ISBN paper 0-88132-134-6   300 pp.

Who's Bashing Whom? Trade Conflict in High-Technology Industries
Laura D'Andrea Tyson/*November 1992*
ISBN paper 0-88132-106-0   352 pp.

Korea in the World Economy
Il SaKong/*January 1993*   ISBN paper 0-88132-183-4   328 pp.

Pacific Dynamism and the International Economic System
C. Fred Bergsten and Marcus Noland, editors/*May 1993*
ISBN paper 0-88132-196-6   424 pp.

Economic Consequences of Soviet Disintegration
John Williamson, editor/*May 1993*
ISBN paper 0-88132-190-7   660 pp.

Reconcilable Differences? United States-Japan Economic Conflict
C. Fred Bergsten and Marcus Noland/*June 1993*
ISBN paper 0-88132-129-X   296 pp.

Regional Trading Blocs in the World Economic System
Jeffrey A. Frankel/*October 1997*
ISBN paper 0-88132-202-4   388 pp.

Sustaining the Asia Pacific Miracle: Environmental Protection and
Economic Integration
André Dua and Daniel C. Esty/*October 1997*
ISBN paper 0-88132-250-4   232 pp.

Trade and Income Distribution
William R. Cline/*November 1997*
ISBN paper 0-88132-216-4   328 pp.

Global Competition Policy
Edward M. Graham and J. David Richardson/*December 1997*
ISBN paper 0-88132-166-4   616 pp.

Unfinished Business: Telecommunications after the Uruguay Round
Gary Clyde Hufbauer and Erika Wada/*December 1997*
ISBN paper 0-88132-257-1   268 pp.

Financial Services Liberalization in the WTO
Wendy Dobson and Pierre Jacquet /*June 1998*
ISBN paper 0-88132-254-7   376 pp.

Restoring Japan's Economic Growth
Adam S. Posen /*September 1998*
ISBN paper 0-88132-262-8   212 pp.

Measuring the Costs of Protection in China
Zhang Shuguang, Zhang Yansheng, and Wan Zhongxin/*November 1998*
ISBN paper 0-88132-247-4   96 pp.

Foreign Direct Investment and Development: The New Policy Agenda
for Developing Countries and Economies in Transition
Theodore H. Moran/*December 1998*   216 pp.
ISBN paper 0-88132-258-X

Behind the Open Door: Foreign Enterprises in the Chinese Marketplace
Daniel H. Rosen/*January 1999*
ISBN paper 0-88132-263-6   344 pp.

SPECIAL REPORTS

1   Promoting World Recovery: A Statement on Global Economic Strategy
    by Twenty-six Economists from Fourteen Countries/*December 1982*
    (out of print)   ISBN paper 0-88132-013-7   45 pp.
2   Prospects for Adjustment in Argentina, Brazil, and Mexico:
    Responding to the Debt Crisis   (out of print)
    John Williamson, editor/*June 1983*
    ISBN paper 0-88132-016-1   71 pp.
3   Inflation and Indexation: Argentina, Brazil, and Israel
    John Williamson, editor/*March 1985*
    ISBN paper 0-88132-037-4   191 pp.
4   Global Economic Imbalances
    C. Fred Bergsten, editor/*March 1986*
    ISBN cloth 0-88132-038-2   126 pp.
    ISBN paper 0-88132-042-0   126 pp.
5   African Debt and Financing
    Carol Lancaster and John Williamson, editors/*May 1986*
    (out of print)   ISBN paper 0-88132-044-7   229 pp.
6   Resolving the Global Economic Crisis: After Wall Street
    Thirty-three Economists from Thirteen Countries/*December 1987*
    ISBN paper 0-88132-070-6   30 pp.

WORKS IN PROGRESS

Explaining Congressional Votes on Recent Trade Bills:
From NAFTA to Fast Track
Robert E. Baldwin and Christopher S. Magee
The US - Japan Economic Relationship
C. Fred Bergsten, Marcus Noland, and Takatoshi Ito
China's Entry to the World Economy
Richard N. Cooper
Toward a New International Financial Architecture: A Practical Post-Asia Agenda
Barry Eichengreen
Economic Sanctions After the Cold War
Kimberly Ann Elliott, Gary C. Hufbauer and Jeffrey J. Schott
Trade and Labor Standards
Kimberly Ann Elliott and Richard Freeman
Leading Indicators of Financial Crises in the Emerging Economies
Morris Goldstein and Carmen Reinhart
The Exchange Stabilization Fund
C. Randall Henning
Prospects for Western Hemisphere Free Trade
Gary Clyde Hufbauer and Jeffrey J. Schott
The Future of US Foreign Aid
Carol Lancaster
The Economics of Korean Unification
Marcus Noland
International Lender of Last Resort
Catherine L. Mann
A Primer on US External Balance
Catherine L. Mann
Globalization, the NAIRU, and Monetary Policy
Adam S. Posen

DISTRIBUTORS OUTSIDE THE UNITED STATES

Australia, New Zealand, and Papua New Guinea
D.A. INFORMATION SERVICES
648 Whitehorse Road
Mitcham, Victoria 3132, Australia
(tel: 61-3-9210-7777;
fax: 61-3-9210-7788)
email: service@dadirect.com.au
http://www.dadirect.com.au

Caribbean
SYSTEMATICS STUDIES LIMITED
St. Augustine Shopping Centre
Eastern Main Road, St. Augustine
Trinidad and Tobago, West Indies
(tel: 868-645-8466;
fax: 868-645-8467)
email: tobe@trinidad.net

People's Republic of China (including Hong Kong) and Taiwan
(sales representatives):
Tom Cassidy
Cassidy & Associates
470 W. 24th Street
New York, NY 10011
(tel: 212-727-8943;
fax: 212-727-9539)

India, Bangladesh, Nepal, and Sri Lanka
VIVA BOOKS PVT.
Mr. Vinod Vasishtha
4325/3, Ansari Rd.
Daryaganj, New Delhi-110002, India
(tel: 91-11-327-9280;
fax: 91-11-326-7224)
email: vinod.viva@gndel
http://globalnet.ems.vsnl.net.in

Mexico and the Caribbean
(non-Anglophone islands only)
L.D. Clepper, Jr., sales representative
Publishers Marketing & Research
  Associates
79-01 35th Avenue #5D
P.O. Box 720489
Jackson Heights, NY 11372
(tel/fax: 718-803-3465)
email: clepper@pipeline.com

South America
Julio E. Ernod
Publishers Marketing & Research
  Associates, c/o HARBRA
Rua Joaquim Tavora, 629
04015-001 Sao Pāulo, Brasil
(tel: 55-11-571-1122;
fax: 55-11-575-6876)
email: emod@harbra.com.br

Canada
RENOUF BOOKSTORE
5369 Canotek Road, Unit 1,
Ottawa, Ontario K1J 9J3, Canada
(tel: 613-745-2665;
fax: 613-745-7660)
http://www.renoufbooks.com/

Central America
Jose Rios, sales representative
Publishers Marketing & Research
  Associates
Publicaciones Educativas
Apartado Postal 370-A
Ciudad Guatemala, Guatemala, C.A.
(tel/fax: 502-443-0472)

Western and Eastern Europe (including Russia), as well as the Middle East and North Africa
The Eurospan Group
3 Henrietta Street, Covent Garden
London, England
(tel: 011-44-171-240-0856;
fax: 011-44-171-379-0609)
email: orders@eurospan.co.uk
http://www.eurospan.co.uk

Japan and the Republic of Korea
UNITED PUBLISHERS SERVICES, LTD.
Kenkyu-Sha Building
9, Kanda Surugadai 2-Chome
Chiyoda-Ku, Tokyo 101, Japan
(tel: 81-3-3291-4541;
fax: 81-3-3292-8610)
email: saito@ups.co.jp

Puerto Rico (School/College/Academic markets)
David R. Rivera, sales representative
Publishers Marketing & Research
  Associates
c/o Premium Educational Group
MSC 609 #89 Ave. De Diego, Suite 105
San Juan, PR 00927-5381
(tel: 787-764-3532;
fax: 787-764-4774)
email:drrivera@coqui.net

Visit our website at:
http://www.iie.com

E-mail orders to:
orders@iie.com

The role of FDI in dev.
FDI and natural resources